COME ALONGSIDE

Other works by Susan Habegger

A New Song
Our Journey Toward Healing

A New Song
Our Journey Toward Healing
Leader's Guide for Small Group Study

COME ALONGSIDE

A Cross-Cultural Guide
to Help Shepherd Individuals and Small Groups
Toward Healing

Susan Habegger

COME ALONGSIDE
A Cross-Cultural Guide to Help Shepherd Individuals and Small Groups Toward Healing
©2025 Susan Habegger. All rights reserved. Do not duplicate.
No portion of this book, including text and images, may be copied except for personal use. No portion of this book, including text and images, may be copied and distributed or used in new creative expressions without prior permission of the author.

ISBN: 979-8-9902797-6-6

Cover Design by Mikel Allen, Mikel Allen Designs
Cover Art *The Path Forward* by Brandon L. Byrd
Book Design by Mikel Allen, Mikel Allen Designs and Susan Habegger
Book Illustrations by Brandon L. Byrd, Glen L. Byrd, Shiloh W. Byrd

All Scripture quotations, unless otherwise indicated, are taken from the Holy Bible, New International Version®, NIV®. Copyright ©1973, 1978, 1984, 2011 by Biblica, Inc.™ Used by permission of Zondervan. All rights reserved worldwide. www.zondervan.com. The "NIV" and "New International Version" are trademarks registered in the United States Patent and Trademark Office by Biblica, Inc.™

Scriptures marked ESV are from The ESV® Bible (The Holy Bible, English Standard Version®), © 2008 by Crossway, a publishing ministry of Good News Publishers. Used by permission. All rights reserved.

NOTES FROM THRIVE LIFE SKILLS BOARD LEADERSHIP

Thrive Life Skills' teaching on how to move forward from trauma has helped scores of individuals who had been mired in the woes of past suffering to make peace with what has happened to them and then to have the tools needed to build a positive, God-driven path to a new and productive life. I am privileged to hear the reports and testimonies from the many locations God has taken us so far and see evidence that this teaching is a highly-effective, God-centered resource.

Jean Nystrand, Retired Thrive Life Skills Board President
Retired Executive Director BSF International

Over the past decade, Thrive Life Skills' teaching about how to move forward from trauma has helped a multitude of people from around the globe learn to move from the crisis of trauma toward hope, peace, healing, and relief. Those who hurt are learning and experiencing healthy ways to deal with the pain and suffering as they discover their value and identity apart from it. As a Thrive Life Skills board member, I have been greatly blessed and encouraged by heartfelt responses:

> From Ukraine—"In the midst of chaos, we need these reminders that our value and identity is from God and nothing can destroy it."
>
> From Ethiopia—"This teaching helped me realize my internal hurt and how to find relief. I don't need to be carried away by the suffering. It helps to know that I'm held by God's love and goodness."
>
> From India—"Thrive's workshop was a pivotal moment for me. The words spoke to my mind and to my heart, allowing me to see the truth of how I was responding to my suffering. It was a lifeline at a time when I had no hope."
>
> From the USA—"I uncovered pain that I had kept hidden for many years, pain that was keeping me from a close relationship with my God. I feel free now to trust and interact with Him in a new way."

These responses are more than encouraging words—they are a testament to the healing that God brings as Thrive Life Skills acts in obedience to "come alongside."

Patty Yoss, Thrive Life Skills Board President

I was privileged to witness a three-day seminar in Jos Nigeria, with Susan Habegger teaching people to help others "move forward from trauma." This time was transformative for me and for the attendees. With eight to ten people per table—most strangers to one another—we learned by doing. With the acknowledgement that everyone has suffering in their lives, Susan explained that trauma is like a skin wound that would get infected, fester, and cause sepsis if only bandaged but not cleaned and effectively treated. The connection was made—people tend to put suffering in a box, cover it with a lid, and hide it deep, allowing emotional sepsis to occur. It was amazing how quickly God took the lids off those boxes—broke down barriers of shyness, self-protection, and embarrassment—and opened hearts to vulnerably share some of their deepest hurts. This nudge to identify suffering and the feelings that accompanied it was the first step of many during the seminar as the participants began to move forward toward healing.

Linda Musfeldt, Thrive Life Skills Board Secretary

RESPONSES FROM AROUND THE WORLD TO THRIVE LIFE SKILLS' TEACHING ABOUT SUFFERING AND TRAUMA

"The people of Northern Uganda have suffered much and carry the memory burden of great atrocities and pain. Thrive Life Skills' course about moving forward from trauma helped my people feel a difference in their lives. The people of Northern Uganda heard truth that gave us a way forward:

- To get back on your feet due to trauma one must first accept that someone or something that gave meaning and joy to life is gone—we must recognize the loss.
- We want to feel normal again but it takes time to get back to one's original self and this can only take place through the recovery process.
- It's better to face the source of our pain directly—with all our mind and senses working.
- We were assured that shame is not a part of our healing or our identity.

One man told me, "Neither is there enough alcohol in the world to make pain disappear . . . I only realized this after the teaching. I found a new way to heal."

Because the teaching is relevant and bears fruit in our lives, we look forward to each return visit from Susan and Thrive Life Skills.

(Fr. Simon Menya, Spiritual Leader and Director of Northern Uganda Self-Sufficiency Project, Gulu, Uganda)

"Your training on moving forward from trauma was extremely useful and insightful. Susan explained the complex aspects of trauma in an accessible way, combining theory with practical tools. The exercises that helped consolidate knowledge were especially valuable. She created a comfortable atmosphere where everyone could express themselves freely. Her professionalism and empathy were impressive. This training expanded my professional skills and gave me a new perspective on working with trauma. I recommend the training to anyone who works with people who have experienced difficult situations."

(Victoria, Workshop Participant, Ukraine)

"I did not know how to express my feelings until I saw the pictures provided in one of the lessons. I could say, "*This. This is how I feel*" with no more words needed."   (Workshop Participant, Thailand)

"Trauma casts a dark cloud over us and we become blind to everything good in our lives, including the presence and power of God. However, God never leaves us alone in our suffering. He always provides help. For me and others who attended the workshop, *Moving Forward from Trauma* in January 2018, God provided help. He came through the cloud of trauma with a ray of light and hope. Susan's teaching, along with the manuals, set us on a path of victory over the battle with trauma and the associated suffering. I highly recommend this manual to everyone dealing with the issues and troubles of life."
(Dr. Yaks Usman, Workshop Organizer and Participant, Nigeria)

"You helped me. You helped my people. You opened yourself and laid it all out on the table. Please tell your board that your work here was very good and that you have our blessing."
(Pastoral Leader and Workshop Participant, Ethiopia)

"I admit that I was still looking back at the pain with my shoulders down. Now, I am able to accept that pain—but also, look forward with hope."   (Workshop Participant, Ethiopia)

"God sent you to us. We have learned so much for ourselves and how to help our people. No one has ever come to us like this."   (Spiritual Leader and Workshop Participant, Uganda)

"I did not understand that I was experiencing the effects of trauma. Now, I can recognize it and refuse to live under its control. I have tools to move forward with courage."   (Workshop Participant, Nigeria)

"The flow of the lessons leads the participants gently through the steps of opening the conversation. Each step also moves forward in levels of trust. It was powerful."   (Workshop Participant, Nigeria)

"The *Moving Forward From Trauma* workshop was exactly designed for me for this season of my life. This experience has brought me closer to God. My favorite part of the workshop was the handouts and the activities. This workshop was a huge eye-opener for me—to know I'm not alone in this journey even though it's so hard and challenging. God is leading me."   (Workshop Participant, India)

"This course helped me to see that it is not necessary to hide suffering. I came to learn how to serve others, but I learned how to serve myself as well. I am able to see my past and expand my vision to the future. I learned that I can be free from the control of the trauma. Healing is a journey and there is beauty in suffering—when we include God."   (Workshop Participant, Ethiopia)

RESPONSES FROM MISSIONS ORGANIZATIONS AS THEY AND THRIVE LIFE SKILLS WORK TOGETHER TO HELP THOSE WHO SUFFER MOVE TOWARD HEALING

I have been serving for 20+ years in Northern Uganda where civil war, poverty, and disease have ravaged the land and the people. My primary focus has been medical—however, I was very much aware of the great need for help with trauma and healing from the psychological suffering that everyone carries. I met Susan, the director of Thrive Life Skills, and the connection was immediate. Our hearts were on the same path to come alongside those who struggle to find some way forward. Now Thrive Life Skills enables *Lift Up Uganda* to fulfill its vision more completely. Susan has traveled with me to Uganda multiple times to hold workshops and seminars, including Moving Forward From Trauma, Discovering Our Identity, Entrepreneurship, Small Business Training, and Women's Retreats. As leaders of nonprofits, we long to provide for the needs we see—needs that often go beyond our focus or expertise. Thrive Life Skills comes alongside to assist *and* provides experienced training for the nationals so they can minister to their own people. Thrive Life Skills and Lift Up Uganda will continue to work together for years to come —*together* we can follow God's call to bring hope to the hopeless.

Sue Nelson, FNP-C, President and Founder of Lift Up Uganda, Inc.

When Holding Ukraine was faced with the overwhelming requests for trauma and PTSD training, we turned to a trusted source, Susan Habegger from Thrive Life Skills, for her extraordinary dedication and compassionate service. The training from Thrive Life Skills has been a beacon of hope for countless Ukrainian women and men, guiding them through the harrowing aftermath of war. The unwavering commitment to help those who suffer overcome trauma and find solace in their faith is truly inspiring.

Thrive Life Skills not only provides essential life skills but also fosters a deep sense of community and spiritual healing. Susan's ability to connect with individuals on a personal level and support them in their journey toward recovery and faith is unparalleled and has a profound impact on the lives she touches. The efforts of Thrive Life Skills are a testament to the power of empathy, resilience, and faith.

We wholeheartedly recommend Susan and Thrive Life Skills for their invaluable contribution to the well-being and spiritual growth of those affected by the conflict in Ukraine.

Dave and Kathy Rohmfeld, Founder/Director of Holding Ukraine

We are really happy to be part of this great God's project and accept you here in Ukraine. "God is good" —we repeated all the time during the trips to Krakow and back, during the seminars, and during some rest time. These days were a real blessing with lots of useful information, communication and sharing from heart to heart. The material everyone got is really helpful for everyone personally and for serving people in home groups and different ministries in the local churches. In their feedback papers all the participants thank the organizers for the seminar— true and actual information. In the afternoon women had their private time with sewing and telling their stories. It was a very inspiring time and two communities have already had the idea to organize sisters' ministries in such a way with different handicrafts and sharing their stories. It's so powerful! God blessed us so much. We look forward to our future common missions and projects!
Clear Vision Charity Foundation, Ukraine

I have used Thrive Life Skills teaching on trauma and healing in my counseling practice with individuals and families. The information and tools have also been helpful to give further confidence to our professional and lay counselors in their work with those who experience trauma.
Mary Paul, Accredited Christian Counselor South Asia, Founder/Director Vathsalya Charitable Trust, Founder Kutumba

This book is dedicated
to the ones who open their hearts . . .
to the ones who tell their stories . . .
to the ones who invite me in.

Different cultures
Different languages
Different experiences

Yet we meet on the pathway of pain.
My suffering takes on new meaning
as it connects with yours.

Gaining courage from each other,
we embrace the journey of healing.
Now, *together* we reach out to others
with the message of hope and peace
from
. . . the God of all comfort, who comforts us in all our troubles,
so that we can comfort those in any trouble
with the comfort we ourselves receive from God. (2 Corinthians 1:14)

CONTENTS

NOTES FROM THRIVE LIFE SKILLS BOARD — i

RESPONSES FROM AROUND THE WORLD — iii

RESPONSES FROM MISSIONS ORGANIZATIONS — v

THANK YOU — xi

PREFACE — xiii

INTRODUCTION — xvii

HOW TO GET THE BEST USE FROM THIS BOOK — xix

SET THE FOUNDATION

Chapter

1. PREPARE YOUR HEART AND MIND — 3
2. BUILD AND PROTECT A SENSE OF SAFETY — 5
3. FIND COURAGE, GRACE, AND PEACE — 15

PREPARE FOR THE JOURNEY

4. LOGISTICAL INFORMATION ABOUT THE LESSONS — 21
5. RECOMMENDATIONS FOR LEADING THE LESSONS — 25

MAKE THE JOURNEY

SESSION

1. INTRODUCTION — 31
2. BEGIN THE STORY — 39
3. OUR COMMON RESPONSE TO SUFFERING — 45
4. HOW DO I FEEL? — 59
5. BECOME FAMILIAR WITH SUFFERING — 65
6. A PICTURE OF SUFFERING — 73
7. LIFE AS IT WAS; LIFE AS IT IS NOW — 77
8. DISCOVERING LOSS — 81
9. THE EMOTIONS OF LOSS — 89
10. TELLING GOD ABOUT MY SUFFERING — 95

11	REASSURANCE	103
12	I AM NOT CONSUMED	111
13	A BEGINNING AND AN END	115
14	A NEW PERSPECTIVE	123
15	WHY?	133
16	WHERE IS GOD IN THE SUFFERING?	139
17	WHY DID GOD ALLOW THIS TO HAPPEN?	145
18	HOPE	155
19	OTHERS IN OUR STORY	163
20	THOSE WHO CAUSED THE HARM	167
21	FORGIVENESS	173
22	MOVE FORWARD	183
23	TRUTH AND UNTRUTH	191
24	DISCOVER THE NEED FOR PROTECTION	199
25	SET BOUNDARIES	205
26	A STRONG PROTECTION: IDENTITY	215
27	VALUE: WHERE DO I FIND IT?	223
28	TETHERS	229
29	THE REALITY OF FEAR	235
30	ALONG THE WAY	241
31	REDEEMED	249
32	IS THERE PEACE?	253
33	MY GUARDED HEART	261
34	HOW SHOULD WE NOW LIVE?	265
35	OUR EMOTIONS: WHERE DO THEY TAKE US?	275
36	LET THERE BE JOY	283
37	A NEW SONG	289
38	THE PERSONHOOD OF CHILDREN	295
39	A CHILD'S RESPONSES TO SUFFERING	301
40	OPEN A SAFE DOOR FOR CHILDREN TO SHARE THEIR STORY	309
41	NONVERBAL WAYS TO OPEN THE DOOR	319
42	BODY-BASED WAYS TO COPE WITH ANXIETY	339
43	SPIRITUAL REASSURANCE	349
44	DISCUSSIONS FOR DEEPER UNDERSTANDING	355
	APPENDIX B	359

THANK YOU

This book is the culmination of years of writing, teaching, listening, and revising—*repeat*. The Thrive Life Skills Board of Directors stayed with me through it all. God sent each one of you to me for specific reasons. You have the same heart and hear the same voice. And yet, you bring varied gifts and perspectives that add to the fullness of the work. You wept with me through the journey that made this book come to life. You rejoiced with me as we watched God use pain for His glory and the good of others. You encouraged me forward toward seemingly impossible tasks. I love each of you and consider *Coming Alongside* an expression of our concerted and collective effort.

A book of this kind, intended for the good of others, is nothing without the invitation and acceptance of those for whom the work is intended. Thank you to the many precious women and men who invited me in. You opened your homes, your churches, and welcomed me under the mango tree. You drove hundreds of miles and crossed borders to bring me to your place of need. You cared for me in delightful ways that fed my stomach, my mind, and my soul. You told me your stories. You shared your pain. You held out your hand and allowed me to step into your culture, your world, in order to come alongside for some moments. You taught me and strengthened me. You gave life to the words on these pages.

My heart is full of gratitude. I hold each story close. I treasure the hours and minutes we had together. As I remember your faces, I earnestly say:

> I thank my God every time I remember you . . . I long to see you . . . so that you and I may be mutually encouraged by each other's faith. (Philippians 1:3; Romans 1:11-12)

PREFACE

The seeds of this book were planted more than thirty years ago, when I lived in Nigeria. Since that time, I have worked in multiple countries around the world with people who endure various types of trauma—war, poverty, displacement, abuse, trafficking, and more. These people suffer tremendous emotional pain and yearn to find a way out, but they face financial and political challenges, along with social marginalization, which limit the solutions available to them.

As a result, I shifted my focus away from things I could do to fix their problems and, instead, found ways to come alongside them *in the midst of their problems*, to encourage them toward hope.

It was then that God filled my mind and heart with this vision:

We must come alongside and walk with those who are disadvantaged and oppressed and who suffer—in the circumstances under which they must live their lives—so that the cycle of despair is broken. We must give them tools to thrive where they are and help them to discover hope for a courageous and peaceful way forward.

In 2010, this vision led to the development of Thrive Life Skills, a 501(c)(3) nonprofit humanitarian organization. God opened doors in Africa, Asia, and Europe for Thrive Life Skills to come alongside missions organizations, church leadership, community leaders, counselors, and individuals who had a heart for those who were hurting. In the first few years of Thrive Life Skills' ministry, we provided training in varied life skills. *Health and Wellness* taught people the basics of how their bodies work so they could make wise choices and care for themselves properly. *Introduction to Business* and *Entrepreneurship* provided training in how to start a business and sustain it with integrity and skill. *Learning To Teach* gave opportunity to many who wanted to serve as teachers in their churches and communities. The courses in *Family Relationships* and *Foundations of Parenting* provided encouragement in the home. A favorite was *Sewing*, beginning with the basics and building expertise through three levels. Of course, *Scripture Studies* was a foundation for learning the truth about God and His relationship with us.

During this time, many hurt souls shared with me that they felt there was an unspoken expectation to keep conversations about suffering quiet—*if we share our pain we are weak or have little faith.*

It seemed that those of us in the church offered help—and even the expectation—to heal, but we did not offer the space or opportunity to give pain the raw, unfiltered expression—and time—that was necessary for healing.

I knew that much of the church's hesitancy settled on the fact that we did not have a safe, applicable, and well-planned format in which to offer such a conversation. We had no program or curriculum, for example, that would address the topic of suffering and accommodate various cultural perspectives. No clinical study on trauma or personal story of victory would meet these needs, and no Bible study offered the kind of help we required. And to simply invite people to discuss their pain, without having a plan in place, could be dangerous. So, repeatedly, I set the issue aside, with the intent to revisit it "in the future." Little did I know the future would lead me directly into the path of my own trauma—and that this experience would shake my entire life.

I was no stranger to trauma. I had invested years of my life working with people around the world who had endured it. But it turned out that I did not truly know trauma until my experience with it took a personal turn. For the purposes of this book, it is not necessary to explain the circumstances that led to my suffering, but I must mention this experience because it was pivotal in both my life and the formation of this course. It brought me face-to-face with the *actuality* of suffering—and at that moment, I realized that my previous *expectations* of suffering and how to handle it were *not* realistic. My perspective of how to walk through pain—and through potential healing—imploded and completely transformed.

This transformation began even while I was suffering, when God strongly encouraged me to put my thoughts and experiences on paper. I was reluctant to start this task—the words and images that landed on the page were far more personal than anything I had expressed before—and yet, I now felt an urgency to connect with others in the confusion that inhibited healing. As I followed through, I learned much in the process. I learned that the spiritual component of handling trauma—the journey we take through suffering with our Good Shepherd, with its ups and downs, its doubts and reassurances—must be real and not fake or forced. I also learned that true healing happens only when we experience every part of the journey honestly. In spiritual settings, we tend to want to jump quickly to healing and peace—solving the problem; but I realized that it could be through our very openness to pain that we become true examples of life and redemption at its fullest.

As I continued to learn and write, God compelled me to turn this work into a course called *Moving Forward from Trauma*, which I could use to train nationals to help their own people through healing. Soon, lesson titles emerged, such as "The Way Life Was/The Way Life Is Now," "Becoming Familiar with Suffering," "Discovering and Mourning Loss," "Consumed," and "The Reality of Fear"—and the course began to take shape.

After 1 year, *Moving Forward from Trauma* was finally complete and ready to present internationally to missions groups and churches who were open to having the conversation about suffering. I held the first training sessions in 2015 at Meh Lah refugee camp in Thailand, followed by multiple places in India. The response to these initial sessions was positive but also surprising, as an interesting pattern arose: without fail, these church and community leaders who gathered to learn to help others would begin to change their focus to instead deal with their own pain. They expressed emotions, asked questions, and recounted experiences. And within hours, I would hear statements such as the following:

> "We have suffered for so many years. How do we recover?"
>
> "We have never talked about our suffering. How do we begin?"
>
> "Is there hope? How do we encourage others to share their stories?"
>
> "I do not know how to respond when someone tells me about their pain."

In this way, training workshops became profound moments of personal connection that gave participants a more subjective awareness of how to meet others in pain. These connections proved to me that the time and place for such a conversation were right.

Over time, word spread, and God brought requests from others. This resulted in return trips to Thailand and India, followed by visits to Uganda, Nigeria, Ethiopia, and Ukraine. Every place we went, the response was overwhelming—hearts were open, words and emotions began to flow, and hope and healing felt attainable once again.

In one memorable trip to Northern Uganda in 2022, I used the lessons to help survivors of a horrific twenty-year civil war. The war had been marked by the displacement of civilians, the abduction of children to be used as soldiers, and the determination to wipe out an entire group of people. The survivors I worked with had been children during the war and were now clergy and laypersons in the religious community—but they still carried the trauma of what they had seen and experienced to the present day. Not long after we started the course, their personal stories began to flow, and healing began.

"No one else has ever come," one man said.

This comment surprised me, as I knew that many had gone before us to help in this particular area. So, I questioned what was different about this visit.

"We have been told that this experience is our identity and that we must simply work harder to overcome it—survive and be stronger. We were told to forget it and make a new life," he said. "But you have shown us that the trauma is *not* our identity. You have helped us to look at the suffering straight on and recognize how trauma is attempting to control our lives. [We now know the trauma] is only part of our story and that there are ways to put it in its place, so that we can live in a healthy way—remembering the suffering but not under its control. I feel such release from what I have carried all these years."

Many others have responded in a similar way:

> "I have heard so much about suffering and forgiveness. I have been told again and again to forget about my past. But my past was having a lot of impact on my present, so I just didn't understand how I could pretend that I wasn't going through what I was. I learned to acknowledge my suffering and be kind to myself. I learned that I don't have to let the suffering take over my life. I received a lot of clarity about myself. It was like meeting myself and hearing about my life." (India)

> "I always felt that I was to hide my suffering. Now I feel the freedom to express my emotion and embrace God's compassion. He wants to hear my pain!" (Uganda)

> "This course helped me to realize my internal hurt and how to find relief from that. It is not necessary to remain with the hurt, suffering is not the whole story, but part of my life. It helps to know that I don't need to be carried away by the suffering—I'm held by God's love and goodness." (Ethiopia)

> "I received answers to questions that I was afraid to ask. The teaching helped me tell my own story and also to listen to others in a caring way. We learned how to stand firm on our legs and help others." (Ukraine)

I now take this course to multiple international locations each year, and the positive responses continue. At the same time, the need for such relevant, practical training has only seemed to grow. The number of people who have expressed the desire to live out the reality of their suffering in a healthy way continues to grow. And so, it is time to expand the reach of this course by making it available to others—which brings me to the reason for this book.

At the heart of these pages, you will find the original lessons that I developed, along with revisions and added materials that, together, create a comprehensive, standalone guide that will help guide this conversation of pain. Because the purpose of this guide is to walk *you* through training other leaders who want to help the hurting, its title has also been updated, from *Moving Forward from Trauma* to:

Come Alongside:
A Cross-Cultural Guide
To Help Shepherd Individuals and Small Groups Toward Healing

In addition to revised and expanded training sessions, this book now includes the following:

- Principles to help train leaders
- Helpful discussion prompts
- Suggestions for lesson application
- General helps for the teacher
- Worksheets and tools for teachers

Thrive Life Skills' main intent for this book is to provide you, or your missions group, church, or organization, with a tool that will help you meet the needs of those you serve. I know what it is like to experience the stress and conflict of being on the field, so busy with meeting immediate needs that there is no time to develop a new program. I hope this guide alleviates some of that stress by giving you what you need—complete and ready to use—now. In addition, this book has been intentionally written and edited toward ease of translation.

As a final encouragement, I want you to remember that we need not be afraid to talk about suffering—even with those around the world whose lives are so different from ours. The reality of pain is not an obstacle to our message of hope. In fact, this conversation is an open door to our good news. It is clear that people from all cultures want connection in their suffering—connection to themselves and to their communities and, perhaps, even to God. The topic of suffering can be an inroad to such connection—because, despite our differences in culture and language and location, suffering is one of our most common earthly experiences.

Feel free to connect with me, as well! If you have questions or comments or would like me to provide long- or short-term training sessions in some capacity, you may contact me directly through the email address given below. I would be happy to hear from you and discuss the possibilities.

Susan Habegger

Director and Founder, Thrive Life Skills

susanh@thrivelifeskills.org | thrivelifeskills.com

INTRODUCTION:
HELP FOR A DIFFICULT CONVERSATION

Suffering is a universal experience—it is familiar to all of us. Yet, we often find it difficult to talk about on a personal level.

Even when we long to share our personal stories, we often struggle with sharing the painful parts. We wonder what information we should share and how. We worry that we will share "too much" or "do it all wrong." We fear that we'll be judged or misunderstood.

Sometimes, we gather the courage to share, but we hold back part of the story and put on a brave face that says, "Yes, I have problems, but I have everything under control." Or we unload our whole story at once, leaving a mess of details behind.

Regardless of the situation, sharing pain is uncomfortable—which means that any conversation that involves sharing pain is usually difficult. Understandably, then, we tend to be leery of these conversations. Many of us even go out of our way to avoid them altogether. Or we believe they should be reserved for professional counseling—after all, "everyday people" don't want to hear or talk about personal problems.

The fortunate reality, however, is that many *are* open to such a conversation. A *number* of people, in fact, desire to not only come alongside the hurting but also to walk through their difficult stories with them, so that they can find a path toward hope.

The fact that you are reading this book suggests that you are among these people willing to help. Maybe you belong to one of the many churches, ministries, or community organizations working to rescue and restore hope to those in devastating circumstances; maybe you have walked through difficulties in your own life and want to use that experience to help others; or maybe God has simply given you compassion for the hurting. Whatever your situation, you take the call to come alongside the suffering seriously. But there is a problem: although you are *willing*, when the doubts and questions come, you wonder if you are *able*.

For example, maybe you have considered starting a small group for people who have experienced trauma, but you're not sure where to start or what to expect. Do you simply invite people to come and share whatever they want, whenever they want, for as long as they want? How do you help people overcome the discomfort and worry that come with sharing pain? Then after pain is shared, how do you respond in a way that's helpful? How do you then guide people onto a path that leads to hope and inner peace?

Those in missions organizations face additional challenges, such as limited resources and fieldwork that consumes enormous amounts of time and energy. In many cases, these groups find that the immediate need for rescue is followed quickly by the provision of urgent and everyday necessities. They want to be more intentional in helping nationals process their emotional pain and move toward healing, but the everyday work takes over. In addition, these groups do not have the time to develop programs that will facilitate these necessary conversations about pain in a way that is safe and organized, let alone in a way that is culturally relevant.

All around the world, organizations, communities, ministries, and churches are full of people whose willingness to help the suffering is hindered by these types of unresolved questions and doubts—and the unfortunate result is a deficiency in opportunities for people to talk openly about the deep hurt that longs for healing.

This is where *Come Alongside* enters the picture. This book provides guidance for those who want to conduct safe, relevant, and organized conversations around the difficult topic of suffering and to offer hope to the hurting. This book will equip individuals and groups with . . .

- the encouragement to speak about pain openly and without fear;
- the foothold they need to provide companionship and a safe space for those who long to travel a path toward healing; and
- the opportunity to bring the Good Shepherd, the perfect companion to us all, on the journey.

I hope that you come away from this book knowing that we do not need to be afraid to talk about suffering. After all, it is one of our most common experiences. No matter who we are or where we are from, our stories long to be told, our hearts yearn for the for the permission to express disquiet, and our spirits cry out for the gentle reminder that we all have a reason for hope.

For that reason, I pray that this book will not only help us to live out the following reality but also help others do the same:

> He put a new song in my mouth,
> a hymn of praise to our God.
> *Many will see* and fear the Lord
> *and put their trust in him.*
> —Psalm 40:3, emphasis mine

HOW TO GET THE BEST USE FROM THIS BOOK

Come Alongside is based on personal life experience, decades of practical application in international ministry, and input from professionals who serve the hurting, both in the United States and internationally. Although based on experience and truth, It should not be read or offered as a counseling course. Neither should the discussion sessions in this book be presented as therapy. Rather, this book offers a framework around which individuals and organizations can build safe, organized, intentional opportunities for people to talk openly and productively about their experiences of suffering.

The materials presented in the pages that follow were originally intended for use in training groups of leaders who would, in turn, shepherd their own small groups on the journey of processing pain and trauma. Although the book continues to be suited to this purpose, it can also be adapted for individual use by anyone who feels called to walk with the hurting, whether in a group setting or one on one.

With that in mind, know that *the way you use this book will depend on your intended purpose*. The section that follows will give you a better understanding of how the book is organized, so that you can approach the material in a way that is most usable to you.

It is advised that a copy of this manual be provided for each leader who will guide a small group or individual. The manual is *not* given to the individual or participants who are part of that small group.

When training those who will, in turn, shepherd other small groups, provide the manual at the completion of the training sessions. Permission is given by Thrive Life Skills for this manual to be translated and/or duplicated for this particular purpose.

HOW THE BOOK IS ORGANIZED

This book is divided into three sections:

- **Part 1: Set the Foundation: Basic Principles to Help Shepherd Others through Pain.** This section prepares the willing leader with concepts and values they can use to form the basis of their walk with others through pain. This section discusses the importance of a leader's motives and goals; the role of preparation, commitment, and consistency in providing a safe environment; best practices for listening and responding to stories of suffering; and advice on how to find grace and peace in the midst of this often difficult work.
- **Part 2: Prepare for the Journey: Recommendations to Help Lead the Sessions.** This section equips leaders with the specific information and advice they will need to facilitate the discussion sessions that appear in Part 3. This section covers the more logistical aspects of conducting discussion sessions, such as how to read the session template and how to appropriately use the script to lead discussions.
- **Part 3: Make the Journey: Discussion Sessions to Light a Path Toward Hope.** This last and largest part of the book provides a curriculum of 37 discussion sessions, along with activities and worksheets. This curriculum will help you to confidently join the hurting on their path through pain, while gently guiding them forward to a path of hope.

Your personal goals will determine the way that you read and use each of these parts. In other words, someone training leaders to use this book with their own small groups will read the information differently than someone planning to directly lead a person or small group.

FOR LEADERS

If your goal is to adapt the book for your own personal use—to help you directly lead a person or small group on the journey through processing pain—you will use the material in Part 1 and Part 2 for your own reference and then use the curriculum in Part 3 to guide discussion sessions to mentor others. You will most likely present one Session from Part 3 for each meeting time.

FOR THOSE WHO WILL TRAIN LEADERS

If your goal is to train leaders to shepherd their own small groups, you will present to them the general leadership principles in Part 1 and the logistical recommendations in Part 2; then you will treat the discussion sessions in Part 3 as shortened teaching examples, in which you model their future role as small-group leaders and they step into the role of their future mentees. For the sake of time, you will include more than one Session from Part 3 during each training time. This process will give them a sense of what their upcoming sessions will look like, and they will gain empathy as they put themselves in the participants' shoes.

Appendix A: Optional Sessions to Come Alongside Children in Suffering. This additional section focuses on children—their response to suffering and our connection with them in their pain and their healing.

Because you will need to present material from all parts of this book, it will be to your benefit to create lesson plans, which you then organize into a schedule, ahead of time. **Appendix B: A Lesson-Plan Outline and Ideas to Help Train Leaders** will assist you with this process.

PART 1
SET THE FOUNDATION:

Basic Principles To Help Shepherd Others Through Pain

CHAPTER 1

PREPARE YOUR HEART AND MIND

Each conversation that you have about suffering will come to life in unique ways, based on the personalities, situations, and cultures of the people involved. Still, there are a few common foundational principles you can rely on to make every conversation as beneficial as possible. In this chapter, we will focus on the first principle, which forms the basis of all the others: *Prepare Your Heart and Mind*.

PREPARE YOUR HEART

To help others is a good and right task, but it is not easy. You will face times of uncertainty and stress, and you may even feel like you want to quit. Fortunately, you can prepare yourself to persist through the trials, and this preparation begins with a fairly simply task. That task is to know your heart's purpose.

You probably have this book because you believe that it is important to walk with people through their trauma. But why? Before you read further, ask yourself the following question and take time to consider all of the possible answers:

> "Why do I want to take this training and become involved in people's lives in this way?"

A GREATER PURPOSE

Each of us has personal reasons for getting involved with those who suffer, but as Christians, we clearly have a biblical motivation, as well. God asks us to help those who are suffering, both for *their good* and for *His glory*. His Word speaks compassionately about the hurt and oppressed, and it shows that He often intervenes to walk with them and protect them. God also sent Jesus as the definitive Healer and Good Shepherd. So, when we come alongside the hurting, we both follow in Christ's footsteps and do the will of the One who sent Him.

In fact, this is one way that we most bring glory to God and show His character—to humbly set ourselves aside and enter another's place of pain, all while pointing to Jesus as the ultimate Savior of us all. This is what God says about such an endeavor:

> You have been a refuge for the poor, a refuge for the needy in their distress, a shelter from the storm and a shade from the heat. For the breath of the ruthless is like a storm driving against a wall. (Isaiah 25:4)

When we keep this greater purpose in our minds and hearts, along with our personal reasons to offer help, we are more likely to endure through the challenges that will inevitably cross our path.

PREPARE YOUR MIND

> Whatever you do, work at it with all your heart, as working for the Lord, not for human masters, since you know that you will receive an inheritance from the Lord as a reward. It is the Lord Christ you are serving. (Colossians 3:23–24)

Whatever we do for God, we want to do well. And to do well, we must prepare—not only our hearts but our minds, too.

To ensure that our minds are prepared to present this course, we must plan ahead. In other words, we must intentionally set aside time for our mental preparation, not only now but before each and every session. This means that you should plan to devote a certain amount of time and attention to the material in this book, both *during* meetings and *outside* of them. You must expect to read through each lesson, contemplate on it, pray about it, and put your mind in the "right position" even before each session begins.

There is no rule book to tell you how to mentally prepare for sessions, but there are a few responsibilities that are essential to the process. So, remember to account for these as you set your expectations for the road ahead:

- Read the entire lesson and then read it again, until you become familiar with the content. To spend that time now will protect you from confusion and forgetfulness later, during the session.
- Think carefully about the goals of the lesson.
- Think about how you will share the truths of the lesson with the participants. What necessary words in the lesson might be new to the participants? Take time to be sure you are familiar with the vocabulary in the lesson.
- Think about possible questions the participants might have as well as your potential responses to them.
- Pray for God's protection and provision during the discussion session.
- Set your mind to think about others more than yourself.

You may refer to this list of responsibilities to help you prepare before every session, or you may refer to it before the first few sessions only, using it less and less often as your preparations become more routine. You may also add items to this list as you see necessary.

The main thing to remember is this: Plan to be prepared! And as you do, remember your higher purpose. You are not preparing to make yourself look good or to invite praise. You are preparing because you want to follow Christ's lead—and you want to have the best chance of doing the job well for His glory.

CHAPTER 2
BUILD AND PROTECT A SENSE OF SAFETY

Wherever there is emotional pain, there is usually also a sense of unsafety. That is because suffering is often related to experiences of fear, betrayal, instability, and vulnerability. No leader can undo these experiences; neither can they impose a sense of safety onto others. They can, however, create an environment in which wounded souls gradually rebuild their sense of security. This leads us to the second leadership principle: *Build and protect a sense of safety.*

To apply this principle requires three basic steps: (1) understand your role and boundaries as a leader, (2) show commitment and consistency, and (3) protect the physical and emotional environments in which you will hold discussions. We will look at each of these steps in more detail below.

UNDERSTAND YOUR ROLE AND BOUNDARIES

The discussion sessions in Part 3 will light a pathway through pain and toward hope. To travel this pathway, participants will need to take an honest look at suffering—a process that sometimes requires courage, as they recall painful memories, share vulnerably with others, and learn to see pain for what it is. Your role is to come alongside them as a companion on this journey and to nurture an environment of safety along the way. In other words, your main job is to try to make the road safe.

Although that may sound simple, it is not uncommon to face situations that will lead you to question your role and the specific actions you should take. There will be times when the expectations on you will suddenly seem blurry and the terms "companion" and "safety-keeper" will seem hard to define. During these times, it can be deceptively easy to wander outside the boundaries of your role without even noticing—and to thereby cut off any sense of safety and companionship.

It will be helpful and important for you, as the protector of the safe space, to have a clearer picture of your role and its boundaries, so that you can refer back to it during these moments of uncertainty. The following outline of responsibilities that lie both within and outside your role as leader will help to paint such a picture for you.

As a leader, your role **is** . . .

- to encourage and reassure those who are hurting.
- to provide stability for those who are feeling nervous or unsure.
- to walk the sometimes difficult line of leading without directing.

As a leader, your role **is not** . . .

- to fix people or their problems.
- to get someone to the place you feel they should be.
- to present the discussion sessions as therapy or counseling or to refer to yourself as a counselor (unless, of course, you are licensed or certified as a therapist or counselor).
- to encourage participants to have emotional or advisory dependence on you or other members. Inevitably, a bond will grow between you and the participants, and that is okay, but be careful not to allow this bond to grow into co-dependency.

As you continue to read, you will learn more about how to enforce some of these boundaries in your role as the guardian of the safe space.

BE COMMITTED AND CONSISTENT

What you do as a leader speaks volumes. This means your actions can go a long way in building and protecting an environment of safety—and this is particularly true of actions that communicate commitment and consistency. When you are genuinely committed to the participants and process and show consistency in your actions, expectations, and responses, you provide stable footing for the path ahead.

There are many things you can do as a leader to show commitment and consistency, but the following actions will be of utmost importance:

- **Commit to attend group sessions regularly.** Over time, participants will become accustomed to your presence and guidance, and your consistency will establish trust. So avoid frequent or unexpected changes in leadership, which upsets this sense of security.
- **Commit to be prepared.** The previous chapter discussed the importance of being prepared in heart and mind. To aid in this preparation, commit to take time to go through the list of actions in Chapter 1 to mentally prepare before each discussion session.
- **Commit to keep everything that is shared in confidence.** It is imperative that you commit to hold others' stories safe and protected. This means that you must not repeat or "process" what has been shared in the sessions with your family, friends, or other leaders. There may be times when you want assistance from another leader about how to handle a particular experience or member in your group. In this case, it is acceptable to share about the situation as long as you keep names and details private. You could say, for example, "I have a participant who is finding it difficult to stay on topic and is giving long narrations of events in her life. How can I handle this situation in a way that is good for the entire group?" Or, "I have a participant who seems to need serious help with a particular event of suffering. How can I provide her with the support she needs?" It is also acceptable to ask a participant with a particular question or concern if you may have their permission to seek guidance from someone outside the group.
- **Commit to nurture the physical and emotional environment.** To *nurture* something is to care for it in such a way that it gets stronger and healthier. To nurture the physical environment in which

discussion sessions will take place, commit to find a room or area where participants will feel safe physically and emotionally and where meetings can occur consistently. Then commit to arrange the area to make it welcoming. This will help set the tone for the sessions and communicate that you care for and value those who are involved.

In addition, commit to nurture a safe emotional environment through your listening, your responses, and the boundaries you keep in place for all participants.

The next sections will help you to follow through on these commitments by offering a more detailed discussion of actions that will nurture the environment both physically and emotionally.

PROTECT THE SAFE SPACE PHYSICALLY

Before you can hold discussion sessions, you must identify a good, consistent place in which to meet regularly. You might meet in a classroom, in someone's sitting room, or even outside under a tree. Your meeting place does not need to be fancy, but it does need to offer a few things:

- The participants should feel physically safe. They should feel sure that no harm will come to them during the session time.

- The participants should also feel emotionally safe. As such, it is not advisable to hold sessions in a place where your conversations can be overheard or frequently interrupted by outsiders walking through. To have a room with a door that can be closed is the best option, but if that is not possible, a curtain can be hung as a boundary for privacy. Think of it this way: participants will be able to share about their painful experiences more openly if they have a place where the world "disappears" for a time.

- The area should be consistently available during the regular session time you set.

Once you have identified a good location for your meetings, assess the area and consider how you will arrange it. Also consider what, if any, accommodations you may need. Ask yourself, "What will make this place safe, comfortable, and welcoming?" and as you consider how to answer, keep in mind the following:

- How will you arrange the seating for class time? People from varying cultures will have differing ideas as to how they feel the most at home. Are they comfortable sitting at a table? On chairs? Or would they prefer to sit on the floor?

- A table is nice, because some session activities ask participants to draw and write, but these activities can be done on the floor or on a clipboard, as well.

- When you use chairs, avoid placing them in rows, as you might do in a classroom. It is best to arrange the chairs either around a table or in a circle, so that everyone can hear and speak freely to others.

- Sessions will offer opportunities for sharing, so it is best to sit at eye level with the participants rather than to stand and look down on them. Although you will guide the discussions, you will not

be the only one who speaks—and you will want others to feel welcome to speak, which is more likely when everyone is at the same eye level.
- As the leader, plan to arrange yourself so that you always face the door. This will allow you to see anyone who enters and to care for any interruptions carefully and quickly.

Once you have determined a location, commit to arrive there thirty minutes or more *before* your scheduled meeting time. This will give you enough time to make sure that everything is in place before the participants arrive:

- Sweep dirt and debris from the floor.
- Clear the area of any supplies or belongings that were left.
- Note the temperature. If it is uncomfortable, adjust it, if possible: turn on a fan, open windows, or change the thermostat.
- Turn on the lights.
- Set up any tables, chairs, or supplies, so that it is clear where the participants are to sit.

These physical preparations will contribute to the success of your sessions. The extra time and effort that you spend getting the area ready will communicate that the sessions are important to you and that you care for and value those who are involved. In this way, you open the door for sharing before the session even begins.

PROTECT THE SAFE SPACE EMOTIONALLY

Although one way to nurture the emotional environment is to attend to the physical area, the work does not stop there. Protecting an emotionally safe space is a continual process that begins when you lay the groundwork during your very first session.

✦ COMMUNICATE EXPECTATIONS

It is not wise to assume that everyone in your small group will know what is expected of them. So, from the very outset of your initial meeting, you will want to clarify these expectations. More specifically, you will want to communicate that you expect every member to offer respect, kindness, and confidentiality during the sessions—and to listen as others speak. This will tell each person that their time of sharing is protected. It will also show that you have invested forethought and planning into this process and are committed to the group's success.

You may use the following dialogue suggestions to express these expectations during your first discussion session:

- "We show respect to everyone in the group. Someone may be of a different tribe, social or economic standing, religion, or race, but during our time together, we see each other as fellow human beings who have suffered. In that way, we all belong."

- "We show courtesy while another person is sharing. We show courtesy and kindness by not laughing at someone's feelings or making light of another person's suffering. We show courtesy by listening without interrupting while another person speaks."
- "We show respect to others in our story by not sharing names and details that would be embarrassing or inappropriate. We do not want to reveal details that we might regret later."
- "We keep everything shared in this group confidential. We do not tell others in our family or community what we hear in our group. We must all feel safe to share without fear that our story will be spoken outside this group."

Even after the first session, you will need to continue to remind everyone of the expected etiquette. You can do this before each sharing time by clearly repeating at least one or two of the etiquette guidelines.

By the end of the session, if the group has done a good job following the guidelines, reinforce and encourage this behavior by expressing gratitude. You might say something like, "Thank you so much for the respect you show each other as you listen and share. This has really become a safe place for all of us."

✦ GUIDE THE DISCUSSION

Even after laying this groundwork, you may face challenges. As a leader, you will encounter many different personalities and people who have various levels of familiarity with how to share and listen to personal details responsibly within a small-group setting. This means that some participants will require more graceful guidance than others.

For instance, how do you respond to a participant who wants to share in response to every question? Or what do you say to a person who shares too personally—perhaps with family details that are not appropriate? What do you do when the sharing goes off topic, following trails that can quickly divert and even unsettle the sharing time?

Here are a few ideas for how to handle these common sharing challenges:

- If a speaker veers off topic or shows no sign of stopping soon, you may need to gently interrupt them and say something like, "Mary, this topic really got you thinking in many directions. Before you go further, though, let's come back to the question. Is there a way that you can relate your story to our topic today? Was there a truth you discovered in the teaching that speaks to this struggle?"
- If a participant is eager to share in response to every question, you might need to set a boundary and say something like, "Mary, I see you want to share on this question, as well. I'm going to ask you to wait for now, though, so that others who might want to share also have a chance. I'm sure you understand. Thank you so much." You could also approach such a participant one-on-one, outside of group time, with, "Mary, I need your help. I can see that you feel very comfortable sharing often and in detail. I am grateful that you feel safe in this group. Unfortunately, some of the other participants do not have that level of comfortableness in sharing yet. So, I need your help to provide the opportunity for others to share. For the next session, if you could, just look at

the questions for sharing and choose one or two that relate to you. At the next session, focus on sharing in response to just those questions, and then we will give the time to others on the remaining questions."

- If a participant begins to share too personally, perhaps with names or details that are not appropriate, you might say, "Please remember that we do not want to talk about people by name and in detail, because we don't want to reveal details that we will regret later. Thank you so much for your help."

Usually, members will respond to your input and adjust for the good of the group. But some may become frustrated and not want to return if they are not allowed to speak as often as they want. In these situations, it is possible to give grace while also ultimately maintaining that your role is to lead the group for the *good* of the group. This means that in situations where an entire group of people miss an opportunity to take the path of healing because one person takes over, your responsibility is to *the majority of the group*—even when it is uncomfortable.

Beyond needing guidance to share, some participants may need direction on how to listen and respond well. One basic rule in this regard is never to allow a discussion in which multiple participants are advising another. As we will learn in the next section, responses given in the form of advice or even stories about "how this worked out for me in a similar situation" actually discourage people from sharing and inhibit their sense of safety.

This is not to say that participants cannot respond at all. For example, validating responses such as, "Thank you for sharing that," "I have felt a similar betrayal," and "I'm sorry that happened to you," are acceptable. However, the intention of this time is to give people the opportunity to express a part of their stories in a safe place. As such, the focus of that time should be on participants' opportunity to *speak*—not on their opportunity to respond.

In addition, as we will also see in the next section, the primary "responder" in the group should be you, the leader. You are the protector of this opportunity for people to bring their pain into the light without comparison, shame, or expectation.

✦ COMMIT TO LISTEN AND RESPOND WELL

One of the most important things you can do to nurture the emotional environment is to listen and respond well. In this section, we will look at principles to help you do both. We will start with a discussion of actions you can take to listen well and then move onto how you can respond.

WAYS TO LISTEN WELL

As a leader, you will spend much of your time listening. This may seem like a simple task, but to listen correctly can actually be difficult. For instance, it's not unusual to realize, while in the middle of a conversation, that you have been distracted or have in some other way neglected to do this "simple" task. So, as you fill the role of protector of the safe space, keep in mind the following:

- **Listen with eye contact.** Give the speaker your full attention. As you listen, think about what is being said. It is not helpful to spend your "listening" time planning what you will do that evening or what you will say to the next person. Do not choose that moment to search for a pen or notebook or to whisper instructions to a fellow participant. As you listen, give your full "mind-attention" to what is being said.
- **Take note of nonverbal communication.** As you listen to a person's words, you are also "listening" to their nonverbal communication. You can tell a lot about a person's emotions by their facial expressions, hand movements, and body posture. Also note these signals in those who are listening. For example, watch for those who seem to want to share but have trouble initiating by raising a hand. All of this is part of "active listening."
- **Model good listening to the group.** You are responsible for modeling good listening to the group and nudging them in the right direction, if needed. For example, if a participant jumps in with assurance and advice for the person who is sharing, this can feel demanding and uncomfortable for everyone, especially for the one sharing, who is now expected to *do* something. In this situation, be ready to redirect by saying something like, "We are so grateful for your sharing, Mary. Our hearts connect with your pain, and we so want to fix it. However, we know that we can't. So, for now we stand with you; we hold your story safe."

WAYS TO RESPOND WELL

Because our responses can open—or shut—the door to more sharing, the way that we respond is important. But it can be difficult to know what to say when someone shares about a difficult experience. Our first response is often whatever we think will make the person feel better. So, we say things like the following:

> "You are going to be okay."
>
> "Everything will get better."
>
> "So many have felt the same way you do."
>
> "We know God has a plan."
>
> "I know exactly how you feel."
>
> "We know that all things work out for good."
>
> "Someday, you will understand why this happened. For now, just trust."

When we really stop to think about these words, however, we realize that some may not be true, and some might simply serve the purpose of pacifying the person in the midst of great pain. In either case, the responses are not helpful. So, how should we respond instead? Here are some guidelines to follow:

- **Avoid the inclination to quickly reassure the person who is sharing.** We often feel an urgency to respond or offer reassurance when people share difficult information. But in our hurry to reassure, we give the impression that we have heard enough and want the sharing to stop.

Our desire to "help" in this way can even sometimes lead us to interrupt the person sharing and speak over them. When we interrupt, we break the speaker's pattern of thought and give the impression that what we have to say is more important than what is being said. It is as if we are stepping on the speaker's words to get to another purpose that we feel is more important.

One exception to not interrupting is when the speaker continues on and on and does not give any indication that they will soon come to a stop. In that case, you might need to make a comment that brings the sharing to a close for that time. You might say something like, "Mary, I can tell that you have much to share about this event. I want to hear more, so I am grateful that we will be spending more time together at our next session. But for now, we need to give others an opportunity to share. We all want to go away today having told a part of our story. Thank you again for trusting us enough to share."

Otherwise, when you feel the urge to jump in quickly with reassurance, one of the best and most basic things you can do is just to mentally pause and think carefully before you respond. If the moment is right for a particular response, it will still be there in a few seconds.

- **Do not be afraid of silence.** Sometimes a participant will take a long pause to collect their thoughts before they continue to share. That silence is okay. Often, when we fill that silence, we break the flow of sharing and sometimes even cause the conversation to go in a different direction.

- **Empathize with the speaker's feelings.** To *empathize* is to share the feelings of another person by putting yourself in their place. However, to empathize is **not** to say, "I know how you feel." Remember that we cannot *know* how a person feels. Even if we have been through the same experience, there will be differences. We will each look at an event from our own viewpoint, and that viewpoint will be based on things like personality, upbringing, education, culture, and so on. This means that each person will have unique feelings and emotions, even about the same event. None of us can empathize—or look at an event from another person's perspective—perfectly, but we can try to come as close as possible. And we will come closest when we set aside our own viewpoints and expectations.

- **Avoid talking too much in response.** It is easy to get involved in giving a response and realize you don't know how to stop! So be mindful and stop yourself when you have the chance.

- **Do not feel that you are expected to give a "spiritual" response.** In a church or religious setting, it is tempting to always give a spiritual response: a verse, a spiritual principle or truth, an example from the Bible, or a personal experience of trust and healing. Avoid this tendency. Although the Bible is our foundation for guidance and hope, these types of "biblical" responses begin to feel like quick answers or even an assignment or expectation. They send the message, *If you do this, all will be well.* Or, *If you do as I did, you will heal in the same way,* and this may not always be true. So, instead, let truths come naturally, as they will, through the sessions. Then allow the participants to discover them and to affirm their own healing steps.

- **Notice your nonverbal responses.** A nonverbal response is one that does not use words, but certainly communicates to the speaker. Consider our facial expressions, for example. While another person is talking, our facial expressions show whether or not we are listening and even how we are listening. These expressions can send messages that are encouraging or unhelpful and even discouraging. Yawning, frowning, and laughing inappropriately are just a few nonverbal expressions that a listener could display that would discourage the person who is speaking. Conversely, a gentle smile, eyes of concern, and even a genuine tear are all positive, encouraging nonverbal responses. You can also respond nonverbally by making eye contact, nodding to show that you understand or hear, or leaning forward.

- **Know that short responses are often enough.** The following are some short responses you can give while a person is sharing to demonstrate that you are invested in their story:
    - a nod of the head
    - a smile or an encouraging look
    - a simple "yes," "hm-m-m," "uh-huh," or "you're doing well"

- **Remember that this time is not about fixing problems.** You are not expected to give the answer to a person's struggle. Rather, think about this time as a gift that you can give to those who are hurting—a gift of permission to express their suffering and find a path forward. Their journey over that path will take time and, on occasion, might even feel uncomfortable, but eventually they will discover truth and help along the way.

- **Do not respond with stories about yourself.** When a person shares a painful experience, we tend to think it's reassuring to tell them we have gone through something similar. There might come a time for such a connection, and this type of connection can sometimes be helpful, but especially in the beginning, people tend to be very protective of their own stories. After all, an event that causes suffering is personal. The pain is personal. The loss is personal. So, when someone is sharing about that pain and loss and another person jumps in and begins to tell their story instead, it detracts from the original speaker's experience, and comparison begins. The person might wonder, "Is my story less traumatic?" Or, "Did they make a better choice?" When we share our own story as a response, we do not intend to create those difficulties for the other person, but they still happen.

- At some point, usually later in the journey, you will likely have the chance to make a simple statement that expresses that you have experienced something similar. Perhaps something like, "Yes, the feeling of being betrayed by someone you love is painful. I remember that I felt great loss." Or, "I hear what you are saying. At one point in my life, I did not think I could go on."

- As you make such a statement, avoid the urge to add "but"—as in, "but then I trusted God, and I gained strength," or "but I let the pain go, and now I am feeling so much better." Those types of responses do not so much encourage as create the expectation for that person to come to where you now are.

- Other opportunities to connect will be revealed as well. God will open doors to these connections at just the right moment—perhaps even in one-on-one situations outside of group time. But as the leader, you must ensure that your story always remains in the background. If not, the door becomes closed to the participant—and opened to you.

Now that we have discussed some inappropriate ways to respond, we can move on to responses that are positive. Here are just a few examples:

"Mary, thank you for trusting us enough to share those feelings."

"I can tell that those were not easy things to share with us. Well done."

"Thank you for sharing those feelings out loud. I'm sure some of us can connect with you."

"Thank you for trusting us with part of your story."

"I can see that this particular lesson really spoke to you."

Often, such positive replies will come naturally in response to something particular that a person has shared. For example, someone may share an event or encounter that compels you to say, "That was something you did not expect in your life. Thank you for speaking it clearly to us." Or, "That is a difficult situation. I don't have words that feel adequate to respond to your pain. Just know that we are so glad you are here with us." And many times, a simple "thank you" is enough, followed by an open invitation for another participant to share: "Who will follow Mary on this question?" As you continue through the sessions and gain experience and confidence, your ability to give these kinds of natural responses will grow.

DISCUSSION QUESTION

Leaders in training should both personally consider and discuss the following question:
Which of the following scenarios do you struggle with most as you listen and respond to others?
- I want to fix the problem or give a quick answer that will reassure.
- I want to share a personal experience that will "help."
- I struggle to set aside all other thoughts to really hear what the speaker is saying.
- I talk too much in my response.

CHAPTER 3
FIND COURAGE, GRACE, AND PEACE

You probably already know that a leader's responsibility to their group is important. But it might surprise you to know that, as a leader, you also have a responsibility to yourself. Like the members of your small group, you are human, which means that you are prone to make mistakes and feel frustration and experience hardship—and as a leader, you face additional expectations and challenges. So, just as you have committed to care for your group, commit also to take care of your well-being. This chapter will show you three ways to do that: you can protect your mental health, give yourself grace, and even find courage and peace along the way.

PROTECT YOUR MENTAL HEALTH

You might not expect it, but it is not uncommon for participants' stories to affect their leader's emotional health. Particularly if you are empathetic, you will feel the pain that is shared, and in many ways, that pain may become a heavy burden. Even the apostle Paul had this experience. In 2 Corinthians, after going through beatings, shipwrecks, rejection, sleeplessness, and many other struggles, Paul says,

> *Besides everything else*, I face daily the pressure of my concern for all the churches.
> (2 Corinthians 11:28; emphasis mine)

Paul felt the pressure of his concern for the people. He felt that burden with a similar intensity that he felt the beatings and the sleeplessness.

Similarly, when we open the door to other people's pain, the awareness of that pain walks into our lives. The crisis is not our own. It is not part of our story in the same way that our own experiences are. But now we are aware of that pain, and it has an impact on us. So, we must figure out what to do with this awareness.

It is helpful to remind yourself of the following truths so that you can lead and encourage others without becoming overwhelmed with their pain:

- "This is someone else's story. Because it is someone else's story, I do not have the provision to carry it as they do. If I take this story as my own, I will add details and layers of pain that come from my own life perspective that may not be connected to the other person but can still affect my own life."

- "If I take this story as my own, I will begin to direct this person rather than walk alongside them."

- "The only one who can handle the transfer of pain and suffering from another person onto themselves is Jesus Christ. My job is to encourage the participant to place her pain and suffering on Him. Thus, my immediate reaction when the pain is placed in *my* 'hands of awareness' should be to open my hands to Jesus and immediately leave it there."

These truths can help us to step back and experience an *awareness* of the pain without taking on the *burden* of that pain. They also help us to move forward *in step* with the participant rather than trying to direct them from afar.

Another reason that you can feel burdened by a participant's story is that you have similar pain in your past. When the participant shares, your memories come flooding back, and along with them come the emotions you felt during that time. Some tears might even flow. That is okay. This response will connect you to the person telling the story, and they will be able to tell that you understand.

Of course, as leaders, we cannot become puddles on the floor. In a sense, we must hold ourselves together. So, if we are emotionally triggered in this way while someone shares, we can immediately seek God's help to keep our connection with the participant rather than retreat into our own pain or take over the story. God can help you do this.

Later, in private, you might need to spend time casting your emotions onto God. Your story is important. Your journey through pain and suffering toward healing is important. And we are all on this journey together. God will help you work through your own suffering as you take the hand of another who is in pain.

GIVE YOURSELF GRACE

As leaders, we want to do our best—not for our personal glory, but for God and for our group. I will assure you now, however: you will not always do your best. You will not always say the right thing or be the best listener or interpret others' stories correctly. No one does. There will be times when you leave a session and think, *Why did I say that?* or *What was I doing?* Give yourself grace.

Most times, when you make a mistake, you can simply move on and learn from the experience. But if your error was serious and you need to rectify the situation with a participant or the group, do so. It's okay to say, "I did not respond the way I wanted to. Let me think about this again."

You will not lead perfectly, but you can lead graciously. That includes accepting imperfection—in the participants and in yourself.

RECEIVE COURAGE AND PEACE

You are reading this book because you feel God's call to come alongside those who are in pain. But you may still wonder if you are ready for the task.

Know that it is normal and right to have some concern and hesitation. In fact, there may even be times while you are leading when you question your ability or feel intimidated by the responsibilities ahead. Remind yourself during these times that you do not need to rely on your own strength; rather, you can depend on the Good Shepherd, who has called you and who is the only one who can bring true healing. He will provide you with courage and peace for the journey.

Perhaps, you can pour out your heart to Him in a prayer such as this one:

I hear Your voice calling me to listen to the pain of others.
Yet, I have my own pain.
I hear You telling me to offer my hands to others as they find their way.
Yet, there are times when my own footsteps are unsure.
I know that I am to offer the truth of Your words to others in their suffering.
Yet, sometimes in the dark, Your voice seems far away and I feel my own doubt.
Perhaps, it is because of my own pain, stumbling steps, and uncertainties that I
can come alongside my brothers and sisters and tell them what I know to be true:
In our pain, we cry out to You and find You there, offering comfort.
When we stumble to find the way,
You shine light on the next step.
When we express our doubts,
You reassure us that You are God.
Help me now to offer myself, but only as a vessel that leads others to You.
Help me to offer reassuring words, but only as they are truth from You.
Help me to offer hope for the future, but only the sure hope of a future with You.
Prepare me, strengthen me, and protect me for my good, others' good, and Your glory.
Amen

PART 2
PREPARE FOR THE JOURNEY:
Recommendations To Help Lead the Sessions

CHAPTER 4
LOGISTICAL INFORMATION ABOUT THE SESSIONS

Now that we have considered the foundational principles that will help us lead, let us shift our focus toward preparing for the small group discussion sessions in Part 3. We will start by looking at logistical details such as when, where, and how often to hold sessions. Then we will discuss how to read the template in which the sessions are presented.

SESSION FREQUENCY AND TIMING

Use the following information to help you develop a session schedule:

- This course has 37 sessions. These sessions provide a foundation on which you can build a plan to suit your needs. (There are seven additional sessions related to children in suffering.)

- The recommended time between each session is 1–2 weeks; however, note the following:

    Experience has shown that 2 weeks is a long time between sessions. If a participant misses a session, it seems extremely long. 1-week intervals keep everyone on task and give the ability to share what is happening through the lessons without too much time passing.

- Avoid including too much in a session or moving too quickly. The gift of the journey will be lost if it feels like an assignment or a quick healing plan.

- The recommended length per session is 1.5 hours.

SMALL-GROUP LOGISTICS

As you begin to think more about the setup of your small group, keep these considerations in mind:

- The recommended size of a small group, which is optimum for sharing, is 8 to 10 people.

- Be aware that there is no coursebook available for participants. However, it is highly recommended that each participant have a notebook for personal use. This will give them a place to take notes and to express their own thoughts and feelings in response to the REFLECTION AND APPLICATION sections. This notebook will also become a source of encouragement and a reminder of truth after the course has ended.

- The sessions in Part 3 should *not* be copied and given to participants as a textbook or workbook. This is because, as you will learn in the next section, portions of each session are intended only for the leader. However, the student worksheets featured among the sessions in Part 3 *should* be copied for group members, if possible.

- As mentioned in the previous section, make sure to choose a location for your small group that is separated from areas where people are walking or congregating. If group members have the perceived threat that others might hear them, they will not feel as free to share.

REMINDERS

The discussion questions and topics in each session have been carefully chosen to provide participants with safe opportunities to tell their stories. Therefore, it is best to keep to the suggested script. This might require a couple of things:

- Be wary of the temptation to hold an open discussion about "whatever is troubling you tonight." Such conversations can quickly lead down a path that actually hinders the progress of healing and destroys the intentions of the group.
- Whenever the conversation strays, gently bring it back. Have the confidence to say, "We are going to stick to the topic of the session and to the questions provided."

Finally, remember that this is not a counseling group. The author does not claim to have counseling credentials, and small-group leaders are not required to be counselors. So, do not present the group or the sessions this way.

THE SESSION TEMPLATE

When you get to the discussion sessions in Part 3, you will notice that they are presented in a specific format. This consistent format is the session template. It is meant to provide you with a gentle, but stable, pathway for leading discussions. The standard layout of this template appears on the next page, along with an explanation for each section

SESSION
SESSION TITLE

GOALS FOR PARTICIPANTS
- This section of the template will provide information to help you prepare to lead the session:

    The direction in which you want to gently guide the participant for that session

    The truth or principle that will be beneficial to healing

    The tool or experience that can assist the participant to move forward with courage and peace

MATERIALS
- Here you will find a list of any items recommended for the session. All participant worksheets and teaching tools listed here will be included at the end of the session.
- Though it will not be listed in each session, it is recommended for each participant to always have their notebook (provided from the start of the class) for taking notes during the lesson.

VOCABULARY
- This portion of the template will introduce words in the main lesson that participants may need a pronunciation and definition to understand, particularly if their first language is not English.

GREETING

This section will prompt you to welcome the participants to open the meeting time. The greeting you use will be unique and personal to each group.

REVIEW

You will use the script provided here to remind participants of the basic themes and lessons discussed in the previous session. Participants may also share any experiences they had as they applied those truths since you last met.

LESSON SCRIPT

The main lesson will appear in this section, written in conversational language to help you share the material in a tone that is informal and comfortable. All of the information for the lesson will be included here, which means no additional research will be necessary.

REFLECTION AND APPLICATION

This part of the lesson provides an exercise such as a worksheet, group discussion, or personal reflection, through which the participants can apply the principles from the lesson to their lived experiences.

COURAGE AND PEACE

This final portion will help you bring the session to a close with calmness and confidence. Because people's minds can become confused and muddled after discussing so many details related to pain and where to go next, this section will suggest words to use to recenter participants and encourage them to continue forward.

> Dot-framed boxes provide information meant only for the session leader—for example, notes on timing, or ideas on how to present certain materials.

> Framed boxes with lines provide space for the leader to write notes
> that will be helpful during the session or to make notes during the session.

The conversations about suffering can be stressful. Some sessions will be more intense than others. This image will alert you that it might be time for a short break—a cup of tea, a walk outside, a song—something to distract the mind and emotions for just a bit. These breaks are not required—use them as you feel necessary for your group.

CHAPTER 5:
RECOMMENDATIONS FOR LEADING THE SESSIONS

As a session leader, you want to create a setting for your group that feels relaxed, unrushed, and welcoming; but you also want to use your time wisely, which means keeping sessions directed and orderly. The trick to balance these two goals is in how you use the session template.

The previous chapter showed you how to read and interpret the various parts of the session template. Now, you will learn how to use those parts, separately and together, to guide sessions in a way that is consistent and predictable but also sensitive to the needs of your unique group.

HOW TO USE—AND NOT USE—THE TEMPLATE

Much of the session template consists of material that you will present directly to the participants—for example, talking points that you will use to teach the lesson or discussion prompts that you will pose to begin a group dialogue. However, the first few sections of the template are meant for your personal use only. These sections, to be read before the session, will help you to prepare.

SECTIONS FOR PREPARATION

As discussed in Chapter 1, if you want to lead well, you must be prepared. For this reason, the first three sections of the template—GOALS FOR PARTICIPANTS, MATERIALS, and VOCABULARY—are devoted strictly to this purpose. You will want to read through these first three parts well before the next scheduled session to make sure that your heart, your mind, and your meeting area are ready at the appointed time.

The GOALS FOR PARTICIPANTS portion can help you prepare mentally for the session ahead. This section brings the upcoming lesson into focus by highlighting its main objectives. Make sure that you understand these objectives up front and then keep them in mind throughout the session, to ensure that the lesson and discussion stay on track.

The second section, MATERIALS, lists the resources that you will need for participants by the time of the meeting. It will tell you, for example, if you should make copies of worksheets or provide writing materials before the session. Make sure to read this section well in advance of your next meeting so that you have enough time to gather the materials you need. It is recommended to provide a notebook for each participant so they can take notes during each lesson. Though this will not always be listed, encourage them to bring this to each session.

The VOCABULARY portion of the template provides a list of terms from the upcoming session that participants may need to have clarified. This list is *not* meant to be read aloud to the group during the meeting; for example, do not simply announce the vocabulary words at the beginning of the lesson. Instead, incorporate the definitions into the lesson, making participants aware of each term and its meaning as you come across it. This will allow participants to connect the definitions with the lessons they learn and understand the terms in a more personal way.

SECTIONS FOR PRESENTATION

The GREETING section is the first section in the template to be used *during* the session. Although it does not provide specific talking points, this section prompts you to start the meeting by greeting participants in a way that is meaningful to them—by talking about a common experience or a recent event, for example. Some ideas for greeting participants include: discuss the weather, mention a challenge in getting to the meeting, or talk about a connection you made to the lessons in daily life.

Next is the REVIEW portion of the template. This section provides specific materials and talking points to be presented directly to participants—in other words, it provides a *script*. *Note that the script is not meant to be read aloud, word for word. Rather, it is intended to provide concepts and wording that you can use to present the material in your own way.*

The script in the REVIEW section will give you words to say to highlight the main ideas of the previous lesson. It will then prompt you to ask participants (1) what they felt and thought in response to the previous lesson and (2) how they applied its truths to their everyday lives. This review should help draw people's minds away from their busy lives and bring them into a calm, focused, common mindset for the session. Make sure to watch the time spent on the review, however; if you remain here too long, you will run out of time to present the new lesson.

The LESSON SCRIPT, which appears next, contains the new material that you will present. Again, do not read the script word for word. Instead, use the thoughts that are given and make them your own. If you need to add to the script, to make it more personal or applicable to your culture, feel free to do so—just be careful not to change the meaning or intent of the truths provided.

After you present the lesson, you will initiate the REFLECTION AND APPLICATION portion of the meeting. This is the time when participants will have the opportunity to express the heart of their stories in a safe place. The script in this section of the template will help you to guide participants through reflection questions, written activities, discussions, and times of sharing.

As such, it might be helpful to start this part of the meeting with a review of the sharing etiquette outlined in Chapter 2. For example, you might quickly remind participants that (1) the focus of this time is on the opportunity to *speak* and not to receive responses or advice, and that (2) although advice and *assumed* connections ("I know how you feel") can discourage further sharing, expressions of sympathy

("Thank you for sharing that" or "I'm sorry that happened to you") are acceptable. We all need these reminders from time to time, but they will become especially important as group members become more familiar and comfortable with one another.

Whenever you pose reflection questions, encourage the participants to write them down in their notebook, so they can refer back to them throughout your discussion and sharing time. (As a bonus, they can also reflect on the questions once the session is over.) Not every participant will respond to every question, and that is okay. Often, our minds and hearts need more time to reflect on these very important conversations. It is *not* helpful, however, to go around the circle, asking each person to share; this only builds anxiety and becomes burdensome to everyone.

Note that, as the leader, you may share periodically during this time, but it is not wise to share in response to every question. When you do share, keep your time brief and without too many details. It is good for the group to get to know you and feel your connection with them; however, this time of sharing is intended to be primarily for them, so it is best to respond only now and again, as it seems appropriate. Also be mindful of the passage of time during this part of the session, and feel free to draw the discussion **to a close as needed.**

The final COURAGE AND PEACE portion will help you bring the session to an end. Through the script, you will encourage participants, in the days ahead, to look for ways that the truths from the session come to life. You may also invite them to reflect on these experiences and to write them down in their notebook, both for their own growth and to share in the next session, if appropriate. For example, did they face a challenge to which they could apply the truth they learned? Or did they experience one of the emotions discussed—and, if so, how did they respond?

The conversations about suffering can be stressful. Some sessions will be more intense than others. This image will alert you that it might be time for a short break—a cup of tea, a walk outside, a song—something to distract the mind and emotions for just a bit. These breaks are not required—use them as you feel necessary for your group.

HOW TO GUIDE TRANSITIONS AND TIME THE SESSION

Do not "announce" when you are ready to move to the next segment. For example, do not say, "Now I am going to do the REVIEW." Rather, transition smoothly from one part of your time to the next so that the gathering feels like a conversation with friends, not a regimented course.

It is also helpful to mentally note the time you spend on each segment. You can do this by noting on paper the estimated clock time at which you want to begin the teaching time and the application time. The teaching time is very important but the time of sharing is necessary for each participant to truly take the journey of healing, rather than simply hear about it.

We care for the participants and their healing journey by caring for their time with respect. Various cultures have different perspectives on "keeping time." It is recommended that the leader be specific in setting a start and end time for the session and then keep to that time. If you have stated that the session will begin at 7:00 p.m. then, as the leader, you must be there and prepared to begin at 7:00. This course will not be effective if the sessions repeatedly begin late and do not keep to time. Experience has proven that if you set the standard of time, the participants will follow your lead.

Related to this idea of timing, you may tailor the length of each lesson and set your schedule to meet your needs. If you are meeting daily, it is recommended to take more than one day per lesson. Too much information in a short time can be confusing. When you use this course to train leaders it is important to give "practice" time to the future instructors. You will need to allow for that in the timing of your training.

As the leader of a small group, you may feel the freedom to adjust the sessions as you observe the participants. Perhaps one lesson is of particular interest and you are aware that the participants need to consider that information, make application and have conversation for longer than just one session. As the leader, you may feel freedom to adjust and take time where it is needed. The session guide is for the benefit of the participants—not a schedule to be strictly kept. In some ways this course is alive—and as such, it can be adjustable as it is used to accomplish the goal of moving forward. Sometimes the pace of forward movement must be flexible.

PART 3
MAKE THE JOURNEY:

Discussion Sessions To Light A Path Toward Hope

SESSION 1
INTRODUCTION

GOALS FOR PARTICIPANTS
- Share our names and one or two details about ourselves, including how long we've lived in the current area
- Understand how to interact with others who will also share details of traumatic events
- Connect with some part of Naomi's story

MATERIALS
- This lesson

VOCABULARY
- **apprehensive** (ap-ri-HEN-siv): uneasy or fearful about something that might happen
- **confidential** (kon-fih-DEN-shul): intended to be kept secret; private
- **falter** (FAWL-ter): to hesitate or waver; to move unsteadily
- **numb** (NUHM): without feeling or emotion
- **similar** (SIM-uh-ler): in common
- **unique** (yoo-NEEK): the only one of its kind; unlike anything or anyone else
- **vulnerable** (VUHL-ner-uh-buhl): open to easily being hurt or attacked

GREETING

> Each session begins with a greeting. This will be unique and personal to each group. Because this is the first session, consider the following as an example:

We are happy to be together for the first time. Much preparation has taken place for us to come to this point. You might still have some questions and even concerns about what our time together will look like. Be encouraged. This is a safe place and you will not be pressured or made to feel uncomfortable. In time, we hope to become trusted friends. It is my hope that you will look forward to our time together.

REVIEW

This is the first lesson, so there is no review.

LESSON SCRIPT

We will get to know each other more as we spend time together over the coming weeks, but for now, we will begin our time by each sharing our name and one simple fact about ourselves. I would also like each of us to share how long we have lived in this area. Maybe some of you have just arrived, and some have lived here all your life.

I will begin.

My name is _____. I have lived in _____ for _____ months/years. *(Make this personal, for example, I started to sew when I was young and I like to sew clothing for women.)*

Take time for each participant to share. This time should not be rushed. However, be aware that there can be a tendency to share added information—and soon the person does not know how to stop. Guide as necessary to keep to the specific questions.

Thank you all for sharing a little about yourselves. As we continue to meet, we'll have opportunities to share more about ourselves and why we're here, but right now, I'd like to expand on this idea of where we come from and where we are going and how those details are a part of our stories. We all have different life paths and different stories, but we also have some things in common. For example, from the time we were all young, each of us had expectations for life—for events we would experience and relationships we would have. As we grew older, however, we were compelled to acknowledge that our expectations would not always be met. In times when they were not met, maturity taught us to accept, adjust—and *move on*. Our survival demanded it, others demanded it, and the constantly changing world around us demanded it.

Even now, as we live day to day, it seems that everything is constantly pulling (or pushing) us *forward*. For some of us, however, it's as if something in our lives refuses this movement forward. Something seems stuck in place—something that, try as we might, we cannot seem to move past. That something is *suffering*.

Some of us have difficulty acknowledging that we have truly experienced suffering. We minimize the experience with words like, "My suffering is not that bad, compared to others,' so I don't want to complain" or "It's okay; it's over now" or "I don't have time to deal with it." But the truth is, there is no scale of suffering by which we can determine its merit for attention. There is no time limit on the effects of suffering. Neither is there only one type of experience to which we can give the title of suffering. Painful experiences include disappointment, betrayal, abuse, grief, unfilled expectations, loss, abandonment, rejection, illness, and more.

Our suffering is our suffering—and by that only, it deserves attention. This is the reason for this study. It gives us the opportunity to acknowledge the suffering in our lives and then to explore it further. You might wonder why we would want to come together to talk about our experiences of pain. We will discuss this more as time goes on, but for now, the short answer is this:

- We know that memories and hidden hurts from our past are causing us pain and trouble in the present.
- We want to rediscover peace and joy.
- If we are to move beyond the suffering, we must care for the wound that is causing the pain.

Unfortunately, it can be frightening and difficult to talk to others about the painful parts of our lives: we might feel that the events that caused our pain are not important enough to talk about, we might be afraid of what others will think about us or our family, or we might simply feel uncomfortable speaking about personal matters. For this reason, we will use the next several sessions to learn how to do the following:

- Value our own stories and the stories of others
- Encourage one another
- Provide a safe place to talk about these difficult topics

Think of this group and our time together as a gift to each of us. The gift is of time and a place of safety where we can share things that are important to us.

Think of it this way: Each person in this group, including you, has a story to tell. Each of those stories is important. Your story and your life are important. *You* are important. And you alone will decide which of your story's details you will share and when you will share them. The other people in the group have stories and lives that are equally important. They will decide the same things about their stories as you will—including when and how much to share. For this reason, we must remind ourselves that *each person's story is theirs alone to tell.* This means that other people's stories are *not ours* to tell. Rather, whatever is shared here must remain **confidential,** or private—it should not be repeated to others outside the group, including to our families or friends.

A person's story is a valuable possession, and when they share it, it is an act of trust. The response to that trust, in turn, can be crucial to that person's healing. Most of us have had the experience of sharing with someone, only to be ridiculed, accused, or ignored. We know how that feels—such negative responses impose guilt and self-consciousness and make us want to slam the door to our hearts shut and never be so foolishly **vulnerable** again. On the other hand, when someone responds to us with respect, patience, compassion, and trust, it creates an emotionally safe environment in that relationship—one where we feel encouraged to share more. And as we share more and trust more, this helps promote our healing.

The ability to share our stories and to listen to other people's stories is a privilege. We must not take that privilege for granted. Rather, we must commit to be trusted "keepers" of others' very special stories. When we do that for one another here in this group, we create an emotionally safe space that protects us all.

This brings us to some guidelines that will help us respect and care for one another as we share our stories and have difficult conversations together:

- When you share parts of your story, be careful not to share details about others that you might regret later.
- Do not respond to others who share by giving advice, comparing their story to yours, or critiquing their ideas. And for sure, not one of us wants to be afraid that someone will ridicule or laugh at us.
- Hold in confidence the stories represented in this room. Do not talk about them even with other participants. This is a gift you give to others—the same gift that others give to you.

When we apply this code of conduct during our sharing time, the results look something like the following:

- We can feel safe that nothing we share will be repeated to others.
- We can be assured that nothing we share will bring rejection, condemnation, or shame.
- We can expect that we will not receive advice on how to fix the situation.

To help us keep this code of conduct, we can remember that the purpose of this group is to offer us the chance for companionship on this journey. Each of us has a healing journey that is one of a kind. We travel at different speeds, encounter different obstacles, and respond in different ways, and we will make many choices on our own as we proceed through this course. Our emotions and challenges are **unique** to each of us, but at the same time, they can be **similar** to what others experience, especially others in this group. And so, we take our individual healing journeys together. We become companions on the same road.

As companions, our job is not to pull each other forward but to walk alongside one another. We do not try to fix or advise each other; rather, we simply become compassionate witnesses of each others' stories. We each focus on our own journey while offering a reassuring presence on the path that we all travel together. So, as we glance around from our unique positions on the path, we see familiar, compassionate faces on the road with us.

Our time of sharing in each session will help us practice our code of conduct and foster this companionship. In addition, each time we meet, we will have a lesson and then some kind of activity to help us apply the lesson to our unique situations. Each meeting will follow a similar program: We will start with a review of the previous lesson, during which time you may share a way that you put that lesson into practice or raise questions you uncovered as you reflected on it. After that will be the time for teaching the new material. And then we will reflect on and apply the new lesson in some way. Sometimes we will work alone on the reflection and application portions of the meeting, and other times we will work on them together. Finally, we will end each lesson with a word of encouragement.

To get the most out of this class, you are encouraged to attend every session. You are not required to complete that session's application in order to attend; however, keep in mind that you will receive from this journey in proportion to the effort and time you give to it. In addition, safety and trust within the group will grow through the consistency of our attendance and sharing.

Are there any questions about the sessions or the **sharing guidelines before we move on?**

Now that we have discussed the particulars of the small-group setting as well as the value of each person's story, and particularly the role of pain in each of our stories, let's look at a story of suffering about a woman named Naomi.

Naomi, just like you, had a story to tell. When Naomi told her story, she didn't wrap it up in a pretty package. She didn't pretend to have answers for her pain. Instead, she delivered it with honest emotion and truthful words. She opened her heart and let it spill forth.

Her story, told in the biblical book of Ruth, is one of sadness and loss. It starts with fearing starvation for her family and then being obliged to her husband's decision to flee to a foreign land. Packing up and leaving everything behind—their family, friends, community, and culture—they travel with two small sons and set up a new home in a hostile environment. Later she becomes a widow. And in time, she experiences the death of both sons.

Left on her own, Naomi goes back to her homeland. And there, she tells her story:

> "Don't call me Naomi," she told them. "Call me Mara, because the Almighty has made my life very bitter. I went away full, but the Lord has brought me back empty." (Ruth 1:20)

Naomi spoke the raw truth about her pain and emotions. Essentially, she said,

"My loss leaves me feeling empty."

"The events of my life taste bitter to me."

"I feel afflicted, burdened."

"I remember how I used to feel, and now that blessing is gone."

Afflicted. Alone. **Apprehensive**. These words describe Naomi's new identity.

Maybe you have felt that way. Maybe you feel that way today. Life tastes bitter. Emptiness invades each day. The despair is tangible.

Listen to these words from Psalms 40:1–3, written by a man named David about his own painful story:

> I waited patiently for the Lord;
>
> he turned to me and heard my cry.
>
> He lifted me out of the slimy pit,
>
> out of the mud and mire;
>
> he set my feet on a rock and gave me a firm place to stand.
>
> *He put a new song in my mouth*, a hymn of praise to our God.

Although this passage does not tell us what happened to David, it does tell us that, at some point, he cried out, lost his "footing," and possibly also lost his "song." It also tells us that God heard his cry, re-grounded him, and gave him a new song—"a hymn of praise."

As we will learn later on, a new song becomes part of Naomi's journey as well, as provision, peace, and even joy reenter her story.

Both Naomi and David express their relationship to God and His presence on their journey—of suffering, rescue, and of healing. Because He is on our journey with us, we will often refer to Him as our Traveling Companion. Watch for ways that He comes alongside to encourage and reassure us. Watch as He gives a firm place to stand and offers the possibility of a new song.

This possibility of having a new song, of having renewed life and hope after suffering, is the foundation for our time together. Without this possibility we would be left to **falter**. We would go through the rest of our days trying to merely survive, when what we desperately long for is to sing again.

If you have experienced deep suffering, you might not see an opportunity to express a new song. You may not think a happy ending to your story is possible. You may even feel **numb**, as if you can experience no emotion at all. Naomi and David would tell you that there are no quick and easy answers; there are no special words that you should say. But there *is* a way forward. You can learn to move away from the pain, through the darkness, and toward hope.

REFLECTION AND APPLICATION

Two important parts of our healing journey are to get to know ourselves and to share our stories. At the beginning of our time today, we started the process of sharing our stories with one another as we told how long we have lived in this area. In revealing other small details about ourselves, some of us may have also discovered ways that we are different from and similar to one another.

Now, let's add to our stories by thinking about this question: When you think of "home," what does your mind see? Is it here in this place? Is it in another place that you have lived? Where is it? Tell us something about that place that makes it feel like home—whether it is in the present or a memory from long ago. These pieces of information help us begin to tell our stories and prepare us for the conversations that we will have together.

> Take time for each participant to share. Always keep watch on the time and guide any participant that does not know when to stop sharing.

Tomorrow morning, each of us will wake up and face our day-to-day life, along with all of its details—schedules and decisions; challenges and joys; work and school; family and community; and much more. Throughout the day, and throughout the week ahead, pay attention to these details as you keep in mind the following questions: What challenges am I facing? What brings joy to my day? What gives me stress? Through this exercise, we can get to know ourselves better, which will give us a good start on our healing journey.

COURAGE AND PEACE

Our time together was good. We listened to each other. We began to tell our stories in a safe place. Listen to this poem that speaks about the importance of why we are here—why your story is important.

>Every person has a story.
>Every story is unique, made of delicately stitched details woven in and out
>with threads of pain, joy, suffering, and comfort.
>Most stories are never spoken:
>unexpressed in human language, never heard by human ears.
>Yet all are valuable. All are known. Treasured and recorded by God.

SESSION 2
BEGIN THE STORY

GOALS FOR PARTICIPANTS
- Begin to tell our story
- Identify positive and negative events in our story
- Understand the meaning of a crisis event
- Identify one crisis event in our story that needs attention and healing

MATERIALS
- This lesson
- Sheets of plain paper; pencils or pens

VOCABULARY
- **calm** (KALM): peaceful; quiet
- **confusion** (kuhn-FYOO-zuhn): the state of not being able to think clearly
- **crisis** (CRY-sis): a crucial time; a turning point; a time of great danger or difficulty
- **relax** (ree-LAX): to rest; to become less tense or anxious
- **scar** (SKAR): a mark left on the skin by a physical wound; a lasting effect of grief or fear left by a traumatic experience

GREETING

Each session begins with a greeting. This will be unique and personal to each group.

REVIEW

Allow participants a few moments to respond after each one of the questions below.

What do you remember about our previous time together?

Last time, we were introduced to Naomi and her story of suffering. Is there any way that you connect with her suffering?

Do you have questions about our time together and why we are beginning this conversation about suffering?

We are starting a journey that is good for our health and well-being. Do you have ideas as to why this conversation about suffering is important for us as we try to find a healthy way forward?

LESSON SCRIPT

I think we can agree that we will need to talk about some difficult experiences and feelings in order to move forward. Gratefully, this group will offer us a safe place to do that. But how do we begin?

If someone asked you to share your life's story, part of your response might be to talk about certain *events* that have happened to you over the years. When we think about it, life is like a story made up of a series of events. One thing after another happens, and there are "ups" and "downs."

> Give each participant a piece of paper and a pencil or pen.
> It is helpful if the leader does this exercise with the participants using paper or a whiteboard.

We understand things much more clearly when we can see them. So, let's draw a picture of the ups and downs of our lives—of our story. Take your piece of paper, and draw a horizontal line across the center.

Now, add a mark at the beginning of the line. This mark represents the day you were born.

Add another mark at the end of the line. That mark represents today.

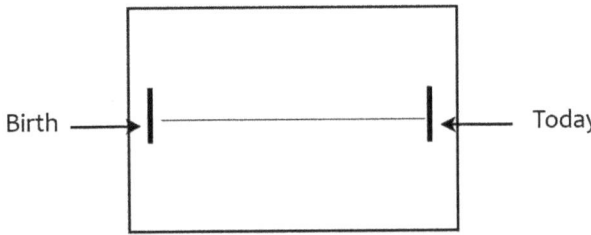

That is a short line for such a long period of time. But it gives us the foundation for our story.

Now, we are going to add some events to this line. Some will be good and some will not be good. Let's all think of one good thing that has happened in our lives, and then write it ABOVE the line. Place it approximately when it happened in your life—early on, in the middle, or recently.

> Allow participants a minute or two to list a good event.

Now let's think of one bad thing that happened. Write that BELOW the line.

> Allow participants a minute or two to list a bad event.

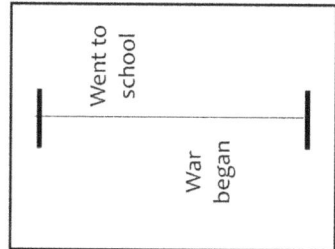

Now do this again for two or three more good events and two or three more bad events. You might be surprised by the moments that are impressed into your memory. Remember, this journey is not about what "should" be or what someone else might think is important. This is your journey, and it is important to respond naturally and truthfully, acknowledging those moments that stir your heart.

> The purpose of this exercise is to help participants see that there have been both good and bad things in their lives. Do not spend time talking about the details of these events. That opportunity will come later. For now, simply have them write the events down.

It might seem strange to put your life on a timeline, and it might seem like a large task to think about all of the events that you have been involved in over years. But now that you have put just a portion of your life on paper, you can really see how each event adds to your story. If you were to tell the entire story of your life this way, the line would be extremely long and you would get an even better picture of how, over time, events shape your life.

It would be nearly impossible for us to tell our entire life's story, however. To try to consider *all* of the events that have happened in our lifetime would be overwhelming. So, as we think about this idea that life is shaped by the events in it, let us try to narrow our focus. In other words, let's zoom in from the immense timeline of our lives to focus on those particular moments that we feel have really left their mark on us.

To do this, I am going to ask you to reflect on some of the life events that went through your mind as you completed your timeline. As you contemplate, I will ask you a series of questions. Do not answer these questions out loud but consider your responses and, if you want to, write them down.

Which moments come up front and center in your mind?

Which events push their way forward, demanding attention?

What *emotions* surface, requiring that you seek out their source?

Are there any moments you recall that seemed to shift you to a place that was unfamiliar—a place where you felt you had no explanations and no answers? A place where you felt you had to scramble for footing, so to speak, but could not seem to find safe, solid ground?

Any moment that you feel put you in such a place is called a **crisis**.

When you are walking through life normally and then something happens to shake you and throw you off balance, that moment is a crisis.

You *feel* it happen. You *experience* it, whether physically or emotionally or both, and it becomes clear that *something* has changed. Whatever words you may try to use to describe this moment, images and emotions like *danger*, *disbelief*, *fear*, and *panic* enter your awareness—and eventually they, too, become part of your story.

In a very real way, life, as you have known it, *stops*.

This is the crisis moment. It is a moment when we are forced to see some part of our lives in a new way —only this new way of seeing feels like a threat to our well-being.

> It is helpful for the participants to have a visual of crisis.
> This particular image will be used in the coursebook.
> You can easily draw a similar image on a paper or white board by crossing multiple lines in the center.
> The participants can draw it as well whenever they want to represent a crisis event.

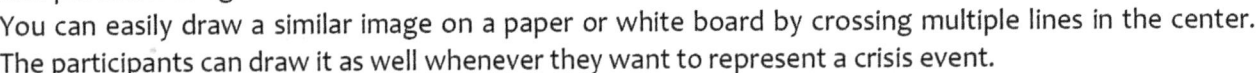

This image represents the crisis moment—the moment that sends shards flying.

> It makes a mark that cannot be erased.

> It grabs our attention.

> And from that moment on, it attempts to consume us.

With this in mind, let's go back to our timelines. As you reflect on your life events, think about what that moment of impact was for you. Let your focus settle on one particular point of impact, one life-shaking event. If you have experienced more than one, try to bring just one of those areas of suffering into focus in this moment, so that you don't feel overwhelmed by several negative events at one time.

As you bring this moment into focus, you may be able to picture when it occurred. If you have not added that event to your paper, you may add it now, below the line. Once you have added it, draw a circle around it to give it full attention. You might want to draw the crisis moment image beside it. Do this by drawing several lines all intersecting in a center point.

> Give group members time to think about this and add an event to their timelines.

This exercise has shown us the truth that *suffering has entered your story.*

Whether your crisis is visible (a shocking event witnessed by others) or invisible (something private that only you know about, so that your lives look to others as if nothing has changed), you know it is there because it has forced you into a new awareness of pain—whether old pain or new pain or ongoing pain that you thought would have come to a close by now. Perhaps this event was many years ago, perhaps, it was recent, or perhaps you are in the midst of it right now. Perhaps, the event happened in the past, but you have only recently discovered how it impacted your life.

Regardless of when and how it happened, you know it is a problem because *something just doesn't feel right*. You *feel* the impact. You are troubled by what has happened. And deep inside, confusion and unrest have taken over.

REFLECTION AND APPLICATION

We have accomplished much today. You have started to tell your story, with its ups and its downs. You have allowed some of your life events to come into greater focus. And you have learned how to identify a moment of crisis.

This attention to crisis and pain can cause us to be anxious. So, now it is time to **calm** our bodies and our minds. To be calm is to become less anxious and more peaceful. It's important to calm our bodies after we think or share about difficult parts of our story, because our minds and bodies have a strong connection. So, when we calm our physical bodies, our minds can also become calm. After working hard we might also use the word **relax**. Our bodies relax—become calm, and then our minds relax—become calm.

It is time for us to learn how our minds and bodies respond to our breathing.

> Mentors, do not be tempted to skip this part of the lesson. This might seem awkward to you at first. This might be totally new to your group members. But experience has proven that participants enjoy and benefit from this time. The breathing exercises will be good for the group members in class and also on their own time.

Anxiety and fear affect the way we breathe. We might not even realize that we begin to breathe more quickly and we take shallow breaths rather than good cleansing deep breaths. This way of breathing actually increases our anxiety and it becomes a harmful circle.

How we breathe impacts how we feel. We can practice how to breathe in ways that help to calm us. Let's think about how we breathe. To inhale is to breathe in and to exhale is to breathe out. Inhale = take air in. Exhale = let air out. When we feel anxious, we breathe more quickly, and sometimes we even hold our breath. We need reminders to breathe in and breathe out, slowly and intentionally.

Maybe you have never thought about it before, but we can control how we breathe. This one simple action can help calm our bodies and our minds.

The following methods can help us take control of our breathing during times of anxiety.

First, put your hand on your chest and feel your heartbeat. Do you feel it? Notice how fast it is beating.

> Now, put your hands behind your head. This opens the large muscle that helps you take air into your lungs. Take deep breaths that fill your lungs and lift your chest. Do this slowly. Continue breathing deeply and slowly. (After about 1 minute)

Put your hand on your chest again and feel your heartbeat. Is it a bit slower?

Now try this:

> Place one hand on your belly and one hand on your chest. Take a deep breath in for four counts and then exhale slowly through your nose for four counts. Notice how your chest and your belly rise and fall when you inhale and exhale. (After about 1 minute)

One breathing exercise uses counting to help us slow down our breathing and calm our bodies when we are anxious.

> In your mind, count to four while you inhale, count to four while you hold that breath, count to four as you exhale, count to four as you hold that breath. Just think 4-4-4-4. Repeat this sequence slowly for two or three minutes. You can repeat this breathing exercise anytime you feel anxiety, fear, or stress.

Inhale	Hold	Exhale	Hold
1-2-3-4	1-2-3-4	1-2-3-4	1-2-3-4

Put your hand on your chest again and feel your heartbeat. Is it a bit slower now?

When we are afraid or under stress, our heart beats many times more per minute than when we are calm. As we took time to breathe deeply and inhale more oxygen, we actually slowed the heart rate—and that is a good thing.

COURAGE AND PEACE

Before we part ways, I want to leave you with a few thoughts to keep in mind over the next several days:

> Every event, spoken or unspoken, is significant.
>
> Every moment, positive or negative, is important.
>
> This life —your life— is valuable.
>
> To become familiar with your suffering will not overwhelm you. You will not be consumed.
>
> Suffering is part of your journey, but it is not your identity.

Before our next session, take some time to look at the timeline you started today. Add one positive and one negative event that happens during our break. And don't forget to breathe!

SESSION 3
OUR COMMON RESPONSE TO SUFFERING

GOALS FOR PARTICIPANTS
- Understand that when we hide our suffering, we cannot heal
- Understand the ways that our bodies respond to unresolved suffering
- Understand that it is okay and healthy to look at our pain
- Understand the meaning of resolution
- Understand that resolution takes time

MATERIALS
- This lesson
- Teaching tool: Crisis to Resolution Parts 1–3
- Participant worksheet: Crisis to Resolution

VOCABULARY
- **infection** (in-FEK-shuhn): the state of being contaminated with disease
- **resolution** (reh-zuh-LOO-shun): the point when a problem is solved; a state of being that is reached when one comes to peace with their problems
- **resolve** (ree-ZOLV): to settle or find a solution to; to bring problems to a place of harmony and peace
- **survive** (ser-VIVE): to remain in existence; to get through or be unaffected by a negative event

GREETING
Each session begins with a greeting. This will be unique and personal to each group.

REVIEW

> Allow participants a few moments to respond after each one of the questions below.

During our last session together, we started to tell our stories by creating timelines of negative and positive events in our lives. Each of us then chose one negative event or feeling that seemed to rise above the rest. How did you feel about that activity? Did you think more about the events on your timeline after that class? Did anything come to mind that you wanted to add? Be sure to keep ahold of your timeline as we continue through this course and feel free to add to it at any time.

LESSON SCRIPT

Last time, we talked about how suffering entered the story of our lives. Ever since that crisis moment, perhaps without even thinking about it, we have probably just done whatever we felt was necessary to **survive,** or to get past the ordeal with as little "damage" as possible.

Usually, when crisis happens, one of our first attempts at survival is to *undo the change*. We desperately want to go back to that place where everything was—or we thought it was—all right. In the midst of our anxiety, we imagine that we must have been safe in that "before" place, and all we want to do is make the suffering disappear. The crisis is there in front of us, but we scramble to make it go away, get it out of sight, or at least put it in a place where it will blend into the landscape.

A common response is to put the suffering in a box, close it, and try to put life back together the way it was—or the way we thought it was.

The process might look something like this:

> Show participants the illustration in Crisis to Resolution Part 1 as you use the script that follows. Point out the parts of the illustration as you refer to them, using the prompts in the script. If you printed copies of the worksheet, you may also hand those out at this point.

You can see the crisis here. It has made a mark that cannot be erased.

As we talked about last time, we know it is there because we feel the impact. Life is suddenly different. It may even feel as if our story has come to a stop. Maybe to others, our lives look as if nothing has changed. But because of what has happened to us, our emotions are troubled. Deep inside, confusion and unrest are changing everything.

One of our first responses is to feel like we want to put our suffering in a box, close it, and set it somewhere out of sight. Then we want to put life back together the way it was before the crisis. Maybe people have even told us to do this. They give the advice, "Just put it aside and move on."

We react this way because we desire **resolution**. *Resolution* is the point when a problem is solved or a person comes to peace with their problem. When we **resolve** something, we make peace with it.

Resolution is a good thing. It is good to come to a place of peace. But, just as important is how we come to that place.

Here is our difficulty: we want to resolve the problem quickly. We want to make everything okay and return to being normal as soon as possible. That way, we can resume living our lives and continue making our story the way we imagined it. There are many reasons we feel this urgency. The most basic reason is that we just want to feel better; it is our instinct to try to avoid pain. Some of us also want a quick resolution for the sake of others—we want to help those around us return to normalcy in their own lives, or we want them to stop worrying about us.

But whatever the reason, the result is that we run so swiftly toward resolution that we don't allow ourselves to truly *feel* the suffering. Rather than making peace with pain, even inviting it into the story, we quickly put it in a box and hide it away, so that we—and others—cannot see it.

This might present a lovely visual to others, but it turns our story inward in a way that prevents our healing and destroys true peace. It leads us to an unhealthy place—an emotional environment that is perfectly suited for infection.

Imagine that you are walking, and you trip and fall. Your leg hits a sharp rock, and it cuts deep. But you do not stop to care for it. Instead, you ignore it and continue with your day. After several days, the wound is infected and sore. So, you put a bandage on it and wear clothing that keeps it out of view, so that no one will see it and be offended.

The skin grows back together, but underneath, the **infection** is still there. Soon, it begins to cause trouble in other parts of your body as well. You get a fever and an upset stomach. Eventually, you seek help and learn that the wound will have to be reopened and cleaned before your entire body can heal. There is no other way to care for your overall health without first giving full attention to *the original wound*.

The same is true for our emotional hurt. If we initially ignore the hurt and do not care for it properly, our hearts and minds and even bodies will respond to the pain in other ways.

For example, we might experience these symptoms:

- Headaches
- Stomach aches or other aches and pains
- Weakness and tiredness
- An increase or decrease in appetite
- Heart problems
- Problems with sleep (too much or not enough)
- Chest tightness and difficulty breathing

This pain can hurt us in other ways as well:
- We may get depressed (always feel sad or not want to live).
- We may no longer find happiness in our work or family.
- We may begin to use alcohol or other drugs too much.
- We might feel irritable or angry all the time.
- We might experience anxiety or a constant feeling of fear.

This means that the emotions we share during our time together may have been hidden inside us for a long time. Perhaps, you have never expressed these feelings to another person, so they remain under the surface, affecting how you respond to others and how you think about your current life.

> Use Crisis to Resolution Part 2 for the next part of the lesson.

It is important for us to understand that *suffering is normal and right following a crisis*. When we suffer, it is because we have allowed ourselves to feel the pain from the wounding event, even though the event itself might be over. It is good and right that we allow ourselves to feel that pain.

And there is no set length of time that we must suffer within. No one can say when our suffering should be over; the experience is different for everyone. Suffering also should not be rushed.

The idea of giving time to suffering might seem unfamiliar to you, even inappropriate. Our natural instinct is to avoid suffering—at all costs! Perhaps your culture tells you that suffering is to be hidden or cared for in secret, or that you must show strength and survival to all who are watching. Although this might sound like a good idea, it does not help us to heal. If we hide our suffering, we will never really be able to **resolve** or come to peace with the crisis that changed everything.

That is why our journey of healing through this course will help us consider how to suffer in a healthy way—a way that is good for us. During this course, we will not rush toward resolution. Instead, we will focus on giving attention to the pain and allowing ourselves to feel it. Only in this way, over time, will we be able to make peace with the suffering. Yes, we will eventually come to resolution, but it will not come as a quick fix. Resolution is not achieved through one determined jump, but through many small steps.

> Use Crisis to Resolution Part 3 for the final part of the lesson below.

Let's look at the path of resolution in this image. Notice that it is not a straight line. Rather, there are ups and downs.

Resolution often begins with small steps. We start by making peace with some part of the suffering, but other parts of it still hold power over our lives. During our journey, there will be times when we feel like we have come to peace with a part of the crisis, but then we suddenly feel confused and angry again. This is a natural part of the process. Eventually, when we do come to peace, it will mean that we are coming to resolution with *the way life is now* and *not the way life used to be.*

We will find how important it is to understand that life will never be the way it was before the crisis. And we will learn that if we continue to try to *re-create* that old way life, we will find ourselves attempting to undo things, hide things, replace things, cover up things, and maybe even rewrite the story of what actually happened—and we will remain stuck in an unhealthy place. In fact, when we try to recreate what life once was, our *new reality* will always, eventually and inevitably, come to the surface, and the crisis will repeat its initial hit, as if the moment of impact is on continual replay: the accusation or disappointment or betrayal will happen again and again.

The good news is, there is a better way. We will know that we are beginning to travel down this better path, that we are beginning to heal in a healthy way, when we are able to make peace *with the way life is now.*

Before we move on to learn about this better way, though, I want you to hear this truth:

The stories of our lives do not stop when crisis comes and things change. The crisis is *part of the story. The suffering and pain are part of the story . . . part of your story.* Even the changes are part of your story. And this story is the one that we must learn to embrace.

REFLECTION AND APPLICATION

Look around the room very carefully. What do you see that is a danger to us right now?

> Give participants time to think and then ask for their responses. Usually, someone will mention a potential danger, saying something like, "There could be a fire on the roof or in the hallway," or "a storm could break the windows."
>
> Listen for the word *could.* Then respond as shown below.

The fact is that *nothing is a danger right now.* Anything that we mentioned that "could happen" is actually not a reality right now. Even if it happened, it would take place in the future. But right now, in this minute, this hour, you are SAFE.

You are safe at this time. You are safe in this building. You are safe with these people.

During a crisis, we are afraid; and there is reason to be afraid. But after a crisis, or a trauma, we sometimes continue to feel afraid. It feels like everything is dangerous. We feel unsafe everywhere we go and with everyone we see.

So, it is important for us to stay in the *present.* We must stay in what is *now.*

God gives us many instructions about fear. Listen to this assurance from God: "So do not fear, for I am with you; do not be dismayed, for I am your God, I will strengthen you and help you" (Isaiah 41:10).

Now, take three long, slow calming breaths. Breathe deeply as we learned last time. Allow the muscles in every part of your body to relax. Listen to the sounds around you. Be very still until I tell you to open your eyes.

> Sit still for three to four minutes. Do not talk to them during this time, but follow your own instructions. Be a model for the behavior you want to see in them. After this pause, continue with the following.

If you feel afraid this week, stop and ask yourself, "Is this really a danger to me right now, in this place?" If you are in immediate danger, get help. If there is no danger right at that moment, then calm yourself. To **calm** is to remove that feeling of fear and to feel peaceful. How can you calm yourself?

1. Remember God's promise to you from the verse we just learned. If you would like, I can repeat the verse so that you can write it down.
2. Do the breathing exercises to calm your body and emotions:
   - Inhale (count 1-2-3-4) and exhale (count 1-2-3-4) slowly and calmly.
   - Pay attention to your body as you breathe.

COURAGE AND PEACE

God knows our tendency to feel anxious and to fear. This is why He speaks to us patiently and often repeats His message to us:

> "So do not fear, for I am with you; do not be dismayed, for I am your God, I will strengthen you and help you" (Isaiah 41:10).

CRISIS TO RESOLUTION PART 1

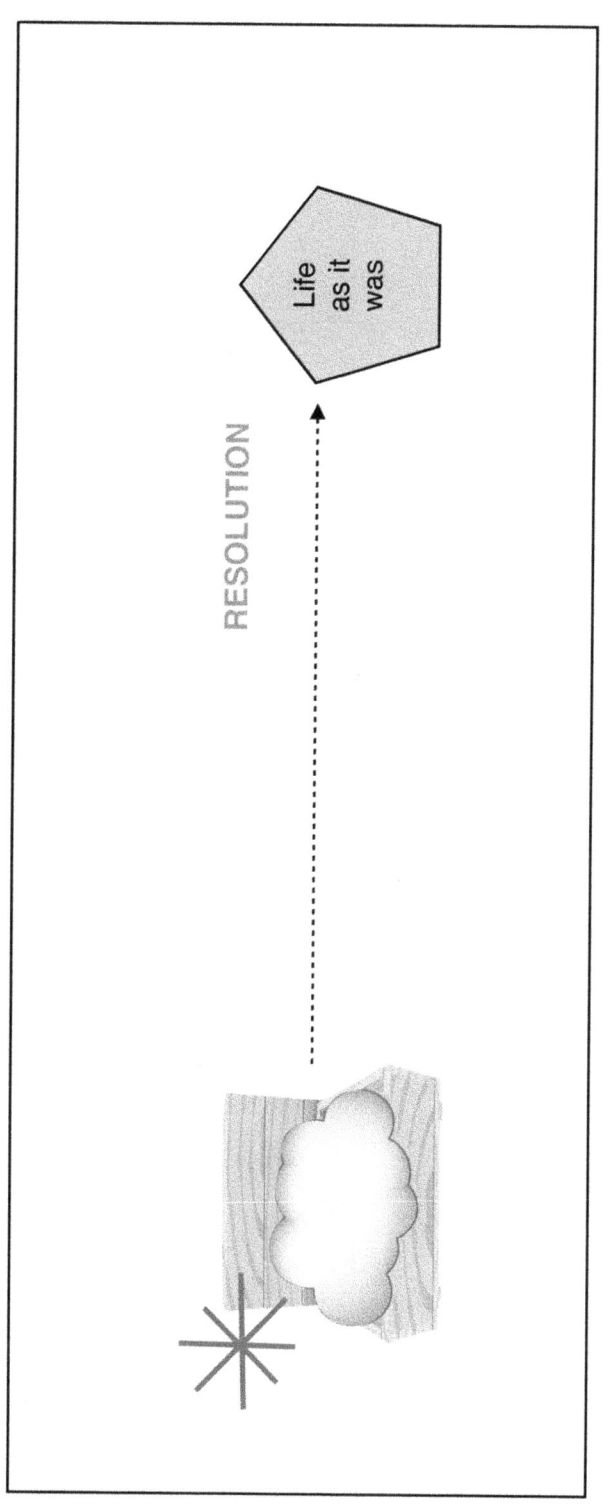

CRISIS TO RESOLUTION PART 2

CRISIS TO RESOLUTION PART 3

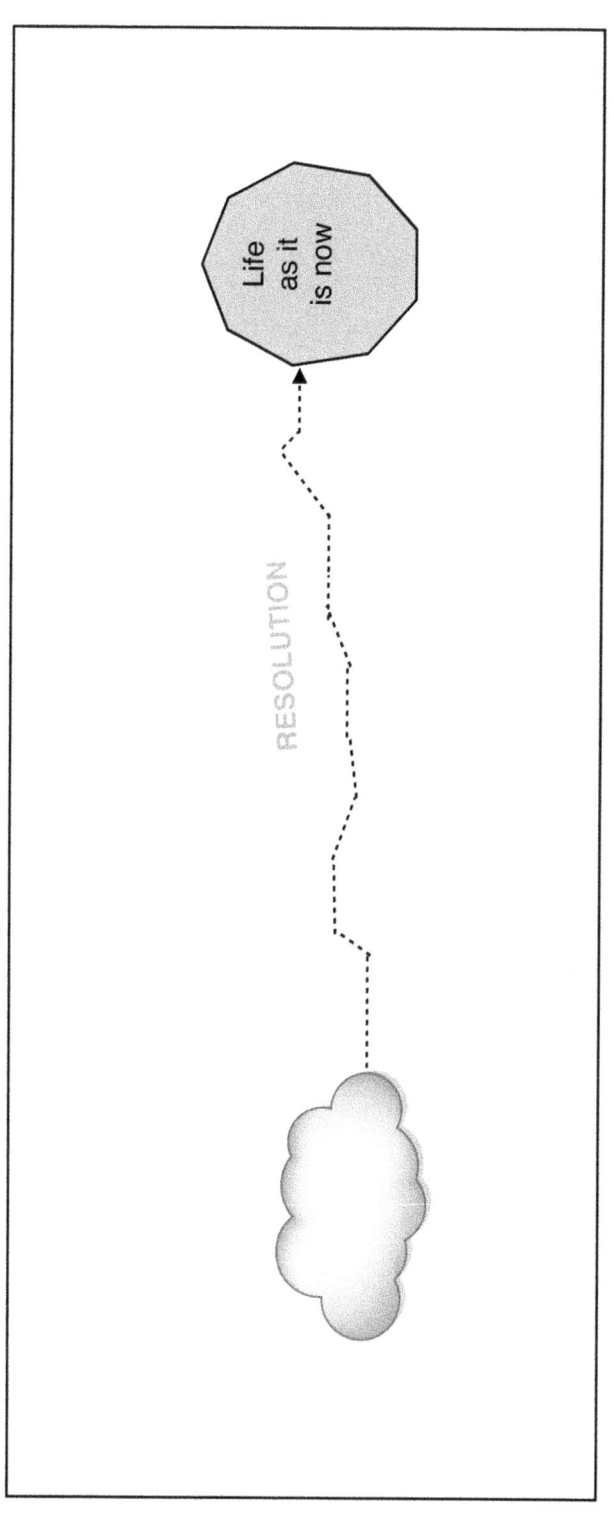

CRISIS TO RESOLUTION

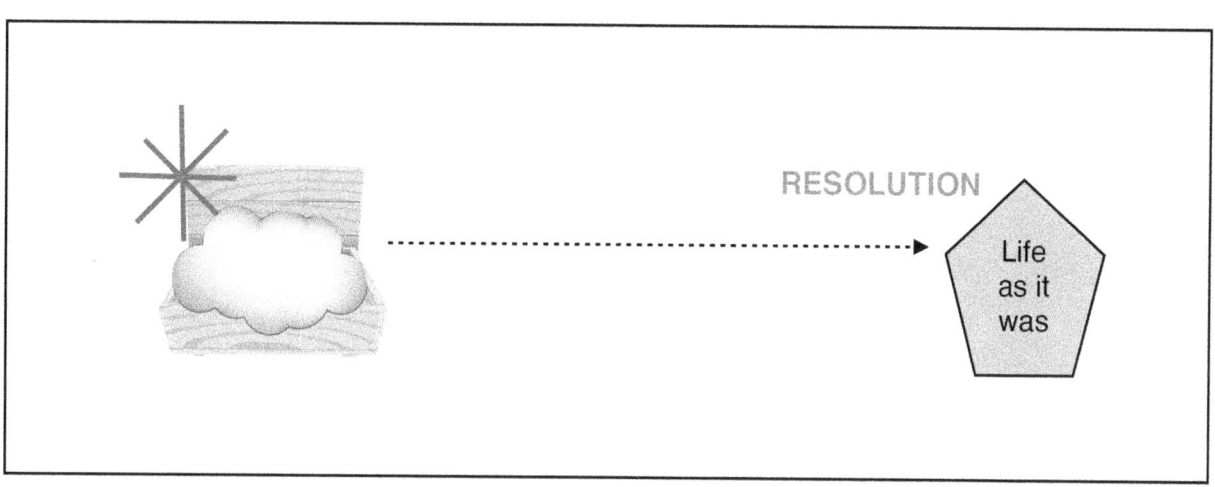

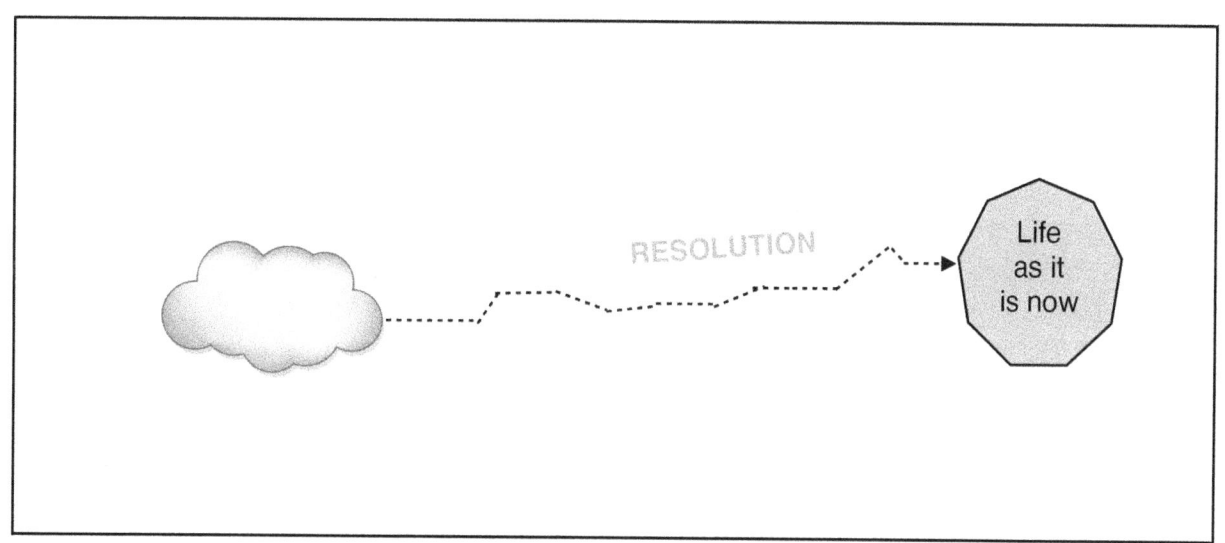

SESSION 4
HOW DO I FEEL?

GOALS FOR PARTICIPANTS
- Use a visual image to identify our feelings of suffering
- Express our emotions in words

MATERIALS
- This lesson
- Participant worksheet: How Do I Feel?

    NOTE: The images in this worksheet are arranged so that you can print one page, front and back, for each participant. If it is not possible to make that many copies, print about half that number and have the participants share. The images in this book are in black and white. If you would like color versions, contact Thrive Life Skills for a free PDF.

VOCABULARY
- **emotions** (ee-MO-shuns): feelings (for example, love, hate, fear, or anger)
- **express** (ek-SPRESS): to show or demonstrate a feeling in words or actions; to communicate

GREETING

Each session begins with a greeting. This will be unique and personal to each group.

REVIEW

Allow participants a few moments to respond after each question below.

The last time we were together, we learned about our desire to resolve our problems, or come to resolution, quickly. Do you recall our definition of *resolution*? Do you remember how it can hurt us to pretend that everything is okay?

It might seem like we should run from or hide our suffering, but what should we do instead, though we might not feel like it at the time? We learned that when we take time to suffer, we can more easily move forward.

LESSON SCRIPT

To allow ourselves to suffer in a way that is healthy, we want to be able to talk about the **emotions** and thoughts we had at the time of the crisis as well as those we have now. But this is not easy. It is difficult to know how to talk about these things.

We may know how our emotions *feel*. We may even be able to close our eyes and *see* what our emotions look like. But we still struggle to **express** those feelings to others. To *express* something is to show it to others, either in words or in actions.

When we try to express our feelings by talking about them, we are often limited by the words we have to choose from, like *sad, hurt,* or *angry*. The words do not do justice to the intensity and depth of what we feel, including what we sense physically, mentally, and spiritually.

This is where pictures can help. Pictures give us a way to express emotions that we cannot describe with words —and, as such, they help us tell our stories.

That's why this part of our healing journey provides images. You can use these images to help open the door labeled, "How do you feel?"

We do not have much teaching time today because we want to give most of our time to sharing.

> Hand out copies of the worksheet How Do I Feel? and then use the script below.

REFLECTION AND APPLICATION

Look through these pictures and silently pick out one or two that you feel express your emotions the best. Then, one at a time, we will tell the group which images we chose.

As you look through these pictures, note the following:

- Allow yourself to connect truthfully to the picture from that place deep within. Your inward responses might surprise you.
- There is no need to study all of the images. Instead, let particular ones speak to you.
- Be compassionate with yourself and encourage self-honesty.
- Avoid correcting yourself. This is a time of true expression, not right or wrong.
- The images portray men and women, old and young, and people from various cultures. Don't let the identities of those portrayed guide your responses. Rather, connect with the action, the perspective, or the feeling that each image opens in you.

- Do not feel the need to explain why the image speaks to you as it does. This experience is meant to simply open a path of connection between your feelings and your words. If it leads to words, good. If not, good. Either way, the connection from suffering to expression has been traveled, and that is the forward movement you want.

> Give the group a few minutes to look over the pictures. When it is time to share, remind the group of the following:
>
> - It is okay if multiple people choose the same picture. If one person chooses the same as you—you can also speak about it on your turn. It is also okay if two people see and feel something very different from the same picture.
> - As each person shares, it is important to listen carefully and to honor their feelings. No feelings during this time are right or wrong—they just *are*.
> - This is not a time to give advice or to correct. This is a time to listen. This is the time when each of us can develop a feeling of safety and confidence in this place.
>
> Allow time for all who want to share. Guide as needed when a participant speaks too long.

COURAGE AND PEACE

The images that we viewed today—which helped us express emotions such as sadness, fear, and even anger—were not what we would call *beautiful*. Some of the images were difficult to look at, and yet, they expressed our emotions so clearly.

Consider the following encouragement that beauty is still a part of your life—even during suffering.

> Read the following poem to the participants.

Even in the emotions of suffering, there is beauty.
The heavens declare the glory, and the skies proclaim the work of the Creator's hands.
Day after day, they pour forth understanding; night after night, they reveal knowledge.
They have no speech, use no words; no sound is heard from them.
Yet, their voices go out into all the earth, their message to the ends of the world:

Beauty has not been destroyed!

HOW DO I FEEL?

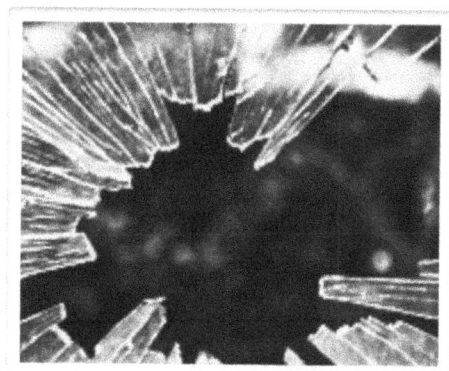
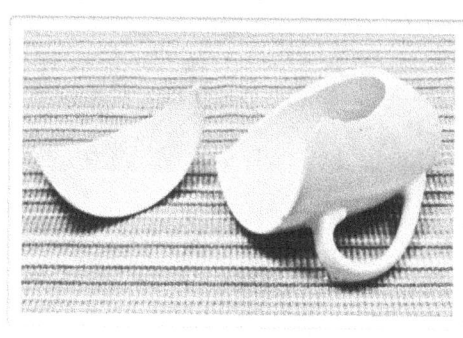

SESSION 5
BECOME FAMILIAR WITH SUFFERING

GOALS FOR PARTICIPANTS
- Understand the meaning of trauma
- Become familiar with the characteristics of trauma
- Recognize the characteristics of trauma in our lives

MATERIALS
- This lesson
- Participant worksheet: The Characteristics of Trauma

VOCABULARY
- **characteristic** (kair-ik-tuh-RIS-tik): a trait or quality that identifies a person, object, or idea
- **familiar** (fuh-MIL-yer): well known, recognizable
- **impair** (im-PAIR): to weaken or damage
- **manipulate** (muh-NIP-yuh-layt): to influence, especially in an unfair way
- **recognize** (REK-uhg-nyze): to identify something or someone through knowledge of its characteristics
- **trauma** (TRAH-muh): the negative after-effects of suffering; one's state of being when suffering overpowers their ability to function in a healthy way

GREETING

Each session begins with a greeting. This will be unique and personal to each group.

REVIEW

We used images to help us express our feelings and emotions about suffering during our last session. Was this new to you? Did the pictures help you express the way you feel inside?

LESSON SCRIPT

To think and talk about our own suffering can be difficult and confusing. That's because our suffering is the result of crisis. Crisis events, by their nature, are overwhelming and cause us not to think clearly. They also make us feel powerless to move forward in life. In other words, these events not only wound us; they also hinder our ability to properly care for those wounds.

As a result, the wound does not heal. Instead, it goes deeper and begins to spread. This deepening wound can affect our sleep, our appetite, our relationships, our work, and even our physical health. When this happens, we experience something beyond the immediate crisis—we experience **trauma**.

Trauma is a word that is commonly used in conversations about suffering and healing, but it might frighten you to think about using it to describe your own experience. For example, maybe you have heard someone say about you, "This person has experienced trauma" or "This person's community has experienced trauma." Perhaps, this word has been used to describe your experience so often, in fact, that you feel *trauma* is part of your identity.

But what exactly does this word mean?

Trauma is the negative after-effects—or the negative "after" picture—of the crisis moment. Think of it this way: the initial crisis event causes the *onset* of suffering, but over time, that suffering deepens and eventually sets into our souls, resulting in pain and confusion that can infect and influence our lives in the days, months, and even years that follow. In this way, the effects of the initial crisis reach areas of our lives that were previously untouched by the event.

TRAUMA = **The Initial Crisis + All of the Pain and Confusion that Follow**

If your suffering not only touches but seems to overpower your responses to current life, then you are experiencing trauma.

Because trauma takes over the control center of our emotions, responses, and decision-making, we become unable to function in a healthy and positive manner in the present. So, even though the initial moment of impact is in the past, we continue to feel its influence now—on our sleep, appetite, relationships, work, and even physical health.

One of the goals of this course is to help us talk about our suffering in a way that is healthy. But what does that mean? How do we know if we are processing pain in a way that is healthy—or not healthy? The answer to that question is found in understanding the role of trauma in our lives.

Let's go back to the example of a physical wound. We know that if we do not properly care for a wound, it does not heal but gets worse and begins to spread. But let's say we do tend to the wound and eventually, it heals—and when it does, it leaves behind a scar. That scar is visible evidence to us that we experienced the wound and that the wound has healed. It is a mark that stays with us for years, sometimes even for life. It also serves as a reminder of our past wound—and the event that caused it. But what it does *not* do is to continue to hurt us in the present.

In the same way, when we care for our emotional suffering in a healthy way, we may be left with emotional, spiritual, and sometimes even physical scars—places in our lives where healing has occurred and left marks. These marks will remind us of our past wounds and the crisis that caused them (and in that way, the crisis will remain a permanent part of our story); however, these marks need not cause us more harm—either now or in the future.

The presence of trauma in your life means that *the after-effects of the initial wound are still causing you harm*. Trauma prevents healing. Trauma reopens the wound time and time again, and then spreads, infecting outlying areas that were previously healthy and causing the pain to feel more intense.

Trauma takes control—and it always wants more. The good news is that when we process trauma in a healthy way, we can begin to take back this control. We can regain control over the areas of our life that are impacted in the present, and we can regain control over the way our story will play out in the future. To do that, however, we must first **recognize** the presence of trauma in our lives—because only then can we call it to accountability. In other words, we cannot deal with suffering until we first accept that it is here.

God's servant Paul, who experienced many crises in his life, shows us a good example of how to do this:

> But we have this treasure in jars of clay to show that this all-surpassing power is from God and not from us. We are hard pressed on every side, but not crushed; perplexed, but not in despair; persecuted, but not abandoned; struck down, but not destroyed. (2 Corinthians 4:7–9)

Do you hear the truth in His words? He admits that there is pain and trouble. He acknowledges that there is suffering and confusion. But he does not let the pain take control; instead, he turns to God for strength and hope.

God, too, knows that we face trials and suffering. That is why He gives us related instructions and encouragement, not only here in 2 Corinthians but in many places throughout His Word.

When we recognize the presence of trauma and pain in our life, we become ready to form one of our best defenses against it—and that defense is to become **familiar** with trauma. This might sound like a bad idea at first, until you consider that the things that are mysterious or unknown frighten us the most.

With that in mind, let's talk about the five main characteristics of trauma and some of the negative ways it affects our lives.

Characteristic #1: TRAUMA IMPAIRS OUR MEMORIES

To **impair** is to weaken or damage. Trauma weakens our memories in a way that can confuse us. This is not to say that we are telling untruth or that we misunderstood or that something didn't really happen. It happened! But trauma tends to dump all of the memories into a large bucket and then challenge us to pull them out in perfect order and detail. In the process, the sequence of events, names, dates, and exact words can easily become intertwined in a way that confuses us and others. Confusion is part of trauma's hold on us, and it often causes us to shut down, losing confidence and clarity.

There is more. Trauma causes us to forget, or set aside, most positive things. We forget our accomplishments. We forget our strengths. We forget our hopes. We forget anything good that happened during the time of suffering, even if it was unrelated to the particular event that caused our pain. We see the past and the future through the invisible veil of pain, fear, and other emotions that suffering created.

Characteristic #2: TRAUMA CHANGES OUR VIEW OF OURSELVES

A common trauma response is to blame ourselves for the crisis event. "I should have done . . . " and "Why didn't I do . . . ?" are common phrases we use in our conversations with others and with ourselves.

We also tend to lose confidence in ourselves and have difficulty making decisions. *Am I imagining this?* we wonder, or, *Am I crazy?* Or, we think, *I cannot trust myself.* We might become overly self-conscious and think that others are looking at us. We might also feel unable to cope with the simplest of tasks and decisions.

Finally, in many ways, we seem not to know ourselves anymore. We can almost feel as if we are on the outside looking in. We struggle to balance self-defense with self-accusation and self-pity with self-anger. One moment, we think, *I don't need anyone,* and the next moment, *I do not want to be alone.*

Characteristic #3: TRAUMA CHANGES OUR VIEW OF OTHERS

Trauma separates us from others. We begin to withdraw into our own world of pain, reasoning, self-conversation, and survival. We also tend to think that everyone else is just fine. *If I could only be in that position,* we think. Or, *No one has ever experienced what I am going through.*

We might avoid sharing with others, because we assume they won't have time to listen or will think we are crazy or looking for attention. Or we might share altered versions of our story to make it seem more acceptable or reasonable to others.

We might define others as foes, using illogical judgment to misinterpret their words or nonverbal behavior to be negative. We might not be able to trust anyone. Or we might trust people too easily!

Characteristic #4: TRAUMA MANIPULATES OUR RESPONSES

Every one of us responds to current situations based on our life experiences. Often, we are aware of this reaction as it is happening and can even control our response. However, trauma complicates things. It can **manipulate** us into responding in ways that we might not otherwise. To manipulate is to influence unfairly.

How does trauma influence us unfairly? The process starts during the crisis event, which we naturally experience through one or more of our senses (smell, taste, sight, touch, and hearing). Whether we are aware of it or not, our brains connect particular sensory experiences—for example, a sound we hear, a scent we smell, or something we touch during the crisis—with that devastating event. Much later, after the crisis has ended, we may hear a similar sound, detect a similar scent, or feel a similar texture, and it can take us mentally, without warning, back to the initial crisis. In an instant, we feel that we are there again.

This sensory connection becomes a trigger that sets off negative emotions, and our response flows from that previous experience rather than from our current reality. Usually, this response is unconscious—that is, it is not a response that we have thought logically about and intentionally decided upon; it is much more immediate, often beyond our control.

Some triggers are obvious and expected; others catch us by surprise, and we have no chance to put up a defense. Either way, things that were harmless before now seem to betray us unexpectedly.

Trauma is clever in its manipulation, but it is illogical—based in past experiences and not in the current reality.

Characteristic #5: TRAUMA'S ATTACKS ARE ROOTED IN FEAR

Trauma's manipulation does not take us to a confident and joyful place. The trigger, the reminder, the confusion—all take us to a place of fear. Robbed of our logic, we feel vulnerable. We become terrified that the same painful experience will happen again. We fear that it will have the same impact and inflict the same suffering, and we think, *I barely survived before. I cannot feel that again.*

Fear can be debilitating, paralyzing. Fear can attack suddenly, or it can grow from a tiny seed that begins with the smallest of reminders. Fear is a powerful tool that trauma uses to undermine and immobilize us. Why? Because, it works almost every time.

These five characteristics create a kind of "profile" of trauma. It is important for us to know these characteristics, so that we can recognize when trauma is using its tactics against us and firmly begin to disarm it.

REFLECTION AND APPLICATION

> Hand out copies of the Characteristics of Trauma worksheet.

Think about the characteristics of trauma that we discussed today.

Which of these cause(s) the most difficulty for you in everyday life?

Which have you encountered recently?

> Allow participants time to respond to the questions above.

Through the coming week, use your worksheet to make a note of times when you encounter some of these threats from trauma. Be specific.

COURAGE AND PEACE

At this point in the course, you may find that you are doing something that you have never done before—intentionally getting to know pain, and particularly *your* pain. As you go through this process, you might feel at times like you are getting weaker, even coming undone.

But the truth is that you are gaining strength. You are gaining courage. You are acquiring truths that will help you move forward, toward healing. So, stay on the journey.

We are not all in the same place on this road, but we can see each other, and we know we are not alone.

CHARACTERISTICS OF TRAUMA

Characteristic #1: TRAUMA IMPAIRS OUR MEMORIES

Characteristic #2: TRAUMA CHANGES OUR VIEW OF OURSELVES

Characteristic #3: TRAUMA CHANGES OUR VIEW OF OTHERS

Characteristic #4: TRAUMA MANIPULATES OUR RESPONSES

Characteristic #5: TRAUMA'S ATTACKS ARE ROOTED IN FEAR

SESSION 6
A PICTURE OF SUFFERING

GOALS FOR PARTICIPANTS
- Look closely at suffering
- Show events and emotions on paper

MATERIALS
- This lesson
- Plain paper; pencils or pens

VOCABULARY
- **embrace** (em-BRAYC): to receive and accept willingly; to hold close
- **emotional** (ee-MO-shuh-nuhl): showing emotions; reacting or responding based upon how one feels rather than upon facts and details
- **intimately** (IN-tuh-mit-lee): a way of being or doing that suggests a close and trusting personal relationship

GREETING

Each session begins with a greeting. This will be unique and personal to each group.

REVIEW

Allow participants a few moments to respond after each question below.

We talked about trauma during our last session. Have you ever been confused about that word in the past? What about now? Did the lesson help to clarify the idea of *trauma*?

We discovered that *trauma* is not the event that happened in our lives. Rather, it is the pain and confusion that settle in after the event and hinder our ability to live in a healthy way. Do you know that feeling? Do you feel there are times when the suffering takes over the control center of your thoughts and responses?

We also learned last week that it is good for us to be familiar with the characteristics of trauma so that we can protect ourselves.

LESSON SCRIPT

We have covered some important ground on our journey so far.

- We briefly visited some events and emotions that have made up our story, both before and after suffering arrived on the scene.
- We became familiar with the idea of suffering and learned that we must allow ourselves to see it and give attention to it in our own lives: *Yes, there it is. I acknowledge that suffering is part of my story.*
- We then became familiar with the characteristics of trauma in our lives. Trauma refers to the prolonged pain, confusion, and upheaval that follows the initial onset of suffering.

Now, it is time to move closer: It is time to connect not only with the *idea* of suffering in our life but with the actual events and emotions of that suffering, as well.

The initial event. Those first emotions we felt. The period of suffering that has followed. How do we begin to express all that is within us?

To start, we must come to know our suffering more **intimately.** In fact, we must learn to **embrace** it. Maybe it seems odd to you that we would want to hold our suffering close. But suffering is an important part of your story. Your suffering is *your* suffering and no one else's. When you become more familiar with it and claim it as your own, then you can learn to talk about it openly and, best of all, without fear.

To become more intimate with our suffering, we can look at it and express it in different ways—in ways connected to our other senses. Last time, we learned that we are connected to our suffering by more than just human-defined words; we are connected through our sensory experiences, as well—this is how trauma triggers negative reactions.

In a previous session, we connected our emotions to pictures. Images help us express our pain. This kind of expression can be **emotional** for us. It can pull up anger, bitterness, fear, loss, and other negative emotions, which is why we often want to avoid it. And yet, it is good to bring those emotions to the surface, where we can experience them and make peace with them.

This time, however, instead of connecting to an image that someone else has created, we will create our own picture.

REFLECTION AND APPLICATION

> Hand out a blank piece of paper for each participant, along with pens, pencils, markers, crayons, and/or colored pencils.

What would it look like if you put your emotions into your own visual image?

Today we will allow our hands to express some of what we see and feel within, using them to create visuals on the page. These visuals might be . . .

- simple pictures,
- words,
- colors, or
- markings on the page that say, "I am here. I feel pain."

Use colored pencils, crayons, markers, or whatever you want to add pieces of your suffering to this page. You might sketch an image of something that relates to your pain. Or you might use only colors and shapes to express your emotion.

There are no rules or requirements. There is no need for others to interpret your picture. This expression of your suffering is for you alone. This opportunity to contemplate and express your pain is *by* you and *for* you. Only *you* need to understand. No other picture can look like yours because yours is unique, just as your suffering is unique to your experience—it is *your* suffering and no one else's.

As you express parts of that suffering in a visual image, you not only become more familiar with it but claim it as your own. You learn to express it openly, without fear.

Listen to your heart and your emotions. Then, allow your hands to draw as you express some portion of your story.

> Allow sufficient time for participants to complete this REFLECTION AND APPLICATION exercise.

COURAGE AND PEACE

As you travel this journey of healing, sometimes you will feel strong and sometimes you will feel undone. No matter how you feel, be reminded of these truths:

> You are a unique and intentional creation by the Perfect Creator.
>
> You are declared valuable by the Perfect Creator.
>
> You are seen. You are known. You are loved.

Later this week, take some time to look at your picture again. Perhaps, there is something that you can add to the image.

SESSION 7
LIFE AS IT WAS; LIFE AS IT IS NOW

GOALS FOR PARTICIPANTS
- Understand the significance of the way life was (or how we thought it was) and the way life is now
- Identify the differences between the way life was (or how we thought it was) and the way life is now
- Understand how we hinder our healing when we try to put life back the way it was

MATERIALS
- This lesson
- Plain paper; pencils or pens

VOCABULARY
- **eventually** (ih-VEN-choo-uh-lee): finally; at some later time
- **hinder** (HIN-der): cause difficulty; delay

GREETING

Each session begins with a greeting. This will be unique and personal to each group.

REVIEW

Last time, we expressed our stories visually, in various ways. Perhaps you do not consider yourself an artist, and yet you were able to put some expression of your pain on paper. Any effort you made was a positive step forward—because every time we reveal a bit more of our pain, we heal a bit more.

We are ready now to look honestly at the reality of life, both before and after the moment of impact. Let's do that together.

LESSON SCRIPT

At one point, we may have pictured our lives—or some part of our lives—in a particular way. We probably had certain expectations and hopes. And then circumstances changed, fears became reality, and those expectations fell apart. Now, we are faced with a life that is no longer as it was—or at least it is no longer the way we *thought* it was. This is a difficult reality to accept, but it is important:

Life will never be exactly the same as it was before the suffering entered our life.

Imagine that you are in your house. You open a door and rush through it into the next room, only to hit your leg on the edge of a table, because the table was not where you expected it. In pain, you stumble, fall to the floor, then look around the room to find that someone rearranged the furniture. You do not like this new arrangement, so you decide to ignore it. You move on and forget that things have changed.

The next time you rush through the door, you repeat the experience—you hit your foot again, get hurt again, and fall again—all because you failed to acknowledge that things were different now. This is what it is like when we do not accept that *life has changed*. We may not like the new arrangement, but if we pretend that things are the same as always, we set ourselves up to stumble and get hurt again.

If, however, we accept this new arrangement, we will know to step through the door more cautiously next time and to survey the room before we enter. We will keep ourselves from repeating the same mistake and feeling the same pain.

This is an extremely simple illustration. It does not begin to touch the levels of pain, destruction, and change that have happened in your life. But it does help to describe an important truth on this journey: If we want to heal, we must look closely and honestly at what has changed in our life, and we must accept that those changes happened. If we deny the changes or live as if nothing has happened, things will continue to stand in our way, make us falter, and cause us pain.

That said, let's spend some time honestly looking at the changes that have occurred in our lives. We must look at them *honestly*, because steps toward healing are built on *truth*. Honesty requires that we set aside the expectations of others and the fears we may have held for many years, and we open our minds to accept truth—because truth is what gives us courage to move forward.

First, let's think honestly about life as it was. Perhaps, that life wasn't truly what we imagined it to be at the time. Perhaps, we only saw it for what we hoped it would be. When things in our life do not look quite how we want them to, it is quite normal for us to readjust those things in our minds to create a picture that we feel is more acceptable. If we want to heal, however, we must take an honest look at the way things were—not at the way we imagined them to be.

Next, let's think about the way things are now. We have already discussed that it is not healthy to put our suffering in a box. Instead, we can honestly acknowledge that it is there and become familiar with it. Once we acknowledge our pain, we find that it is easier to come to peace with the reality that this pain is now part of our story. We do not feel that we need to recreate life as it used to be, but instead accept *the way life is now . . . with the scars, the wounds, and the pain.*

Coming to peace with this "after" picture is important, because, if we to try to *recreate* life as it was or as we imagined it to be—either in real life or just in our minds—we find ourselves attempting to undo betrayals, hide the effects of abuse, replace losses, cover wounds, and rewrite the script of suffering. And as we saw in the example of the rearranged furniture, this actually makes the suffering worse. **Eventually** and inevitably, we end up face-to-face with the reality that things have changed, and the crisis repeats its initial hit. In some cases, the moment of impact seems as if it is on continual replay: Accusation, again. Disappointment, again. Betrayal, again.

In our reflection and application time today, we will do an exercise that helps us to compare life as it was to life as it is now. But before we get to that, let's discuss one final truth that we must be open to accept: that truth is that *resolution is a journey*. As humans, we are naturally drawn toward resolution; we like that feeling of putting things back together again. When we are hurt, we express this by attempting to quickly reassemble our lives so that we can move forward as soon as possible. But rushing to resolution can actually hinder our healing and peace, because it denies the truth that real resolution comes slowly by slowly.

Resolution is a process. To achieve it, we must balance two ways of thinking:

>We want to avoid the demanding expectation to heal—right now!

>We want to avoid giving into despair and defeat—and giving up.

In other words, we accept that this is our journey, while we give ourselves grace for the journey.

REFLECTION AND APPLICATION

> Give each participant a plain piece of paper and something to write with.

Let's talk about how life now is different from the way it was before the crisis. It is important for us to clearly identify the changes that have occurred, because we cannot heal from those things that we do not see or intentionally avoid.

At the top of one side of your paper write THE WAY IT WAS.

At the top of the other side of your paper write THE WAY IT IS NOW.

Look honestly. Do you remember how life looked before—or at least how you imagined it looked? Maybe you can think about how you had hoped it would be.

Now, look just as honestly at the way it is—the way it became after your crisis event. Or, the way it is now that you see the truth. How is life now different than what you had hoped it would be?

Express the differences you see on each side of the paper.

These might be very practical differences, such as . . .
- changes in where or how you live,
- changes in your physical condition or abilities, or
- changes in your job or how you earn a living.

Or these might be differences in . . .
- your relationships,
- your faith,
- what is possible in your future, or
- what you believed to be true.

It also might be changes in what is possible for the future, such as . . .
- special events—weddings, birth of children, graduations

If you don't have words to describe what you are feeling, draw or sketch the changes you are feeling instead. Avoid getting distracted by other questions, such as "Why?" "What if?" or "What do I do now?" Avoid everything but *the honest expression* of the "before" and "after" pictures of your life.

COURAGE AND PEACE

Many things around us are changing—even people are changing. However, we have this assurance about the Good Shepherd who walks with us in our suffering:

> Jesus Christ is the same yesterday and today and forever. (Hebrews 13:8)

It's wonderful to know that we have one thing—one person— that will never change!

SESSION 8
DISCOVERING LOSS

GOALS FOR PARTICIPANTS
- Understand the reality of loss
- Acknowledge loss in our lives
- Understand the need to grieve this loss

MATERIALS
- This lesson
- Plain paper; pencils or pens

VOCABULARY
- **grieve** (GREEV): to feel grief because of loss or suffering; to be sorrowful
- **loss** (LOSS): the act of losing something or someone; the absence of something that has been lost; the feeling of grief when something of value is taken away
- **minimize** (MIN-uh-myz): to make smaller in value or importance
- **mourn** (MORN): to express grief or remember with sadness something or someone that was lost
- **vague** (VAYG): not clearly expressed or felt

GREETING

Each session begins with a greeting. This will be unique and personal to each group.

REVIEW

Last time, we talked about how life is different now than before the point of impact. It is also likely different from what we expected. For some of us, the point of impact was an actual event; for others it may have been a bit of information that we received or a realization we had—something we didn't know before. In either case, it is important for us to see clearly how life is different now.

In our previous exercise, we wrote or drew about the differences in life before and after this point. Maybe since then, you thought of additional ways that life changed, and you may continue to come up with such differences over time. You can add those to your paper as well. The important thing to remember is that we did this exercise because understanding and accepting how life is different now will actually help us move toward the future in a healthy way—without carrying wrong expectations with us. Today, we are going to build on that conversation by looking at one part of the "after" picture that all of us likely have in common: that part is **loss**.

LESSON SCRIPT

We have been talking together about suffering in *our lives*. And although we are all on this road together, this conversation that we have is also very personal to each of us. Consider how many different stories of crisis and suffering there are just in this group. If we were to talk to others around the world, there would be millions more of these stories. Further, the details of each story are very different. And yet, with all of these varying stories and details, there is one consequence that is present in almost every trauma—and that is loss.

Think of it this way: When a crisis occurs, seeds of suffering are sprinkled into our lives. Out of these seeds, roots sprout. Immediately, these roots grasp for a stronghold under the surface, and when they find one, they hold on tightly. Soon, evidence of the seeds of suffering is revealed above ground, through the growth of unique leaves and flowers. Although the resulting plants may resemble one another, no two of them are exactly the same. The tiniest details of their outgrowth express their uniqueness, just as our stories reveal our individual expressions of pain. Under the surface, however, these plants share one particular root of suffering. That common root is loss.

We might recognize it immediately, or it may take some time—but, in every trauma and in every painful emotion, something is gone. It is missing. And in its place is an absence, or a void. This is *loss*.

There is more than one definition for the word *loss*. It can be defined as the act of losing something or someone or as *the feeling of grief that results* when that something or someone is gone. In its most basic form, this word suggests *the absence of* something or someone. But especially when it comes to suffering, that absence is not *nothing*. Absence is *something*. It is tangible to our spirits, our souls, and even our bodies. We can *feel* absence. There is a common expression I learned when I lived in Nigeria: "I went to your house to see you, but all I met was *your absence*." In other words, absence is not merely the lack of something; it is *something* all on its own.

As we begin to recognize and accept that life looks different now than before the crisis, we are likely to discover loss. Loss becomes evident when we compare the "before" and "after" pictures of life and find that, in the latter picture, something valuable is missing.

However, it is not enough for us to discover this missing piece—this absence; we must also try to figure out *what* it is that we have lost. We must look for the thing that is missing.

But if something is gone, why go looking for it? Especially when doing so is painful? Why not just let things be or, better yet, snip that root of suffering—that loss—so it cannot cause us more grief?

Think about the death of a loved one. Can you imagine if we never mentioned that person's name again? If we refused to talk about her, quickly replaced her, and put away anything that reminded us of her? That would be so sad and very unhealthy. By not recognizing the sadness and the loss we felt in her absence, we would hinder our ability to process grief and find healing.

Loss *IS*. Loss demands our attention. If we are to heal, we must identify it and give it the attention it desperately needs. Doing so is neither a statement about our well-being nor an attack on it. Quite the contrary, it is a gift of love and caring that we can give to ourselves when we ask the hard questions: "What am I missing? What was taken from me without my permission?"

Let's acknowledge what is gone. It is a loving conversation to ask ourselves to acknowledge and talk about something that is causing pain in order to help us heal.

So, where do we begin?

1. **First, we must acknowledge and identify the loss.**

It is fairly obvious to us that things have changed since the crisis. But what have we lost as a result? Let's go back to the example of entering the room where the furniture was rearranged. This time, consider that it was a storm that rearranged everything. The first time you rushed through the door to that room, you hit your leg on a table and fell to the floor in pain. Imagine if, instead of leaving the room right away, you decided to stay and try to put everything back where it was before it was rearranged. You push the table back to its original spot, along with the couch and a chair. You re-hang two pictures that had fallen. Then you stand back and survey the room to realize that something is missing. As you try to recall the room's previous arrangement, the details become fuzzy. Was there a second chair? Was there a table by the chair? There are parts of the room that are now gone and some you cannot even remember!

This confusion is a part of our suffering. The missing pieces—whether they went missing after the crisis or were never actually there in the first place—are *our losses*.

Some losses are obvious. It is easy to see what we have lost when a fire takes a house, when war or disease takes a life, or when a thief takes possessions. These losses are visible, and we recognize them clearly. However, such obvious, visible losses—although important—can take over and conceal less evident layers of loss. In order to heal, we must acknowledge the full extent of the loss, which includes all of its many layers.

After a housefire, for example, one might be so consumed with finding a new place to live or with repairing damages that once immediate needs are met, the person assumes the problem is solved. But in reality, additional problems—some hidden, some **vague**—still need attention. **Perhaps the victim suffers from the emotional loss of safety or the disappointment of destroyed items that carried precious memories. There is also the anxiety of change now required to move on.**

If that person goes back to "life as normal" but does not identify the additional areas that need attention, they will cause even more trouble down the road. To identify those additional layers, to identify the true extent of the loss, takes time, honesty, and effort, but it is a valuable part of the journey. It is part of cleansing the wound.

Sometimes, there are no obvious layers of loss. There is no visible expression of what is gone. We cannot point to an item or a person and say, "That was here, and now it is gone." Here are some examples:

- A person who is abused loses a sense of protection, trust, and value.
- A man who must flee for his life as a refugee or displaced person loses his sense of strength and honor as he also loses his ability to defend his family.
- Alcoholism leaves a path scattered with the loss of identity, value, courage, and security.
- The breach of a precious relationship sweeps away one's sense of safety and trust.
- The loss of a child includes the loss of hopes and dreams for grandchildren and momentous occasions.

Such hidden, intangible losses are powerfully intrusive, destructive, and consuming, and the list of invisible losses that we can experience is long and painful, so it is vitally important that we take the time and effort to identify them in our lives.

Perhaps, you have discovered some of these less visible losses in your own experience. Let's take a moment to share. As we do, note that we may have some losses in common, while others may be unique.

Allow the participants to share.

2. **Second, we must respond to the loss without trying to replace what is missing.**

Much of the suffering that we feel after trauma (for example, sadness, anger, and fear) is our response to loss. Perhaps, we lost trust, relationships, or our sense of safety. Maybe we lost hopes and dreams for a future that we feel is no longer possible. Or maybe we feel that we lost years of our life because we devoted them to something or someone that is no longer here. Whatever the case, loss creates intense negative feelings within us, and our instinctual reaction is to defend ourselves against them. This type of reaction is called a *defensive response*.

We have all responded defensively at some point in our lives. It is our instinct to put up a defense anytime we perceive a threat to our well-being. But when we try to protect ourselves against loss and suffering, these defensive responses often play out in one of two ways:

a. We **minimize** or downplay the loss, saying things like,

> "It isn't that bad,"
>
> "I don't need that,"
>
> "I will be fine. I will just rebuild,"
>
> or
>
> "Others have it worse than I do."

> In some cases, we may even minimize the loss of others. A woman may say to her friend who has lost a child, "Be grateful that you still have two other children." Or an adult may say to a girl who was abused, "I know someone who had a much worse experience than you. Be grateful your experience was really not so bad."

> But these types of "assurances" do not calm the ache; they only make people feel guilty. They silence our expression of pain, but they do not silence the pain itself. Deep inside, we still *feel the absence*. Something or someone has been *taken away against our wishes,* and no attempt to minimize it will change that reality.

b. We attempt to replace whatever we lost as soon as possible.

> For example, a mother who has lost a child might want to have another child immediately. Or after the loss of a relationship, someone may quickly try to fill the void. Our instinct is often to swiftly rebuild the house or cover the scars. But when we try to replace what we lost too quickly, we only cover up the pain—we do not heal it. We also make poor decisions when we focus on filling the emptiness. So, the choices that come from this instinctive reaction to protect ourselves actually lead to more suffering.

Defensive responses are natural, but they are not helpful. They only keep us from "seeing" the full extent of loss and suffering. But to heal, we must honestly see the loss and grieve for it. To **grieve** is to *feel the loss* of something or someone. When we grieve, we allow ourselves to *feel the suffering* that we experience from that loss in order to heal from it.

It is normal and healthy to grieve. However, some people feel that grieving is wrong. Some believe that to grieve is to complain or be dissatisfied. Others say that if we truly trust God, we will not grieve or feel loss. These beliefs are *absolutely not true*. How do we know? Let's look to Jesus as our perfect example.

Do you know that Jesus grieved?

We know that Jesus lived a perfect life while on this earth. He did not do anything that was displeasing to God. But listen to this: "Jesus wept" (John 11:35). Why? One of Jesus's dear friends had died. Jesus knew about the resurrection of life after death. Jesus even knew that He was going to bring His friend, Lazarus, back to life that very day! And yet, real tears welled up out of real loss. They flowed from a heart that connected intimately with the pain of others.

Jesus grieved because He felt the *loss* of Lazarus, His friend. Jesus also felt the loss for Lazarus's family and loved ones, as they experienced the absence of their brother and friend. He did not tell Himself and everyone at the grave, "Put on a brave face. There is no reason to be sad!" Jesus *felt* the pain that death brings. He was comfortable to *feel the emotion* and then to *allow the overflow of that emotion to be expressed and seen*.

And this was not the only time Jesus expressed feelings of loss. On the night Jesus was arrested, He was praying to His Father because He knew the betrayal and the physical and emotional suffering that would come upon Him. Listen:

> Then Jesus went with his disciples to a place called Gethsemane, and he said to them, "Sit here while I go over there and pray." . . . Then He said to them, "My soul is overwhelmed with sorrow to the point of death. Stay here and keep watch with me." (Matthew 26:36, 38)

Jesus grieved at the events to come, and to describe His sorrow, He used the words "overwhelmed . . . to the point of death."

Jesus felt loss from the friends and followers who would betray Him, from those who would run away rather than stand with Him in His pain. He felt loss because those who should publicly recognize Him would instead turn on Him and cry out for His death. Loss upon loss befell—even for the Son of God—and He grieved these losses to the point that "his sweat was like drops of blood falling to the ground" (Luke 22:44).

This is a good example of how the heaviness of loss can even press in on our physical bodies, provoking them to respond in unusual and sometimes violent ways. Jesus must have felt a great heaviness from loss and sorrow for His physical body to respond in such a powerful way.

In Jesus's life, just as in ours, suffering planted the seed of loss. When that seed came to life, Jesus did not keep His emotions hidden from others but expressed it in actions and words that resonate with us even now. If Jesus feels and expresses sorrow, then we may feel the freedom to do the same. And more than that, we can connect with Jesus in our loss—because, in His loss, He first connected with us.

This is not the only place in God's Word where the experience and expression of suffering are spoken about. In fact, there are many such references. Take the following verse, for example:

> There is a time for everything, and a season for every activity under the heavens . . . a time to weep and a time to laugh, *a time to mourn* and a time to dance. (Ecclesiastes 3:1,4)

There is a time for us to experience and express the loss—even loss that can seemingly overwhelm us to the point of death. *There is a time* to stop and feel and express. During this time, it is neither wise nor advisable to rush blindly down the road in a desperate effort to escape.

When we grieve, we declare the existence of the suffering. When we grieve, we open a channel for cleansing.

The Word also tells us that when we grieve, we step onto a path where we can encounter *comfort*. True comfort. Not empty promises. Not sweet sayings. Real comfort that touches our soul. What is the source of this comfort? The source is "the Father of compassion and the God of all comfort, who comforts us in all our troubles" (2 Corinthians 1:3–4).

In other words, God wants you to express and communicate your pain to Him so that you can find comfort. In fact, His compassion is how He wants to be known by you!

Perhaps, you have been rebuked for your tears. Perhaps, at times, your tears have even brought derisive laughter and anger from another. Be assured: God will not respond to your pain this way. God's responses to us when we cry out do not incite fear or embarrassment. Neither our pain nor our expression of that pain are unnoticed or discarded. Instead, God responds as He did to Hezekiah: "I have heard your prayer and seen your tears" (2 Kings 20:5).

Listen to the way David wrote about God's response to his own cries: "Record my misery; list my tears on your scroll—are they not in your record?" (Psalm 56:8). In another passage, David wrote, "I am worn out from my groaning. All night long I flood my bed with weeping and drench my couch with tears . . . the LORD has heard my weeping" (Psalms 6:6, 8).

Your tears are not unheeded. They will not be set aside. Quite the contrary, your tears are part of the story—precious and valuable. God reaches for them, holds them, and keeps a record of them in His book.

In fact, God, our traveling companion, captures and protects *all* that we share. Nothing is missed or disregarded. Nothing is left on the floor to be swept away.

Quiet your heart and listen:

> He heals the brokenhearted and binds up their wounds. (Psalm 147:3)
>
> The LORD is close to the brokenhearted and saves those who are crushed in spirit. (Psalm 34:18)

God reveals His compassionate heart by how He sees us: the brokenhearted, the crushed in spirit. That sounds like One who grasps what the suffering has done to your heart, your spirit, and your soul. That sounds like One who knows your pain and is giving you freedom to *feel* those very emotions.

Finally, God not only gives you permission to mourn; He also *feels* the pain of your grieving. He puts Himself in your place:

> For we do not have a high priest who is unable to empathize with our weaknesses . . . Let us then approach God's throne of grace with confidence, so that we may receive mercy and find grace to help us in our time of need. (Hebrews 4:15–16)

REFLECTION AND APPLICATION

In our search for ways to heal and move forward, we must acknowledge loss and take time to mourn it. Let's take some time to think about that.

Maybe you have never thought carefully about what you lost through your experience of suffering. As we explored this idea today, maybe you thought of some things that you had before the crisis that you feel you no longer have. Or maybe you remembered possibilities that you once saw for your future that are now no longer possible. Perhaps, nothing came to mind. Either way, think about your responses to these questions to help you explore loss in your own experience:

- What was once here that is now gone?
- What has been taken from me that I did not willingly give?
- What empty places do I see . . . or sense . . . or feel?
- What do I reach out to grasp, only to find that it is no longer there?
- What might have been possible, but no longer is?

> Give time for the participants to write in response to these questions.

You may not have any or all of the answers to these questions today. That's okay. Awareness can still come in the days and weeks ahead. In fact, our awareness of loss often comes when we least expect it. It can be as simple as walking into a room and suddenly feeling the absence of someone or something. If this happens to you, write it down. It is good and right to give value to these losses by noticing them and even preserving them.

Also know that some losses that come to your awareness might surprise you—however, each one is real and wants your attention. So, do not ignore what comes to mind.

COURAGE AND PEACE

Your path is unique.
Take time to think about the blessings and the challenges,
    the joy and the suffering,
        the bright skies and the dark clouds.
The Good Shepherd is leading you . . . even through great, unexplainable loss.

SESSION 9
THE EMOTIONS OF LOSS

GOALS FOR PARTICIPANTS
- Understand that loss can bring strong emotion
- Acknowledge negative emotions in response to loss

MATERIALS
- This lesson
- Participant worksheet: Emotions of Loss

VOCABULARY
- **absorb** (uhb-ZORB): to take in or soak up
- **deny** (dih-NY): to declare something to be untrue; to refuse to believe or accept that something is true
- Also see the list of emotions within the lesson script

GREETING
Each session begins with a greeting. This will be unique and personal to each group.

REVIEW
Last session, we discovered that loss is a common root of suffering for all of us. We know the feeling of loss. Something was there, it was real, it was at least possible—and now it is gone.

Although we experience different kinds of loss and respond to those losses in different ways, we learned that it is important for us to acknowledge this loss and feel it, rather than try to pretend that all is okay.

We also talked about this in a personal way, putting on paper the losses that we feel. Once we "saw" this loss, we might have experienced some very strong emotions in response! Now it is time to think about what to do with those emotions of loss.

LESSON SCRIPT

Loss brings feelings that might surprise us. These emotions can be difficult to explain. We might even have a mix of emotions that confuse us. It is good for us to talk about these feelings because they affect us every day, even if we are not aware of it. Feelings of loss "stir up" other feelings.

Have you ever seen a ball of string or yarn that was all tangled? One long, connected piece weaving in and out and around. It's a mess!

We can feel that way sometimes—like a tangled mess of emotions. One minute we feel rejected and the next we feel relieved. One day we feel lonely and the next day we distrust anyone who tries to help.

We each have our own tangle of emotions. So, let's try to unravel those emotions a bit and talk about some of the feelings we discover.

> Hand out copies of the worksheet. However, have the participants refrain from completing the worksheet until you complete the following exercise:
>
> Read each word on the worksheet (also listed below). Ask participants to think about the words and notice which ones they feel a connection with. Then ask them to share briefly about the feelings that certain words bring—not necessarily as related to the crisis event, but in general. Many of the emotion words listed in the worksheet will be familiar to them, but some may be new to some participants. Note that the purpose of this exercise is not to help participants learn definitions but to help them connect with the words that describe their emotions. This connection will give them a way to express how they are feeling later in the course.
>
> Note that many of the words listed are similar to each other in meaning, but one word might bring a connection for a person that another would not. For example, one person might connect to *anger* while another might connect more closely with the feeling of *rage*.
>
> The definitions of each word are provided below. You do not need to read the definitions out loud; instead, you may refer to them if participants ask about the meaning of certain words. When you are finished with the exercise, continue with the script below this box.
>
> **Abandonment:** left alone; forsaken
>
> **Anger:** outrage; displeasure; wrath
>
> **Anxiety:** worry; fear
>
> **Betrayal:** deception; a breaking of trust
>
> **Bitterness:** resentment; holding a grudge
>
> **Confusion:** uncertainty; a feeling of not understanding what is happening
>
> **Depression:** a heavy heart; hopelessness
>
> **Despair:** depression; discouragement
>
> **Disappointment:** sadness because one's hopes are not met
>
> **Distrust:** not able to trust others

Dread: to think of with fear; to be anxious or worried about

Emptiness: without hope or purpose

Envy: discontent; a longing for what someone else has

Fear: terror; distress

Guilt: a feeling of having failed or done something wrong

Helplessness: a feeling of being weak and powerless

Hopelessness: without hope; an inability to see the possibility of good

Hurt: pain; injury; agony

Jealousy: resentment of what someone else has

Loneliness: a feeling of being alone, without friends or protection

Loss: the death or absence of something; the experience of losing something; the emotion that results from the absence or death of something

Numbness: a lack of feeling; an inability to express emotion

Pain: suffering; discomfort

Panic: extreme fear

Rage: wrath, extreme anger

Regret: to be sorry about; to feel sad about something that was done

Relief: release; deliverance

So many feelings! These are all emotions that we experience when grieving and healing from loss, but as we can see, some of us feel stronger connections to certain words than to others, depending on our experiences.

We respond to these emotions in a variety of ways. One response we all have in common, however, is **denial**. Denial is not an emotion but it is a reponse to the emotions that we feel. Denial is refusal to believe that something is true. We do this when an event is so painful that we cannot accept it. Denial can be dangerous because there is no way to heal if we deny that the event happened. Some of us might even deny that we are having negative emotions. We then begin to live in a world that we have created in our imaginations—a version of the world that we can accept.

It is better to accept that suffering happened and to feel all the other emotions that come with it than to deny the loss and keep it all in a box. We will never heal until we face the emotions we feel from the loss.

So let's use the worksheet now to help us think about some of these emotions in our own lives.

REFLECTION AND APPLICATION

Look carefully at the words on the tangled ball of emotions. Think about your own feelings and emotions. Use a pencil to color in the space around the words that express how you feel about the loss you experienced. Remember, you may feel many of these emotions. Color all of the words that you connect with. There are also empty spaces if you want to add some words of your own!

After you are done, let's all share one feeling from our tangled ball of emotions.

> Give participants time to complete the worksheet. Then give each participant an opportunity to share one emotion they colored.

Now that we have all shared, write this statement at the bottom of your worksheet and fill in the blank: "Sometimes, when I think about my loss, I feel _____."

COURAGE AND PEACE

You have been working very hard. The emotional and even physical strength needed for this journey is undeniable. That's why we are here to give courage to each other. And although you may not see it, you are growing stronger—we are all growing stronger together.

EMOTIONS OF LOSS

SESSION 10
TELLING GOD ABOUT MY SUFFERING

GOALS FOR PARTICIPANTS
- Understand that we can express our pain to God without fear
- Hear the words that David expresses as he suffers
- Write to God about our personal suffering

MATERIALS
- This lesson
- Participant worksheet: Write A Psalm

VOCABULARY
- **distress** (dih-STRES): great pain, anxiety, or sorrow
- **fathom** (FATH-uhm): to comprehend; to understand; to measure the depth of
- **refuge** (REH-fyooj): a place of safety or shelter from danger
- **stress** (STRES): burden, anxiety, pressure

GREETING

Each session begins with a greeting. This will be unique and personal to each group.

REVIEW

Maybe you did not realize that there were so many emotions until our previous session. Perhaps you had not recognized some of those emotions in yourself until after we last met. Even when those feelings are negative, we discovered that it is good for us to speak the truth about how we feel. The simple statement, "I feel _____" is an act of courage that helps us gain strength.

There is another thing we can do with our innermost feelings to help us gain strength, and that is to share them honestly with God. We touched on this briefly in one of our previous sessions, but we will talk about it in more depth today.

LESSON SCRIPT

We began this course with the encouragement that we can—and should—tell our stories. In various ways, we then took our story out of the box that we had hidden it in and gave it expression—we expressed it to ourselves and then to each other. Now we are going to talk about sharing our story with another who wants to hear it. The interesting truth is that He already knows your story—even better than you do! But He wants to hear your side of the story. He wants to hear about your pain and fear in your own words. He wants you to connect with Him and to draw strength from Him. And He can listen to and understand you in a way that no one else can. This "other," of course, is God.

In His Word, God reminds us often that He sees our suffering and cares about our hurt. He also gives us the privilege and permission to share our deepest feelings with Him. Take a look at this passage from Isaiah:

> Do you not know?
> Have you not heard?
> The LORD is the everlasting God,
> the Creator of the ends of the earth.
> He will not grow tired or weary,
> and his understanding no one can fathom.
>
> He gives strength to the weary
> and increases the power of the weak. (Isaiah 40:28–29)

These verses give us four good reasons to talk to God about our hurts, fears, and concerns:

- God is not limited by time or circumstances. (He is "everlasting" and the "Creator" of all things.)
- God will never grow weary of listening to us. ("He will not grow tired or weary.")
- God's understanding of all things—including our pain—is greater than any person's. (His "understanding no one can **fathom**.") A *fathom* is actually a way to measure the depth of water. God uses this word to tell us that we cannot comprehend how "deep" His understanding is for us, especially in our pain and suffering. His understanding is beyond measure.
- God has the power to give us strength in our weakness. (He "gives strength to the weary and increases the power of the weak.")

God is the perfect listener: He *wants* to hear. He *understands* what we are saying—and even what we are not saying. And He has *power* to help us.

In addition, when we share with God, it is different than when we share with our human companions:

- To share with people that are close to us sometimes causes them **stress**. They might worry about us and the situation, and this worry might even begin to affect their life. Sharing with God is different. When we share with God, we do not create stress for Him. The things we share about our suffering will touch His heart, but they will not cause Him to worry. He can handle the most terrible feelings that we have, and He will never get overwhelmed or stressed with the details. A crisis to us is *not* a crisis to God!

- When we share with others, we can sometimes be afraid of how they will react. We might fear that they will be mad, walk out of the relationship, view us unfavorably, or tell others things that we don't want to be told. But when we share with God, we can express our pain without fear. God not only provides us with a place of safety. but He also *IS* our safety—the Bible says He is our refuge. He will not become angry or offended when we share, and He will not betray our trust.

- Unlike our human companions, God knows what we are feeling, even when we may not have the words to express it. God can listen to our hearts and thoughts. He can "hear" our tears and quietness. And when we do speak, He can understand the words that come out of our **distress**.

Perhaps you have been told that you should not share negative feelings with God. But the truth is that He knows our hearts before we even speak them; so, when we share, it does not change His thoughts or affections toward us. The Bible provides many, many examples of people who share their pain, fear, and doubt with God, along with His favorable responses. Take these verses from Psalms, for instance:

> Then they cried out to the LORD in their trouble, and He brought them out of their distress. (Psalm 107:28)

> Trust in Him at all times, O people; pour out your heart before Him; God is a refuge for us. Psalm 62:8

"Pour out your heart before Him . . ." Have you ever wanted to "pour out your heart?" What does it mean to "pour out your heart?"

> Allow the participants to share.

We have talked about the way we often try to hide our feelings. We say, "Everything is okay," even when our emotions don't feel okay. Sometimes those emotions feel like giant waves in a storm that will carry us away. And when we hide them, those emotions settle into our minds, hearts, and even stomachs! It is as if our fear, anger, sorrow, and tears all seep down into a vessel, deep inside. The feelings are still there, but they are contained and hidden. Once in a while, a few tears or words slip out in conversation with another person or at night when we are alone.

How wonderful it would be to tip that vessel over and pour out its contents freely!

Most of us have wanted to pour out our hearts, but we think, "Who would listen? Who would care?" Maybe you even feel like one woman who said, "I am afraid that if I begin to cry, I will never stop." But the truth is, our Creator will listen and care. He will hold our tears.

In the Bible, David provides numerous examples of what it looks like to pour out our hearts to God. He did not hide his feelings of suffering or his negative thoughts. Instead, he talked to God about them, and those conversations are recorded in the book of Psalms.

In a minute, we will look at some of these Psalms to see what we can learn from David about sharing our emotions and stories with God. As we do, notice the following details:

- David knows God well and is able to share his real feelings with Him, including his fears, his anger, his loneliness, and his despair.
- David expresses feelings of anger and revenge against those who have harmed him, those he loves, and those who have acted against God.
- David speaks truthfully about injustice and cries out for God to stop the evil, rescue the victims, and destroy the evil-doers.
- God never gets angry with David or reprimands him for these expressions.

> Hand out copies of the worksheet or write the verses from the worksheet on a large board or sheet of paper, where they will be visible to all members. Read the verses out loud and ask the group to listen for words and phrases that describe David's feelings. Allow the participants to share first and then add thoughts as needed. This activity will help them later on, when they create their own psalm.

Now that we have looked carefully at David's prayers, let's answer the following questions together:

1. Which of David's words describe intense emotions (for example, *fear, trembling, horror, anguish, terror*)?

2. Which action words in these passages describe David's pain and longing (for example, *overwhelmed, fly away, flee, hurry, vanish*)?

3. Which visual words describe David's pain in way that paints a picture for us (for example, "horror has overwhelmed me," "my tears have been my food," "my bones suffer agony," "my foes taunt me," "my heart is in anguish")?

4. What questions does David ask God? ("Will the LORD reject me forever?" "Will he never show his favor again? "Has his unfailing love vanished forever?" "Has his promise failed for all time?" "Has God forgotten to be merciful?" "Has He, in anger, withheld His compassion?" "My God, my God, why have you forsaken me?" "Why are you so far from saving me, so far from my cries of anguish?" "Why have you forgotten me?" "Why must I go about mourning, oppressed by the enemy?")

David openly expresses his pain and questions to God. This is an example for us. We can speak openly to God about our pain too.

God is not threatened by our emotions. God knows that we feel different emotions at different times, and He is the *only* one who can fully understand and absorb them.

So, as we reach out to Him and connect with Him in our pain, He will connect with us—both in the many layers of our suffering and in the tapestry of our everyday lives. And we will continue to know more of Him.

We learned from David how to pour our hearts out to God, so now we are going to do the same. We will write a psalm of our own.

REFLECTION AND APPLICATION

In an earlier lesson, we drew pictures of our suffering. Today we are going to draw pictures of our suffering with words, the way David did. We can describe it in ways that come alive to us.

Listen carefully. You do not need to write in complete sentences. It does not need to rhyme or have a pretty sound to it. Rather, think about what would happen if you took a vessel full of fruit and poured it on the ground. Fruit would fall and bounce everywhere. That is how your words might be on the paper.

Simply share the thoughts and words that come to your mind that describe how you "feel" about your suffering; how you felt during the event.

Remember that David described things that he felt in his body, some that he felt in his mind, and some that he felt in his heart. You can do the same.

You may also use words found in nature, like *thunder, lightning, storm, darkness, desert, flood,* or *waves,* among many others. Paint a picture with the words.

Use all kinds of words to give a picture of what you feel. Use questions that you have for God or others. As you express your emotions, the pain and suffering will almost come to life. The words will begin to form a portrait of your experience.

This is your story. Your feelings. Your psalm. Your chance to pour out your heart to God.

> **Use the remaining session time for the** participants to create their own psalm. They may also continue this exercise at home. **Provide a piece of paper or have the students use the back of the handout.**

COURAGE AND PEACE

As we get ready to go our separate ways, remember that your words are precious and valuable to God. He is never too busy. He never becomes weary of you. He is listening before you even open your mouth to speak. He understands and even catches what your words cannot express.

So, tell God about your suffering. Read your psalm to Him every day. Add new thoughts and feelings, if you like. As you practice speaking these words to God, you will become more familiar and comfortable with this kind of conversation with Him. He is the perfect One to hear.

WRITE A PSALM

THOSE WHO SUFFER MAY FREELY EXPRESS THEIR EMOTIONS TO GOD.

Trust in Him at all times, O people;
pour out your heart before Him;
God is a refuge for us. (Psalm 62:8)

Fear and trembling have beset me;
horror has overwhelmed me.
I said, "Oh, that I had the wings of a dove!
I would fly away and be at rest.
I would flee far away
and stay in the desert;
I would hurry to my place of shelter,
far from the tempest and storm." (Psalms 55:4–8)

My tears have been my food
day and night . . . " (Psalm 42:3)

Will the LORD reject forever?
Will he never show his favor again?
Has his unfailing love vanished forever?
Has his promise failed for all time?
Has God forgotten to be merciful?
Has He in anger withheld His compassion? (Psalms 77:7–9)

My God, my God, why have you forsaken me?
Why are you so far from saving me,
so far from my cries of anguish?
My God, I cry out by day, but you do not answer,
by night, but I find no rest. (Psalms 22:1–2)

I say to God my Rock,
"Why have you forgotten me?
Why must I go about mourning,
oppressed by the enemy?"
My bones suffer mortal agony
as my foes taunt me,
saying to me all day long,
"Where is your God?" (Psalm 42:9)

My heart is in anguish within me;
the terrors of death have fallen on me. (Psalm 55:4)

SESSION 11
REASSURANCE

GOALS FOR PARTICIPANTS
- Hear God's warning that suffering *will* come
- Hear God's reassurance that He wants to hear from us during suffering
- Accept God's invitation to cast our cares on Him

MATERIALS
- This lesson
- Participant worksheet: Reassurance

VOCABULARY
- **omniscient** (om-NISH-uhnt): all-knowing; having complete knowledge and understanding
- **omnipresent** (om-nuh-PREZ-uhnt): all-present; being present everywhere at the same time
- **omnipotent** (om-NIP-uh-tuhnt): all-powerful; having unlimited power
- **reassure** (ree-uh-SHOOR): to say something to remove another's doubts and fears; to put someone's mind at rest

GREETING

Each session begins with a greeting. This will be unique and personal to each group.

REVIEW

Perhaps our last session introduced a new idea to you—honestly speaking our emotions of pain to God. We had a good example as we read David's truthful words of pain and fear—even doubt. And then you wrote your own psalm of suffering as an expression to God. What did you learn about your own feelings as you expressed them to God? Did you feel comfortable doing that?

Allow time for participants to briefly respond to these questions.

We will continue this conversation today as we consider God's response to our expression of pain.

LESSON SCRIPT

As we talked about last time, suffering is mentioned often in God's word. This tells us that God *knows* there is suffering. In fact, it almost seems that, through His Word, He *intentionally warns* us about it—not as a threat, but so that when it comes, we will not be overwhelmed to the point of despair. It is as if He tells us to expect it.

At the same time, whenever the Word tells us about trouble and suffering, it also reassures us. To **reassure** is to say something to remove the doubts and fears that we feel. In this case, that *something* is the promise that God is with us and for us.

Fear and doubt can put our minds through such turmoil and unrest; but when God reassures us, He puts our minds to rest. God knows just what we need to hear.

> If you printed copies of the worksheet for each participant, hand those out now. Invite them to follow along with the Bible verses you read as you lead the discussion below.

Listen to these words from God:

> I have told you these things, so that in me you may have peace. In this world you will have trouble. But take heart! I have overcome the world. (John 16:33)

Notice how He tells us that trouble is coming . . . and then directly after that, He reassures us that He has overcome that trouble. He says, "I have overcome the world!"

Now, let's look at the next group of verses written. These were written by David, who we talked about previously. As you know, David experienced much suffering, and he wanted God's reassurance, just as we do. So after we read each verse, we will answer two questions: (1) What words express the truth of suffering? and (2) What words express the reassurance of God?

Here is the first one:

> The LORD is good, a refuge in times of trouble. He cares for those who trust in him. (Nahum 1:7)

> Review the two questions, then allow participants to answer. Listen for the following responses: (1) Words that express the truth of suffering: "times of trouble" / (2) Words that express the reassurance of God: "The LORD is good; He cares."

> Weeping may last for the night, but a shout of joy comes in the morning. (Psalm 30:5)

> Allow participants to answer. Listen for the following responses: (1) Words that express the truth of suffering: "weeping; night" / (2) Words that express the reassurance of God: "shout of joy; morning."

> The LORD is a refuge for the oppressed, a stronghold in times of trouble. (Psalm 9:9)

> Allow participants to answer. Listen for the following responses: (1) Words that express the truth of suffering: "oppressed; times of trouble" / (2) Words that express the reassurance of God: "the Lord is a refuge; a stronghold."

We are grateful for reassurance. And yet, we might wonder if anyone, including God, has the power and authority to reassure us in such a way: "Overcome the world?" Can we actually trust this kind of reassurance?

Three characteristics of God can help us in this conversation; God can reassure us this way, and we can trust Him, because He is all-knowing, all-present, and all-powerful. Let's take a closer look at each of these characteristics.

1. God is ALL-knowing or **OMNISCIENT**.

    God knows all. This means nothing takes place outside of His knowledge, and that includes the suffering in your life. No one can do anything to you that God does not know about. Here are just a few of the many Bible passages that show us this truth:

    Do you not know? Have you not heard? The LORD is the everlasting God, the Creator of the ends of the earth. He will not grow tired or weary, and his understanding no one can fathom. (Isaiah 40:28)

    Nothing in all creation is hidden from God's sight. Everything is uncovered and laid bare to the eyes of him to whom we must give account. (Hebrews 4:13)

    Before a word is on my tongue, you, LORD, know it completely. (Psalm 139:4)

2. God is ALL-present, or **OMNIPRESENT**.

    God is present everywhere. There is no tiny corner where God cannot be. Therefore, God is also present in our suffering. He is not hiding or preoccupied. Consider the following verses:

    "Am I only a God nearby," declares the LORD, "and not a God far away? Who can hide in secret places so that I cannot see them?" declares the LORD. "Do not I fill heaven and earth?" (Jeremiah 23:23–24)

    Where can I go from Your Spirit? Where can I flee from Your presence? . . . If I rise on the wings of the dawn, if I settle on the far side of the sea, even there your hand will guide me, your right hand will hold me fast. If I say, "Surely the darkness will hide me and the light become night around me," even the darkness will not be dark to you; the night will shine like the day, for darkness is as light to you. (Psalms 139:7, 9–12)

3. God is ALL-powerful or **OMNIPOTENT**.

    All power belongs to God. He displays it every day for those who are willing to see. Even all of nature bows to His power and authority. So, we can be sure that God has the power to confront all instruments of suffering. The Word shows us what this omnipotence looks like:

    "I am the LORD, the God of all mankind. Is there anything too hard for me?" (Jeremiah 32:27)

    All the peoples of the earth are regarded as nothing. He does what he pleases with the powers of heaven and the peoples of the earth. No one can hold back his hand or say to him: "What have you done?" (Daniel 4:35)

These characteristics tell us that God, and only God, is ALL. No one else can provide this kind of comfort and security for us, because no one else is all. For this reason, we can accept God's reassurance.

David knew this about God. We hear this in the following words that he wrote to his Creator:

> Though I walk in the midst of trouble, you preserve my life. You stretch out your hand against the anger of my foes; with your right hand you save me. (Psalm 138:7)

David truthfully admits that there is trouble in his life . . . but then he draws attention to God's hand, which is present and able to save him. David trusts God's hand of reassurance because he knows that God is ALL.

As we look at the next couple of verses, let's answer this question together: Which of the three characteristics of God do we see in each verse? What words convey those characteristics?

Here is the first verse:

> God is our refuge and strength, an ever-present help in trouble. (Psalm 46:1)

> Allow participants to answer. Repeat the two questions, if necessary, and listen for the following responses: He is all-powerful (indicated by the words "refuge and strength"); He is all-present (indicated by the word "ever-present").

Now, let's move onto the second verse:

> When you pass through the waters, I will be with you;
> and when you pass through the rivers, they will not sweep over you.
> When you walk through the fire, you will not be burned;
> the flames will not set you ablaze.
> For I am the LORD your God, the Holy One of Israel, your Savior.
> (Isaiah 43:2–3a)

> Allow participants to answer and listen for the following responses: He is all-present (indicated by the words "I will be with you"); He is all-powerful (indicated by the words "they will not sweep over you," "you will not be burned," "the flames will not set you ablaze").

In every verse, God acknowledges the presence of trouble—of suffering—*and* in each verse, God reminds us that He is here and has the power to help, heal, and protect. He *reassures* us! He sees the trouble and unrest in our minds and hearts, then He helps us to remember who He is.

The burden of the suffering would be too much for us to bear if we did not have the promise of God's presence and purpose in it. But we do have that promise, along with the invitation to entrust God with our burdens. Listen to these words:

> Cast your cares on the LORD.

The sadness, anger, fear, loneliness, despair—these are all *cares*. All the emotions of grief and loss are *cares*. The physical responses are also cares. God does not intend for us to carry those cares alone. They are too heavy. The burden is too great. Instead, He says, *Give them to Me.* Oh, but it is stronger than that: to *cast* is to *throw*. Picture a fisherman *casting* his line into the sea. He pulls his arm back and tosses it out with strength—away from himself and into the deep. In the same way, we are to heartily, energetically throw our cares upon Him. He asks it of us! And when we accept this particular invitation, it carries with it a profound promise, one that we desperately need right now: "I will sustain you."

    The invitation: *Cast your cares on Me.*

    The promise: *I will sustain you.*

Have you ever tried to physically throw something heavy? When you do so, it can set you off-balance. The same is true when you attempt to cast off your heavy burden of grief and suffering. You have grown accustomed to the weight of the pain, so when you get rid of it suddenly, it can be unsettling, even destabilizing. The good news, however, is that when you cast that burden onto your Perfect Companion, He is able to sustain and support you through the imbalance, as the weight shifts away from you and onto Him.

And the promise continues: As we encounter pain and turmoil, God sustains us. As we lean on Him, we are upheld and supported by Him— in the midst of the cares and the suffering. He provides strength that we do not have in ourselves. The interesting truth is that when we feel the heaviness of the suffering and cares, His intention is that we give that heaviness to Him! It is then that we discover how strong we are as He sustains us—as He supports us.

    The reality: *God is able to absorb our grief.*

He is able to *absorb* all of it. To *absorb* is to take in, or soak up. Think of a sponge. If you place a dry sponge in water, it soaks up the water. The problem with a sponge is that it can get so full of water that it cannot absorb any more. At that point, it simply overflows and is of no further use. But God is able to absorb every last drop of our loss and pain. He will never say that He can take no more. He will never be overwhelmed by our suffering.

    God sees our cares, our grief, and our loss.

    He tells us to throw that grief onto Him,

    He supports and carries us through our emotional awareness,

    and He absorbs all that we give Him.

    It is never too much.

    And He does not return it to us.

REFLECTION AND APPLICATION

To learn to cast all your cares on Him is an important part of your healing journey. When you cast your cares, you express your intention to move forward but not to carry all of your pain alone. This awareness of God with you—to reassure you and be a refuge—will give you confidence for the future.

To pour out our hearts to God and cast our cares on Him are things that we must do in private. This is not a group activity. So your opportunity to apply this lesson to your life is to decide where and when you will cast your cares on God. Choose a quiet place and somewhere private. As a starting place, you might read your psalm out loud to God, and then continue to express the pain that you feel.

COURAGE AND PEACE

Cast your cares on the LORD and he will sustain you. (Psalm 55:22) The Good Shepherd is waiting to hear and absorb all that you have to share with Him. He values both your spoken words and the unspoken emotions of your heart.

REASSURANCE

I have told you these things, so that in me you may have peace. In this world you will have trouble. But take heart! I have overcome the world. (John 16:33)

The LORD is good, a refuge in times of trouble. He cares for those who trust in him. (Nahum 1:7)

Weeping may stay for the night, but rejoicing comes in the morning. (Psalm 30:5)

The LORD is a refuge for the oppressed, a stronghold in times of trouble. (Psalm 9:9)

Do you not know? Have you not heard? The LORD is the everlasting God, the Creator of the ends of the earth. He will not grow tired or weary, and his understanding no one can fathom. (Isaiah 40:28)

Nothing in all creation is hidden from God's sight. Everything is uncovered and laid bare before the eyes of him to whom we must give account. (Hebrews 4:13)

Before a word is on my tongue, you, LORD, know it completely. (Psalm 139:4)

"Am I only a God nearby," declares the LORD, "and not a God far away? Who can hide in secret places so that I cannot see them?" declares the LORD. "Do not I fill heaven and earth?" (Jeremiah 23:23–24)

Where can I go from your Spirit? Where can I flee from your presence? . . . If I rise on the wings of the dawn, if I settle on the far side of the sea, even there your hand will guide me, your right hand will hold me fast. If I say, "Surely the darkness will hide me and the light become night around me," even the darkness will not be dark to you; the night will shine like the day, for darkness is as light to you. (Psalms 139:7, 9–12)

"I am the LORD, the God of all mankind. Is anything too hard for me?" (Jeremiah 32:27)

All the peoples of the earth are regarded as nothing. He does what he pleases with the powers of heaven and the peoples of the earth. No one can hold back his hand or say to him: "What have you done?" (Daniel 4:35)

Though I walk in the midst of trouble, you preserve my life. You stretch out your hand against the anger of my foes; with your right hand you save me. (Psalm 138:7)

God is our refuge and strength, an ever-present help in trouble. (Psalm 46:1)

When you pass through the waters, I will be with you; and when you pass through the rivers, they will not sweep over you. When you walk through the fire, you will not be burned; the flames will not set you ablaze. For I am the LORD your God, the Holy One of Israel, your Savior. (Isaiah 43:2–3a)

Cast your cares on the LORD and he will sustain you. (Psalm 55:22)

SESSION 12
I AM NOT CONSUMED

GOALS FOR PARTICIPANTS
- Be assured that our suffering will not consume us
- Be assured that all is not lost
- Understand that God preserves our substance in suffering

MATERIALS
- This lesson

VOCABULARY
- **consume** (kuhn-SOOM): to completely destroy or use up
- **threaten** (THRET-n): to declare intention to cause harm; to frighten or cause panic

GREETING

Each session begins with a greeting. This will be unique and personal to each group.

REVIEW

In our conversation about pain and suffering it was wonderful to discover a refuge, a place of safety, where we can express our deepest hurts. We know that God understands. We heard His truthful warning that suffering will come and then the reassurance that always follows. Because He is ALL, we can trust that reassurance and cast our cares on Him. It is necessary for our healing that we understand these truths. In fact, our healing is dependent not only on understanding truth but also on discerning between truth and untruth. So, in this lesson, we will learn about some common untruths that we might face—and some truths we can use to combat them. The untruths we will talk about come in the form of fear.

LESSON SCRIPT

Today we are going to consider two common fears that **threaten** us. Before we do, however, we must make an important distinction: we must remember that suffering is real and trauma is real—but the accusations and *threats* that arise from the trauma are often *untruth*.

One such untruth that tends to threaten us is THE FEAR THAT I WILL BE CONSUMED BY MY SUFFERING. Perhaps, you have said something like, "If I look at my suffering, if I face my trauma . . . it will destroy me; it will **consume** me." Or perhaps, you just sensed this deep inside. To *consume* is to destroy or use up. So, the fear, the threat, is that the pain will destroy you—it will use up all your strength and enter every part of your life.

Long ago, there was a man who seems to have had the same fear. Then he discovered a truth to combat this fear. This is a truth that can help us on our healing journey even now:

> I remember my affliction and my wandering,
> the bitterness and the gall.
> I well remember them,
> and my soul is downcast within me.
> Yet this I call to mind
> and therefore I have hope:
> Because of the LORD's great love we are not consumed,
> for His compassions never fail.
> They are new every morning;
> great is Your faithfulness."
>
> (Lamentations 3:19–23)

So, how did this man combat his suffering? He started by looking at it clearly and truthfully ("I remember my affliction"). Our instinct is usually to run from our fear—but when we run from fear, it only grows stronger. When we, instead, stop to look carefully at our fear the way this man did, we gain strength and regain some of the control it has taken from us.

The next thing this man did, in the middle of his suffering, was to "call to mind . . . the LORD's great love." He also saw that this love set boundaries to his suffering ("I am not consumed").

Finally, he recalled God's compassions that "never fail," and His faithfulness, which was "great."

For many of us, the ideas of love and compassion and faithfulness have been tainted with bitterness and betrayal. Maybe it was from our relationship with a parent, spouse, child, grandparent, sibling, friend, or someone else, or maybe it was from a combination of relationships, but our expectations of love and compassion and faithfulness—what they are and how they would be expressed to us—were broken, even shattered, and the resulting pain crushed our very souls. The *loss* of right and good and perfect love threatened to completely consume and destroy us. So, it is important that we hear this reassurance:

"Because of **the LORD's** great love . . . we are not consumed" (emphasis mine).

Perhaps, you find it difficult to trust or even accept love. Know that there is One who loves you with a great love. A loyal love. A faithful love. A pure love. And it is because of *that great love* for you that you have not been—and will not be—destroyed.

What a precious and profound truth to carry with us on this journey:

> *I remember my suffering,*
> *and*
> *I am not consumed.*

A second common untruth that invades our thoughts is THE FEAR THAT ALL IS NOW LOST. The words that this fear whispers to our hearts sound something like, "All is lost. You cannot survive. You have already been consumed by your suffering, so there is nothing left to do. *You are undone.*"

Hear this truth: You still *ARE*! Yes, there may be parts of your life that were literally burned up, purified through suffering. There may be parts of your life that are gone just because circumstances have changed. But hear this truth from your good God:

> [My] eyes saw [your] unformed substance; in [My] book were written, every one of them, the days that were formed for [you], when as yet there was none of them. (Psalm 139:16, ESV)

You might wonder, *What is my substance?*

Your substance is that which God created of you, that which can never be destroyed. Your substance is the *you* that He sees and knows and loves and values. Your substance is your story that He wrote and preserved in His book. Your substance is what has survived the fire, because He held it close and protected it.

> You have the freedom to accept that *who you really are—is who you are still.*

Also, understand this: Your suffering *is part* of your substance. Your days of pain are written in God's book, because they are valuable. However, any actions by others that caused you that pain—*those are not part of your substance*. You do not need to carry those forward with you. There were circumstances that held you captive, but they did not destroy your substance. The labels that others might have placed on you are not the words written in His book. But your substance, which God saw *before anyone* else could—that *you* still is!

> *Even after all you have lost . . . here you are; the substance of you.*

You can hold up this truth as a shield when trauma throws its darts of accusation and threatens to annihilate you:

> *You are.*
> *You have not been destroyed*
> *You have not been consumed.*
> *You—the substance of you—exists eternally.*
> *And you are valuable.*
> *Because of the LORD's great love . . .*
> *you are not consumed.*

REFLECTION AND APPLICATION

Think about the two fears that may threaten you:

- Fear that you will be destroyed or consumed by your pain.
- Fear that all is now lost.

What truth did you learn in this lesson that can protect you from these fears?

> Allow participants to respond and discuss.

As we draw to a close, write the following truths on your paper so that you can remember them whenever you have fear and doubt:

> *You are.*
> *You have not been destroyed*
> *You have not been consumed.*
> *You—the substance of you—exists eternally.*
> *And you are valuable.*
> *Because of the LORD's great love . . .*
> *you are not consumed.*

Watch for opportunities to see your value this week. Read the words on your paper out loud once per day. This is one way that you can speak truth to yourself.

COURAGE AND PEACE

Approach the coming days with the confidence that grows from knowing yourself more fully and from being held close and protected by your good and perfect Traveling Companion. Your vision is clearing and your heart is becoming more steady. Take deep breaths, as needed, and feel the strength that is building within. Individually—and together—we are moving in a good direction.

SESSION 13
A BEGINNING AND AN END

GOALS FOR PARTICIPANTS
- Understand that the crisis had a beginning point and an ending point
- Understand the truth that the immediate danger is over
- Experience the relief of this truth that the immediate danger is over

MATERIALS
- This lesson
- Plain paper; pencils or pens

VOCABULARY
- **contradict** (kon-truh-DIKT): to speak the opposite of
- **reality** (ree-AL-ih-tee): the state of things as they actually exist; a thing that is actually being experienced
- **relief** (ree-LEEF): a feeling of reassurance and relaxation following release from distress; comfort; freedom
- **true** (TROO): correct; real; not false
- **truth** (TROOTH): that which is true or real

GREETING

Each session begins with a greeting. This will be unique and personal to each group.

REVIEW

In our last session, we grew more aware of God's reassurance to us as we faced two fears that likely threaten us: the fear that we will be consumed or destroyed by our pain and the fear that all is now lost. Do you remember the truths we learned that will protect us from these fears?

Allow participants to respond and discuss. The answers are given in the script below. Listen for these answers and use the script, as needed, to reinforce these truths.

Whenever we fear that we will be consumed or destroyed by our pain, God reassures us through His Word that His great love for us keeps us from being destroyed. Whenever we fear that all is lost, God reassures us that His eyes and heart see us and that He keeps a record of all that has happened to us. There is also reassurance that the substance of you—who you really are—is held safe by Him. You exist eternally. You are valuable. Therefore, you can remember your suffering in safety: you have not been and will not be destroyed.

LESSON SCRIPT

> This lesson may be difficult for those who are in the middle of an ongoing war or disaster. In this case, focus on the reassurance from Lamentations that we are not consumed. Help them to see smaller events or difficulties within the larger event—challenges which they have accomplished.

With these truths firmly in mind, it is now time to take a closer look at your suffering. This may be one of the more difficult conversations we have, so as we move forward, don't forget to hold onto the reassurances you have from God. Also, be encouraged, because as part of this conversation, you will discover a valuable tool that you can use often to help you on your journey.

This session will look a bit different from our others, as the REFLECTION AND APPLICATION exercise will be part of the lesson. In this exercise, we will think about the timetable of the crisis event. As you can imagine, this will require that you intentionally and clearly think about the *details* of the event, which may, at first, make you fearful; our instinct is to run away from the details, far and fast. But as we have learned, God holds us safely so that we can confront our fears with His truth and reassurance. We can also give ourselves confidence by remembering that this exercise is necessary in order to release ourselves from the control that the crisis still holds over us. And we will be stronger and freer because of it. Together, we will take it slowly, step by step.

REFLECTION AND APPLICATION

> Hand out sheets of paper and writing utensils, if you have not already done so.

On the paper in front of you, you are going to put some of the details of your event on a timeline. To start, draw a line horizontally across the middle of the paper.

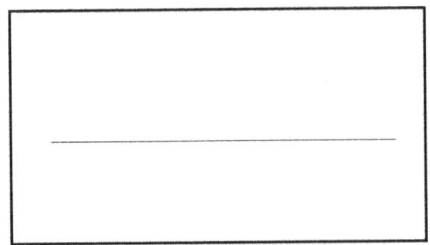

Now, let's think about the timing of the event—the beginning. You might want to remember or look back at the timeline that you drew previously, that showed when the crisis event happened in your life.

As you start to focus in on this event, try to think of the *very first thing* that happened. What *began* your time of suffering? Consider this carefully. It may be difficult, and it may not be obvious. It might help to think about it as the point in time when you moved from feeling *safe* to feeling *unsafe* in your particular situation.

As you ponder this, you may initially feel that you have always been in pain. But remember that the timeline of your crisis event *is not the timeline of your suffering*. Suffering bleeds over the lines, into both past and future. We cannot put a start line or stop line on suffering, although we can learn to rein in its control on us over time. But, we can put a start line on the crisis event.

Perhaps, there was an initial moment of inflicted pain. Or perhaps, there was a moment when you just became aware of your pain—that, too, is a moment of impact. In some cases, there are even multiple points of impact or awareness; for example, there may be an initial impact, followed by new realizations and then new information, and this happens time and again, each time increasing your awareness. Or there may have been the first signs of pain, and then new pain, and then even more pain. Or newly revealed truths opened your eyes to suffering that had been there long before you were even aware of it.

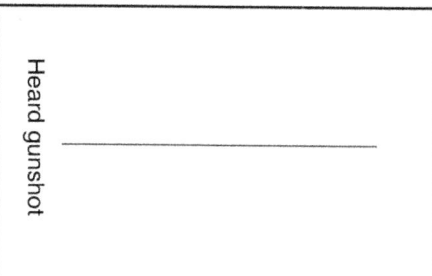

The journey of suffering is often not direct and easily plotted. So, trust yourself.

It might help to ask yourself the following questions and then to listen to your responses with full attention:

When was the first moment I felt unsafe?

When was the first time I felt threatened?

What was my first clue that all was not as it should be?

When the answers come, use just a few words to describe that initial moment at the beginning of the line.

Give participants time to complete the exercise and be prepared to help them define this moment of impact clearly. If they suffered in a war, for example, it might be the first time soldiers threatened a neighboring village, the first time they heard a gunshot, or the first time they saw a soldier. Or if they suffered abuse, it might be the first moment they realized the person was going to harm them, the first movement the person made toward them, or the first touch. In all cases, it will be important for the student to see the point in time when they moved from feeling *safe* to feeling *unsafe*.

Your second step might be even more difficult than the first: to discover the point in time when this crisis event ended.

Now, this is tricky. Remember that one of trauma's characteristics is to keep you in a state of fear and panic, so that feelings of danger, threat, and vulnerability linger even after the immediate event of danger is over. This illogical fear encroaches into everyday life, settling in for the long haul, and impacts you even today. So, to discern the reality, you must often push past these feelings.

Think about the sequence of events in your crisis as follows: *beginning*, *end*, and *response*.

Some events feel like they have continued for a long time—they seem to endlessly unfold, change, and perhaps grow in intensity. Often, it's only later that can we look back and discern the moment when the actual *threat* of the event came to an end and our response began. We then begin to understand that the threats that remain are not real; instead, they are based in the fear that comes from trauma. The remaining effects of this fear are now *responses* to the actual event. Will some of those responses turn into their own crisis events? Yes. But those merit their own individual timelines, each one with its own beginning and end.

> So, think very carefully. At what moment did the immediate threat diminish?
>
> Or at what moment did the action of the crisis event end?
>
> This might be when the actual physical threat to you came to an end
>
> or it might be when some final bad news was given to you.

In just a few words, describe that moment at the end of the line—the moment when the immediate threat came to a close and you were safe again.

Allow time for participants to complete the exercise and be prepared to address any questions. In no instance should you suggest the moment an event ended for a person, because it will be different for each person. For those in war, the event might have ended the same day it began, if they fled and arrived in a safe village shortly thereafter. Or it might be months later, when they arrived at a refugee camp or when enemy soldiers were defeated. For those in abuse, the event might have ended years after the relationship started, when the person moved away from their abuser; or it might have ended when the abuser was arrested just a week after they met. The end of each person's crisis event will be as unique as each story: it is simply the moment a person goes from being *unsafe* to being *safe* again.

This might get a bit tricky, especially for those who felt unsafe even after the actual danger was over. Some participants might even continue to feel unsafe in the present. For these students, review the conversation in Session 3, about how to reflect on what is happening in the moment, and ask them to consider whether they feel unsafe because of what *could happen* or because of what is *presently happening*. Guide them to think about the event and, if possible, help them to see when the *probability* of danger ended. For example, if the feeling of unsafety involves soldiers, point out the present truth that the soldiers are not here. Then ask, "When did the soldiers leave?" The moment they left is the moment the danger ended.

These types of individual conversations should be slow and gentle. They should not provide "the answers" but should, rather, guide the participant to discover the truth on her own. This is part of the healing process.

Now, look at the paper in front of you. There was a time when the crisis event began, and there was a time when the crisis event ended. It is important for us to see this reality, this truth: there was a beginning, and there was an end.

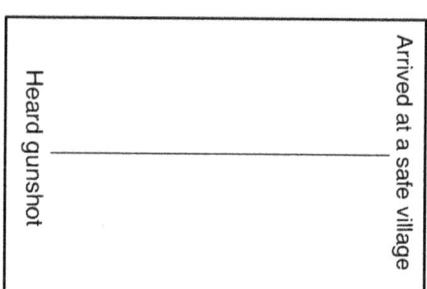

Even though the pain and the suffering and the memories may have continued, the actual event began at one point and ended at another point. This is encouraging.

When we experience an event of great suffering, the pain and fear of that event linger in our minds. By looking at this picture, we can remind ourselves of the truth that, even though the pain of the event still remains, the immediate danger may be over.

What if the suffering of the event is still ongoing? Then it is helpful to discover smaller beginnings and endings within the event. Perhaps, there was a difficult confrontation that was necessary, a particular physical challenge, or even an especially distressing day of "life as it is now." Maybe there was a time when relocation was necessary or acknowledgement of a loved one's death.

Make small timelines for these and note the beginning and the end of each.

- That confrontation that you had to face? It had a beginning, and it had an end. You need not carry it forward with you and remain under its threat or control.
- That long walk you had to make? It had a beginning and it had an end.
- That long night of waiting for news of your loved one? It had a beginning and it had an end.

Does it help you to see that the time of the immediate crisis has an end? What emotions do you feel when you look at the beginning of the line? What emotions do you feel when you look at the end of the line and know that the immediate danger is over?

Allow time for participants to briefly respond to and discuss the questions.

It is important to recognize these moments of experience and closure. It protects us from being held in place by months or even years of suffering, as we wait for some definitive moment of relief that never seems to come.

The effect of the event—the pain—will continue for some time. However, the fear and anxiety that comes when we continue to live the event over and over does not need to continue.

Relief is a feeling of reassurance and release from distress.

Let's do something that will help us understand the feeling of relief.

Raise (scrunch) your shoulders up, as if you are trying to touch them to your ears.

Hold your shoulders there. Do you feel the tension? It is uncomfortable, and you have to work at holding them in this position.

Now, allow your shoulders to fall down and relax. Let them hang comfortably without stressing your neck. This feeling you have when you allow your shoulders to relax is *relief*.

Scrunch up your shoulders again.

This is how crisis events make us feel. In fact, we might begin to walk around with our shoulders and neck very tense as we think about the potential danger around us. Even after the danger is past, our bodies may stay in this tense position.

Our minds also feel this stress and take on "a position" of tension. As a result, our thoughts and emotions become tense and stressed.

Now, feel the relief of dropping your shoulders into a relaxed position again. *Ahhh*, relief! We can let our bodies and our minds let go of the tension, because we know that the immediate danger is over. Relief is a wonderful feeling.

It is important for us to see our suffering in this way so that we can speak truth to ourselves about what is really happening at any particular moment. This is *reality*. **Reality** is something that is actually happening right now. Reality is not something that "could" happen. Reality is not something that we wish would happen. Reality is not something that we are afraid will happen. Reality *is* happening. Reality is **truth**.

When we experience severe pain—emotional or physical—reality can become cloudy. Our fears cause us to think about things that *could* happen, our anger causes us to think about what we think *should* happen, and our longing for peace causes us to think about what we *wish* would happen. So, it becomes difficult to separate what "is" from what "could be" or "should be" or from what we "wish." But, reality is what actually *is* happening.

You have worked hard today. It is not easy to remember the details of an event that caused much suffering, but you did it, and this work will help you to move toward a place of healing. You discovered that there was a beginning and an end to the crisis event, which will help you to see the reality that *is* and offer you the chance to experience relief. Otherwise, if you don't see the end to a crisis, you may live as if you are still in the middle of it—and that is an unhealthy and stressful place to live.

Do you remember the words of the man in Lamentations? He was suffering but saw reality clearly:

> I remember my affliction and my wandering, the bitterness and the gall. I well remember them, and my soul is downcast within me. Yet this I call to mind and therefore I have hope: Because of the LORD's great love we are not consumed, for his compassions never fail. They are new every morning; great is your faithfulness." (Lamentations 3:19–23)

This man *remembered* the details of his suffering clearly, just as you did today. But he also saw the LORD's goodness during the suffering and acknowledged that there was a limit to it: "We are not consumed . . . his compassions never fail . . . great is Your faithfulness."

COURAGE AND PEACE

Close your eyes for a moment. Put your hands loosely in your lap and breathe deeply. Pay attention to any place in your body that is tight or hurting. Focus on that part and try to relax it.

Now, scrunch up your shoulders to your ears as we did earlier. Hold it. Slowly release them and relax your shoulders. Feel the relief.

Imagine the "end" point on your timeline, the time when the event ended. Allow yourself to feel the emotions of that reality, that truth.

Think about God's love and compassion. Think of these words: *I remember my suffering. I am not consumed.*

Feel the truth that God is with you right now. You are safe in His care.

> Give participants a minute to sit quietly and rest. Then ask them to open their eyes.

Repeat this relaxation exercise anytime you feel afraid or stressed this week. Watch for stressful situations in which you can see a beginning and an end. This might help you to practice releasing events instead of holding onto them, as if there is no end.

As you leave today, realize that you have been given the opportunity to step away from the all-consuming control of the initial pain you felt at the moment of impact. This means that the resulting trauma also no longer needs to be in control. We will discuss this more in future sessions. But right now, let's rejoice in our movement forward.

SESSION 14
A NEW PERSPECTIVE

GOALS FOR PARTICIPANTS
- Identify a positive truth about our suffering
- Recognize the potential for good amid suffering

MATERIAL
- This lesson
- The crisis timeline created in the previous lesson
- Participant worksheet: A New Perspective

VOCABULARY
- **dominant** (DOM-uh-nuhnt): controlling everything; most powerful
- **imagine** (ih-MAJ-in): to create an image in our mind; to invent something that is not real
- **perspective** (per-SPEK-tiv): point of view; the way in which we see and interpret the meaning of things
- **validate** (VAL-ih-dayt): to confirm; to prove valuable; to justify

GREETING

Each session begins with a greeting. This will be unique and personal to each group.

REVIEW

Our suffering often speaks fear into our lives—even when the immediate threat is no longer a reality. Last time, we did some hard work and thought carefully about the details of our suffering. We looked for evidence that the actual event had a beginning and an end. We learned that even though our responses and the effects of the suffering are still in process, the event itself is over. This truth keeps us from living under the same fear that we felt when the event first happened. Even if a part of the suffering is still ongoing, even if there were other crises, we can recognize that there are moments of beginnings and endings, so we need not live under the full impact of the pain. We need not allow it to harm us over and over again or to hold us in fear. Did this truth help you this week? If so, how?

Give participants a few minutes to respond to the questions.

LESSON SCRIPT

Even though we recognize that the event itself has ended, we may continue to feel as if we are constantly under its attack. It is natural for us to want to defend ourselves from attack. With this event however, because all of our senses, life circumstances, thoughts, and emotions connect to the pain, every part of us—body, soul, and spirit—also wants to respond in self-defense. The pain takes over. As a result, we can see no good in anything. In our conversation, either with others or with ourselves, we find ourselves saying things like the following:

> "All is lost."
>
> "No one cares."
>
> "Everything is a mess."
>
> "Nothing is turning out the way I expected."
>
> "No one understands."
>
> "Nothing can make this better."
>
> "I will never trust anyone for the rest of my life."

And on and on our complaints go. We can see no good in anything, because the pain has taken over. Even if moments of "right" and "good" occur, they disappear into the background, overwhelmed by our feelings of "wrong" and "bad," while the focal point of suffering continues to stand front and center.

It is as if our bodies and minds respond so defensively to the feelings of attack that they throw out a blanket of protection that covers all parts of our lives, whether those parts are relevant to the crisis or not. This blanket can even extend so far as to cloud our memories of good things that happened *before* the crisis—including things completely unrelated to the event.

And so, suffering disturbs our acceptance of anything good or positive, even about ourselves. Any acknowledgement of good feels disloyal. Any positive response seems to signal pardon for or weaken the accountability of the pain attacking us. And *trauma is never satisfied*. It continues to eat away at every "good" in our story until it appears to us that the only thing left is "bad."

But this image that we are left with is not truthful. The *truth* is that there is more to our story. Part of moving forward and taking back control from the trauma is uncovering the defenses we've put up to create this distortion of truth.

To start this process, we must gain a new **perspective.** In other words, we must help ourselves look at experiences in life with new eyes—eyes that allow us to see the positive. We must give ourselves permission to *remember the good*.

But listen carefully: This is much more than simply attempting to look at life with optimism. We are not just trying to make ourselves feel better. We do not want to simply offset the negative with positive thinking—because there is no positive that can undo the negative that has happened! Neither are we saying that the positive things that happened "outweigh" the negative things. In other words, to acknowledge that something is positive does not mean that we ignore what is negative. It also does not mean that the suffering we feel will go away or be any less.

Further, we do not want to rearrange the details of the event in our minds to try to produce some evidence of good; neither do we want to **imagine** what good could come from our suffering in the future. It is not wise to create a brilliant story of God's intention to inject good into our story in a way that somehow **validates** our suffering. Doing so attempts to speak the mind of God without true knowledge and to balance the crisis against some form of pretty outcome—and in the end, it feels like we are saying that the evil was acceptable in order to accomplish some form of good.

So, what *do* we want to do?

> We want to intentionally recognize *the truth* that there is legitimate *good*.

The reality is that *we might not ever be able to identify the good*. But we can embrace the truth that, even when we cannot identify it, *good is there*.

> The challenge is *not* to try to find the good—
>
> but to be ready and willing to *recognize it when God reveals it*.

Joseph was able to do that. If you do not know Joseph's story, it is a good read. In the Bible, it appears in Genesis 37, 39, and 40–45. To summarize, Joseph suffered at the hands of his own brothers and others who accused him falsely—and tried to harm him, imprison him, and take his life. His story includes the following crisis events:

- He was betrayed by his family.
- He was thrown into unfamiliar surroundings.
- He was falsely accused by those who held power.
- He endured physical discomfort and danger.
- He had intentional harm inflicted on him by those who were supposed to protect him.
- He had to hide his identity from his family.

As we read Joseph's story, we dare not hunt around for each negative and attempt to find a positive to balance or even replace it. However, as his story unfolds, we can see the *reality of good:* the events of his suffering changed and moved Joseph into a good place—a place of responsibility and influence. When it was over, Joseph said to those who had tried to harm him,

> You intended to harm me, but God intended it for good to accomplish what is now being done, the saving of many lives. (Genesis 50:20)

Joseph acknowledged that his suffering was real and that intentional harm was aimed in his direction by those he trusted. But, even in *the reality of pain and betrayal*, he was also able to see and speak *the reality of good. Both were present.* One did not cancel out the other. Rather, both were added together to form what would become his unique story.

It is important to note that Joseph's understanding of good, however, did not come until later—only after much of his story became clear. In other words, God's hand was at work in Joseph's story, even when Joseph could not see it.

It is the same with us. God is with us in our story—at *every* point of our story. He assures us that, even in suffering, He is doing a wonderful work in our lives. And although we may not see it at the time, we can look back and see the positives woven as a thread of care throughout our story. God was there. God was involved. We might have many "why" questions for Him, but He wants us to know that He never let go of us. He says,

> When you pass through the waters, I will be with you . . . (Isaiah 43:2)

God will not always reveal the good to us as clearly as He did to Joseph; but we can rest assured that, even in the midst of suffering, He will always work for both our personal good and for the good of His kingdom:

> And we know that in all things God works for the good of those who love him, who have been called according to his purpose. (Romans 8:28)

Notice that this verse does not say that the evil done to us was or is *good*. It says that God is able to *bring good*—even out of the painful events in our story. Although the particular *good* that God brings is unique to each person and story, there are often some similarities in the types of good we see:

- **Eternal good.** The *good* that God brings is always good from an eternal perspective; *it is good* as seen in the heavenly realm. This idea of *eternal good* stretches our way of thinking when trauma deceives us into thinking we dare not see any good at all. It allows us to see the *potential* of good, even in the midst and aftermath of destructive evil. And it is a reality that brings reassurance and helps us move forward on this path.

- **Personal and spiritual good.** Suffering often leads people to a spiritual place where we come to know God and experience His presence in a way that changes our life forever. Somehow, in some small way, it is as though our vision and our thinking begin to connect with the eternal mind of Christ. This is good. Left to ourselves, we would not choose the suffering and sacrifice that led us to have this connection with God. We would not willingly go look for the kind of good that comes only through desperation and unimaginable pain. Yet, now we might hear ourselves say, "I would not trade my knowledge and awareness of God for anything," and in doing so, in some peculiar way, we embrace the suffering. Suffering can also lead us to learn about ourselves and to allow God to transform places within us that would have otherwise remained untouched. This, too, is good.

- **Practical good.** You might also notice provisions, or "practical goods," that come in the midst of suffering: a place to live, food to eat, comfort from others. God often cares for a multitude of such details that, otherwise, could sweep us under.

Now, it is time to acknowledge the *reality* of some positive things in your life. Let's begin this application of our lesson together.

REFLECTION AND APPLICATION

Are you open to good in your story? Are you ready to recognize good *as God reveals it to you*?

Perhaps, you feel stuck. Maybe this truth will help steer your thoughts in a positive direction: You are here! Since the beginning of our sessions, you have begun thinking and talking about your pain. You have been willing to uncover the wound and learn how to clean it, so that it can begin to heal. And now you are ready to see beauty. All of this takes courage.

Now, this is your opportunity to see good. Do not feel the need to *create* good. Just honestly recognize the good that was in your life—as well as the good that is now here, close to you and connected to you.

The lesson showed us that there were probably positive ways that God cared for you through your event that you might not have understood at the time. It also showed that, through your suffering, you may have grown in your understanding of and love toward God. Now, it is your turn to share. Is there anything you have learned in your suffering? What good can you see when you look back on your event? What do you know to be true? Please be courageous as you share.

> Allow time for the participants to share. Do not pressure them with what they "should" have learned; rather, allow them to share whatever comes to mind. If they seem hesitant, you might share a personal lesson that you learned or a *good* that you noticed in your own suffering and let that inspire them to think of their own stories. You could also prompt discussion by asking the group one or more of the questions below.
>
> - Are any of you surprised by some of the things you have done to survive? Are you surprised by some of the things you have done to make it to this day?
> - Describe a few of those tasks, those mountains you climbed, those "How did I?" moments.
> - Who was with you during this experience? Were there helpful hands at any point?
> - Were there encouraging words? Was there uplifting music?
> - What safety net of *provision* can you now see was there, even during the darkest times?
> - Is there anything you know now that you did not know before the event?
> - What truths have come to the surface because of the pain you've endured?

Remember, when you recognize good, that does not mean you deny the evil involved. What it does mean is that you hold evil in its place. It is strong, but it has no right to consume you. It has no authority to wipe out the good.

> Distribute copies of the worksheet A New Perspective.

Look at the worksheet. Do you see the moment of impact? This activity will use the good that you discover to help you gain a more healthy perspective of that moment.

Start by carefully examining this event. Do you see any . . .

- positive moments?
- times of provision?
- blessings that kept you afloat?
- positives in your current life?

They are there. *They are always there,* even when you don't see them. Use some of the previous questions to help you bring the truth to the light. When you're ready, write three of these "goods" in the empty pieces of the puzzle in Image #1.

> Give participants time to complete the exercise.

As you worked on Image #1, perhaps more than three positives crossed your mind. If that happened, add those positives to the blank puzzle pieces in Image #2. You may use the previous positives from Image #1 and then add more.

Do you see what happens to the event of suffering as we acknowledge more positive events, provisions, and blessings? It is still there—it has not changed in any way—but it no longer *consumes* the image. Instead, as blessings are added, the entire image becomes brighter and fuller, and the moment of impact loses prominence. The more blessings are added, the less oppressive and consuming the trauma becomes.

This does not make the trauma any less real. It does not make the effect of the trauma less severe. It does, however, make the trauma a smaller part of the overall picture—in other words, it removes some of the control that trauma has over our lives.

The puzzle images help us see that suffering is a very *real* part of our lives—but it is only a *part*. And this is in step with the rest of our journey up to this point. We have never denied the pain, as that would be unhealthy. Instead, we have learned to face the reality of our suffering and its effect in our lives. Now we are simply *adding the reality* of blessings and provisions, so that we can begin to put suffering in the proper proportion.

We begin to see that there is other subject matter in our picture. There is additional scripting in our story. When we recognize that, the suffering recedes. It exists, but it is not **dominant**. It happened, but it is not our identity.

When we recognize the safety and blessings in our lives, both right now and along the way, trauma's control over us diminishes.

And as trauma loosens its grip on us, it allows us to move forward—away from suffering and toward resolution.

But for all of this to happen, we must first give ourselves permission to *remember the good*. We must train our "eyes" to notice accomplishments and blessings so that we can see through and around the suffering to other parts of our lives.

As we gain this new and healthy perspective, we might find that some problems become solvable. This new way of seeing might also help us to interpret and interact with the world around us in a more positive and productive way. Perhaps, we will even begin to think about our hopes and our future. Look at image #3. Do you think that is possible?

COURAGE AND PEACE

Think about this truth:

The event of our suffering is not the only subject of our story

or the complete picture of our life.

Joy and hope are all around us when we take time to identify them.

A NEW PERSPECTIVE

IMAGE 1

IMAGE 2

IMAGE 3

SESSION 15
WHY?

GOALS FOR PARTICIPANTS
- Be assured that it is okay to ask difficult questions about why suffering happens to us
- Understand that suffering exists because this world is broken from the effects of sin
- Understand that we all experience suffering because we live in this broken world
- Understand that one cannot live good enough or have enough faith to avoid all suffering

MATERIALS
- This lesson
- Plain paper; pencils or pens

VOCABULARY
- **avoid** (uh-VOYD): to stay away from
- **consequence** (KON-see-kwens): the effect or result of something that happened earlier; result; outcome
- **evidence** (EHV-i-duhns): something that makes plain or clear; proof
- **personal** (PUR-suh-nl): related to a particular person; related to oneself

GREETING

Each session begins with a greeting. This will be unique and personal to each group.

REVIEW

We learned to discover good during our last session. This is much more than an attempt to look at life with a positive spirit. We cannot offset the negative with positive thinking, because there is no positive that can undo the negative that has happened! We are, however, intent to recognize the truth that there is legitimate *good*. Did you find *good* as you looked at your own story?

Give participants a few moments to respond.

The truth is that God's hand is at work even when we cannot see Him. God assures us that, even in suffering, He is doing a wonderful work in our lives. And He is with us in our stories—at *every* point of our stories.

But even as we start to embrace these truths and make progress on our journey, it is not uncommon to find that one haunting question continues to stand in our way. That question is *Why?*

LESSON SCRIPT

"Why did this have to happen?"

"Why suffering?"

These questions probably sound familiar to you. Often, when they come, we just want to ignore them and set them aside. But as long as they remain unresolved, they will continue to distract us, trip us up, and hinder our progress.

Although we might not ever resolve all of our "why" questions, today we will discover principles that can help us come to peace with some of the *whys* surrounding suffering. We will start by looking at two specific questions to help us along this part of the journey:

- Why is there suffering in the world?
- Why did suffering happen to me?

But first, listen closely: Our purpose for examining these questions is *not* to seek validation for the evil, injustice, or abuse that occurred. Any answers we find will *not* balance the scale, as that scale cannot be balanced by any human means or from any human perspective. Instead, our goal is to learn truths that we can use to respond to these questions so that we can come to peace with our suffering and, perhaps, with our Traveling Companion. We want to calm the unsettling and disturbing distractions—the *whys*—that keep us from moving forward.

With that in mind, let's look at the first question:

WHY IS THERE SUFFERING IN THE WORLD?

For this discussion, we return to the very beginning—the story of creation. God created a beautiful world and declared it *good*. He then created humanity in His image to live in this wonderful world—and, more specifically, in the garden of Eden. How can we even imagine what that was like? Maybe it's easiest to think about it in terms of things that were *not* there: There were no weeds in the garden. There was no illness. No wars. No pain. No suffering. Adam and Eve, the first man and woman, were blessed. It was a peaceful, good, and right time.

Then came an event that changed everything. God gave instructions: "You are free to eat from any tree in the garden; but you must not eat from the tree of the knowledge of good and evil, for when you eat from it you will certainly die" (Genesis 2:16-17). We need to understand something very important: God always has good reason for His instructions and guidance. It is most often to protect us, to prepare us, or to provide for us. In this case, by His instruction to "not eat," God was protecting Adam and Eve from the destructive **consequences** of this tree's fruit; but more than that, God was protecting you and me and His entire creation from that consequence—the consequence of knowing good *and* evil.

Sadly, Adam and Eve did not follow this instruction meant to protect them and us. Instead, they ate from the one forbidden tree. And their disobedience brought consequences. At that moment, death entered the world. At that moment, illness, pain, and war entered the world. And suffering entered the world at that point, too. Adam and Eve had opened up their knowledge of good—and that was good—but they had opened themselves to knowing *evil*, as well.

This is where *we* enter the story—because at that point, not only did the knowledge of evil enter the world; it also came upon all of humanity. In other words, the consequences of Adam and Eve's disobedience affected everyone and everything from that point forward, including us. The beautiful creation that God had put into place ended up in bondage to decay and suffering (Romans 8:8-21). Further, it brought death—and *death* now touches us all (as Romans 5:12).

Today, because of that one event, the world is broken. There is physical illness and disease. There are wars. There are evil deeds. And there are natural disasters. We also see **evidence** of death all around us—in our aging process, in evil that tries to overtake beauty, in abuse and injustice, and in other destructive measures.

So, let's go back to our first question: Why is there suffering in this world?

There is suffering because this world is broken.

Yes, this world is broken. Evil and suffering are here, and there is no going back. Every day, we see it, we read about it, and we hear about it—and then, sometimes, the world's brokenness impacts *our own experience,* and we are touched by it in a very **personal** way. We experience physical illness and disease, natural disasters, war, and the effects of others' evil deeds. We experience *the knowledge of evil.*

This leads us to our second "why" question:

WHY DID SUFFERING HAPPEN TO ME?

Imagine walking down a road that is newly paved and very clean. There are no potholes, there is no dirt or dust, and there are no vehicles. You can walk freely, wearing your best shoes, and you will not get dirty or hurt.

Then the road changes. The pavement ends and, in its place is a dirt path. The wind blows and sweeps dust into your eyes and onto your shoes. Eventually, it rains and turns the dirt to mud. And when the rain ends, you start to notice potholes in the road. At first, they are small enough that you can walk around them by slightly changing direction, but as you move on, the holes get wider and deeper, and they require much more effort to avoid. After a while, a car drives by, hits one of these potholes, and sprays you with mud. The muck of the road is now on you. *It was bound to happen,* you think. *The road is in such poor condition now that it is impossible to avoid its effects any longer.*

When you arrive at your destination, there is mud on your clothes, your hair is matted, and your shoes are filthy. If someone were to ask, "Why are you in such a condition?" you might respond, "There was no way to avoid it. Mud and rain and giant potholes and cars were all part of the road I had to travel."

The same is true for life. Pain, evil, illness, and disasters are all part of it, and there is no way to completely avoid them. *Brokenness and suffering are part of the road we must travel.* Keeping this insight in mind is not only helpful but also necessary to our healing. It helps us respond to the "Why me?" question with truth. In addition, it helps us to identify responses to this question that are *not* true.

For example, some might say, "If you just do the right thing, God will keep you from suffering." This is not true. In fact, God's word often tells us to *expect* suffering. Consider 1 Peter 4:12: "Dear friends, do not be surprised at the fiery ordeal that has come on you . . . as though something strange were happening to you." No one can live *perfectly* enough to **avoid** suffering, because suffering is already *in* this broken world—and so are we. Even Jesus lived a perfect life, and yet He experienced suffering in this world. Suffering is just part of the road that we travel.

Similarly, others say that you can avoid suffering if you just "have enough faith." This teaching does not appear anywhere in God's word either. Many biblical stories tell us that the men and women who put their faith in Him *definitely do* suffer. In fact, the people God chooses for great works often seem to suffer the most.

So, whenever you wonder, "Why did suffering happen to me?" remember the truth:

Suffering is an unavoidable result of the broken world we live in.

Suffering is simply part of the road we travel. Some of you may feel that this answer is too general or impersonal, because it depicts everyone together on the same muddy road. If this describes you, and you wonder, *Isn't there more to the story?* rest assured that our next lesson will take a more personal look at this conversation.

For now, to avoid getting stuck on the "Why me?" question over and over again, it is important that we understand this basic truth about our common experience: We are going to be touched by suffering simply because we are here.

REFLECTION AND APPLICATION

Let's discuss a question together:

What evidence do you see around you of the world's brokenness? Take time to think about some of the ways that death and the knowledge of evil can be seen in the world today.

> Give participants time to share in response to the question.

Now we have a question that is personal, so we will write our responses rather than share them with each other:

In what way has the world's brokenness touched your own life? What evidence do you have that suffering touches your life as you walk this road?

> Give participants time to write down responses to the question.

COURAGE AND PEACE

Today, we acknowledged suffering as a natural, expected, and unavoidable part of life. This is a difficult concept to accept, and your heart may still be wrestling with it. Yet, you are healing—one step at a time. And there *is* hope.

> God did this so that . . . we who have fled to take hold of the hope set before us may be greatly encouraged. We have this hope as an anchor for the soul, firm and secure. (Hebrews 6:18–19)

SESSION 16
WHERE IS GOD IN THE SUFFERING?

GOALS FOR PARTICIPANTS
- Acknowledge God's presence in the suffering
- Apply the following characteristics of God to this real part of our lives:
    - His omniscience
    - His omnipresence
    - His omnipotence

MATERIALS
- Lesson

VOCABULARY
- **chaos** (KAY-os): a state of utter confusion or disorder; turmoil
- **chaotic** (kay-OTT-ik): confused; disorderly
- **distracted** (dih-STRAK-tid): not paying attention; thinking of other things
- **ignorant** (IG-ner-uhnt): lacking in knowledge; unlearned
- **mystery** (MIS-tuh-ree): something that remains unexplained or unknown
- **theory** (THEE-uh-ree): a proposed explanation
- **tradition** (truh-DISH-un): a custom or belief passed from generation to generation
- **personal** (PUR-suh-nl): related to a particular person; related to me

GREETING

Each session begins with a greeting. This will be unique and personal to each group.

REVIEW

Last time, we began to talk about why suffering happens both in our world and in our personal lives. We discovered that suffering is just part of the road we are on, and there is no one who escapes it. Writings or teachings that say we can avoid the experience of suffering by living life in a certain way or by having a certain amount of faith are untruthful. We know this because God tells us that there will be suffering, and He says that we should expect it.

We discovered this so that we could reply truthfully to two common questions about suffering that tend to keep us stuck in place:

- Why is there suffering?
- Why did suffering have to happen to me?

In our next two lessons, we will discover truths in response to two more questions that can hold us back:

- Where is God in my suffering?
- Why did God allow this to happen

LESSON SCRIPT

We know that suffering is part of this broken world and that we must experience it. But if that's the case, then . . .

WHERE IS GOD IN THE SUFFERING?

If we allow Him, God can be our closest traveling companion and the only one we can completely trust. So, it is good to include Him in all of our conversations along our journey. Perhaps, He is a close companion of yours. Or perhaps, you regard Him as a distant, uninvolved acquaintance. Or maybe He is unfamiliar, even unwelcome.

There is no pressure here to change how you see God. However, it is wise to remain open to the possibilities. After all, who God is—or at least who we choose to believe He is—lays the foundation for all of our conclusions about suffering and life in general. For example, a person who chooses to believe that God does not exist or is not involved in our lives will approach life much differently than a person who sees God as a trustworthy companion and guide.

Often, when we try to define what God does and what He intends, we base our ideas on cultural or religious traditions, philosophies, or our own desires and fears. But it might be wise to also consider what He says about Himself. If we look in the Bible, we see that God describes Himself in multiple ways—too many for this study! So, here, we will discuss four of these characteristics that pertain most to our discussion.

The first three, which we talked about earlier, are about God being ALL in some area:

He is . . .

> omniscient (all-knowing),
>
> omnipotent (all-powerful), and
>
> omnipresent (all-present).

Do you remember these characteristics of God?

We will visit the fourth aspect of who He is in a moment, but first, let's stop here and see how these first three help answer our question *"Where is God in the suffering?"*

If God is all-knowing, then He is not **ignorant**, unaware, or **distracted**. If He is all-powerful, then He is not powerless, with His hands tied. If He is all-present, then He is never far off. The conclusion we draw from all of this is that *God knows our suffering, He is able to help us in our suffering, and He is present with us in our suffering.*

Some might not be happy with this answer. For some unknown reason, many of us feel comfortable including God in the *conversation of healing,* but when an attempt is made to include Him in the actual event—in *the experience of suffering*—we often push back. It is as if we don't want Him in that place of confusion or don't know what to do with Him, standing there in the presence of evil and pain. Maybe we even fear that we will feel angry or bitter toward Him or believe that He has betrayed us.

But if we are to make sense of this conversation, we must embrace truth. Only truth can hold up under the devastating pressure of suffering and withstand our desperate need to come to peace with hurt. We cannot cling to nice assurances that do not follow through to logical conclusions, because they will fail us every time. But if we follow the path honestly, we will eventually come to peace.

With that in mind, it is helpful to know that our minds often create **theories** that explain the *whys* of suffering in a way that keeps God outside the experience. These theories sound good and seem to make sense on the surface, but when we dig deeper, we see that they are actually untruths. Below are two such theories, each followed by a deeper truth that shows us how they are misleading.

Theory 1:

The brokenness of the world has led to **chaotic** events. These are like the potholes in the road. At random times, my life gets caught up in this **chaos**, and bad things happen. It is a bit like being in the wrong place at the wrong time. So, the suffering I experience is at the whim of chaos.

Truth:

It certainly appears that the world is in chaos. However, even the apparent chaos is under the authority of God's hand. Think back to what we know to be true about God. He is all-knowing, all-present, and all-powerful. If chaos rules, then God is not who He says He is. If God is who He says He is, then the chaos has boundaries.

There is a brilliant description of the intricacies of God's power, knowledge, and authority in Job 38-41. It's a good read. It makes us smile, cry, and laugh, and in this crazy world where so many run onto the stage and claim authority and power, these verses reassure us of who is holding the boundaries:

> Where were you when I laid the earth's foundation? . . . Who marked off its dimensions? (Job 38:4-5)

> Have you ever given orders to the morning, or shown the dawn its place? (Job 38:12)

> Does the eagle soar at your command and build its nest on high? (Job 39:27)

Other places in God's Word also assure us that the events of our life are *not* left to chaos; they are not random. Consider this passage in Psalm 139:16: "[His] eyes saw [your] unformed body; all the days ordained for [you] were written in [His] book before one of them came to be."

Theory 2:

God gives humankind free will. In other words, He allows people to choose whether to do right or wrong or even evil. My pain is the result of another person's free will used unwisely.

Truth:

The term "free will" is vague and often misused. It is more accurate to say that God gives us the privilege and accountability of decision-making. That is, He does not treat us as puppets or force or manipulate us into the choices we make. But is our will *free*? Well, not exactly—because the choices we make are often determined by the limits of our physical and mental capabilities, among other things.

Still, it is true that God gives us the privilege of choice. This does not mean, however, that He is at the mercy of our will. In a moment, we might find ourselves unable to overpower or refuse the actions of someone else due to a differential in age, strength, or authority. We might even feel that we are at the mercy of a physical disease or other circumstances. Yet, ultimately, in light of the descriptives *all-knowing*, *all-present*, and *all-powerful* —this truth remains: everything that happens in my life has passed through my Father's "ALL hands." This is true even when I feel at the mercy of something or someone else.

Let's go back to Job for a moment. The evil one had to go to God and request permission to inflict suffering on Job (see Job 1-2), and then God had to set—and remove —the boundaries on this suffering. The same is true in our lives: God does not create evil (remember, we learned how it entered the world in the previous lesson), but He gives permission for it to enter our lives. In the next session, we will discover truth to help us answer the question of why God gives this permission. But for now, it is important to understand that evil *does* submit to Him and cannot step over His boundaries. You are not at the mercy of man's will.

God shows us this in His Word:

> So do not fear, for I am with you; do not be dismayed, for I am your God. I will strengthen you and help you; I will uphold you with my righteous right hand. (Isaiah 41:10)

> Are not two sparrows sold for a penny? Yet not one of them will fall to the ground outside your Father's care. And even the very hairs of your head are all numbered. So don't be afraid; you are worth more than many sparrows. (Matthew 10:29–31)

What truths does this leave us with so far?

Truth 1: There is suffering in the world because it is broken.

Truth 2: We experience suffering because we live in this broken world.

Truth 3: God, being all-knowing, all-powerful, and all-present, is with us in our suffering.

We are not at the mercy of chaos. We are not at the mercy of man's will. *God is with us in our suffering.* This is such an amazing **mystery**. Beautiful. Profound. Mind-stretching. It is the kind of mystery that cannot be solved by gathering clues—it is a spiritual mystery. Spiritual mysteries are concepts that are beyond our understanding. They include the indescribable, incomprehensible, and wonderful aspects of God about which we sometimes have to say, "I can't explain it, but I know in my heart of hearts that it is true."

Our conversation about God's involvement in our suffering must sometimes include such *mystery*, because God's desire is that we embrace His presence in every part of our journey—even in our suffering. Only then can we accept that there is purpose in our suffering. We will talk about that more in the next lesson—but first, let's think about what we have learned today.

REFLECTION AND APPLICATION

It's important for us to take this time for reflection and application after each lesson, because it gives us the opportunity to think about how we can apply the truths that we have discussed. We can say that we believe many things about God, but God only becomes real in our lives when we apply what we believe to our actions. And it is only when God becomes real that we can truly discover how His truths help us along our path of healing.

With that in mind, let's talk about the following questions:

- In what ways have I blamed my suffering on the general chaos of the world?
- In what ways have I blamed my suffering on the will and actions of others?
- How can I open my heart and my mind to the presence of God in my suffering?

Give participants time to share in response to each question.

COURAGE AND PEACE

> Read the following to the participants.

Did God know?

Did He allow it?

Is it part of His plan for me?

As I consider all of the truths about my God and thoughtfully apply them to my life,

I come to a compelling conclusion:

My God is aware of the storm of suffering on the horizon.

He sees. He knows.

My God is powerful enough to prevent it or steer me in another direction.

And often, He does.

There are other times, however, that He takes my hand and,

full of loving intention, says,

> Come, child. We are going to walk into that storm.
> I am coming with you, and I will not leave your side.
> I will cover you with my feathers of protection,
> and under my wings you will take refuge.
> I will whisper direction to you: "Go to the right" or "Go to the left."
> Trust my purpose for you. Trust my goodness.
> Trust my love for you.
> Trust *me*.

Oh dearest Father,

"You hem me in behind and before and you lay your hand upon me. Such knowledge is too wonderful for me, too lofty for me to attain . . . all the days ordained for me were written in your book before one of them came to be. How precious to me are your thoughts, God!" (Psalms 139:5–6, 16–17)

So, this is not my fear; this is my unshakeable assurance:

GOD IS *WITH* ME IN MY SUFFERING.

SESSION 17
WHY DID GOD ALLOW THIS TO HAPPEN?

GOALS FOR PARTICIPANTS
- Apply the truth about God's goodness to the suffering in our lives
- Understand that our suffering has purpose
- Accept God's presence in our suffering as a blessing and as assurance

MATERIALS
- This lesson
- Teaching tool: A Visual of Suffering

VOCABULARY
- **bitter** (BIT-ur): having a harsh taste; distasteful; painful
- **good** (good): righteous, excellent, honorable, for a right purpose
- **purpose** (PUR-puhs): a reason that something exists or happens; an intended result or goal

GREETING

Each session begins with a greeting. This will be unique and personal to each group.

REVIEW

Previously, we talked about some very difficult questions:

- Why is there suffering in this world?
- Why did suffering happen to me?
- Where is God in the suffering?

What answers did we discover?

Allow the students to share. Listen for the responses given in the script below. Then use the script to help reinforce the truths of the previous lessons and to bring the sharing to a close.

Suffering exists because this world is broken by sin.

We experience suffering because we live in this broken world; it is part of the road we travel.

God, being all-knowing (omniscient), all-present (omnipresent), and all powerful (omnipotent), is with us in our suffering.

LESSON SCRIPT

Even as we think about the truth that *God is present with us in our suffering*, another *why* arises: If God knows about our suffering, is with us in our suffering, and is more powerful than our suffering, then *why, oh why, did He not stop it? Why did He allow it? Why did He not intervene?*

This is the perfect time to hear about the fourth characteristic of this One who is on the journey with us.

4. He is good.

> Praise the LORD, for the LORD is good. (Psalm 135:3)
>
> You are good, and what you do is good. (Psalm 119:68)

Although we may say that we believe God is good, God wants us to come to a place where we accept His goodness personally. This can be hard, because His goodness to us does not always *feel* good.

For example, some say God is not good because He allows children to go hungry. Some say God is not good because He allows floods and storms and wars and illness and sorrow of all kinds. Maybe you feel that God is not good because He did not stop the suffering that came into your life.

Remember that He knows all, including our questions and doubts. Listen to what He tells us:

> "For my thoughts are not your thoughts, neither are your ways my ways," declares the LORD. "As the heavens are higher than the earth, so are my ways higher than your ways and my thoughts than your thoughts." (Isaiah 55:8-9)

This does not mean that He thinks little of our pain. The Word tells us that God feels our pain to a great extent. His heart always turns toward the oppressed, the weak, and the suffering.

Rather, God is telling us that there is so much more to our story than even we know. He sees layer upon layer of circumstances and events; He sees into past, present, and future; and He sees the hearts and minds of everyone on Earth. What He knows is far beyond what we can ever know. And He participates in our lives with a purpose that is eternal.

Remember Joseph's story, in Genesis 37-50? Joseph was mocked and slandered by his brothers who, after deciding not to murder him, sold him into captivity in a faraway land. Things got better for a time, but then he was falsely accused of criminal activity, after which he was imprisoned and forgotten. Eventually, through a series of events, he came to a place of authority alongside the king under whose rule he had previously been imprisoned. And it was in this position that God used him to save many lives. Years later, when Joseph unexpectedly encountered his brothers again, this was his response to all of the suffering he had endured: "You intended to harm me, but God intended it for good to accomplish what is now being done, the saving of many lives" (Genesis 50:20).

Do you recognize the four characteristics of God in this story?

God *saw* Joseph's suffering (He is omniscient); God was present with Joseph in his suffering (He is omnipresent); and God had power over those who caused Joseph's suffering (He is omnipotent). God, in His *goodness* (He is good), also allowed this suffering to happen for an eternal purpose that Joseph could not see at the time.

This brings us to a pivotal point in our perspective of suffering:

> *We can know with certainty that God is involved in our lives*
> *in such a way that He will not allow the actions of others to change His plan for us.*

No one is more powerful than God. No one can sneak in and change God's plan for you while He is not looking. No one can fight Him for control of your life and win. Even though people may make decisions that impact your life, it is always done within God's knowledge, sight, and power—within His boundaries.

So, what do we do when circumstances seem unjust or unfair? We embrace the perfect goodness of God and remember that our suffering has purpose.

Early on in our journey, we were introduced to Naomi. Naomi was moved away from her home, family, and culture. She lost her husband, and, then as a widow, she faced the loss of her two sons. Naomi could have given in to numbness and despair, but *she did not*. She did not have every answer and she did not know what new challenges awaited her. She just kept listening to the quiet voice inside that called her forward. And then she took steps to move in and through and away from her pain.

In the process, *Naomi told her story*. And as we listen in on that story, we learn that Naomi lived out this very awareness of God. Remember, she didn't wrap up her pain in a pretty package and pretend to have answers for it. Rather, she told her story of sadness and loss with honest emotion and truthful words. She opened her heart and let it spill forth:

> "Don't call me Naomi," she told them. "Call me Mara, because the Almighty has made my life very bitter. I went away full, but the LORD has brought me back empty. Why call me Naomi? The LORD has afflicted me; the Almighty has brought misfortune upon me." (Ruth 1:20–21)

As she expressed her suffering, God became a natural part of that expression. Naomi spoke the raw truth of the situation while *also* expressing her understanding of who God is. Essentially, she said,

> "My loss has left me to feel empty. The events of my life taste bitter to me, and I feel afflicted and burdened. I remember how I used to feel, and now the blessing is gone—and it all happened by the hand of God."

There are those who say that Naomi *blamed* God; however, it is more accurate to say that Naomi *placed the responsibility* for the suffering on God. There is a subtle but important difference. Blame is often cast upon someone as an accusation of unfairness or neglect. Naomi, however, spoke of God with the highest and most profound worship, while, at the same time, she acknowledged her pain through His hand.

To understand this point more clearly, notice what Naomi did *not* say:

> "Why has God allowed this to happen to me? I don't deserve this suffering! God is not fair. I will no longer trust God because of this. In fact, this suffering proves to me that there is no God."

Naomi did not blame God. She also did not blame chaotic events or wrong choices. Rather, Naomi's words reveal that she saw her suffering clearly—and, more important, that she saw God's hand in it!

Now that we have discussed four big truths that can help us respond to our suffering, let's walk through a visual expression of these truths in our life.

> Use the Teaching Tool pictures at the end of this session to teach the next portion of the lesson. Introduce only one picture at a time as you tell the story. You may fold on the dotted lines to keep other pictures out of sight. The script will tell you when to display each.

These images might bring our expectations—as well as reality—to life. Let's begin with our expectations. Many of us tend to anticipate life's journey to look like this:

> Display picture #1 as you read the following script.

Green grass, blue sky. A few clouds, but nothing too overwhelming. Shade is available, as needed. When there is no immediate crisis, we can typically maintain this image of life.

But then . . . moments of crisis enter the picture.

> Display picture #2.

We experience suffering, and we wonder, *Why?*

Why has this happened? And why me?

How could God allow such terrible events to ruin my previously beautiful image? Is He uncaring or cruel? Is He unaware? Is He weak against evil? I thought He loved us and was looking out for us!

But there is a problem with these questions—their logic is based on an incorrect visual. That's because our original image of life was not based on truth.

You see, as related to suffering, this is the real image of our journey in this world.

> Display picture #3.

The road is muddy and full of potholes. Opportunities for suffering abound. Evil is active, seeking ways to undo us. Thus, moments of crisis are all around. Most of these realities are unseen, unfelt, and unrecognized in our everyday lives. But the truth is, *they are there.*

This is why, after crisis enters the picture, it does not work when we try to put our former image of beauty back into place and move on with life as it *should* be. It does not work because that former image was not based on reality. In reality, life on Earth does *not* look like green grass and blue sky until God, unthinkingly and without reason, allows crisis to enter. Instead, the true image of the world is broken and dirty, tainted by the knowledge and influence of evil—and we are living in the midst of it. The reality is that we are surrounded by moments of crisis from the very beginning.

This picture of reality can feel discouraging and even distressing. But when we look closer, we can see the situation more accurately.

Display picture #4.

Look carefully, and you will see someone present who is very important in this conversation. He is our companion on the journey.

This Ruler of ALL—who sees all, knows all, and is all-powerful—sees every opportunity for suffering that exists in this broken world. And when that brokenness becomes more personal to you, He becomes more involved in your life: He reduces risk, lessens the impact, protects. He attends to every crisis that hovers over you or even threatens from afar. In His perfect knowledge of you, and in His profound awareness of what is good, He allows only particular moments of crisis to touch your life. For each moment of crisis that He allows, there are many others from which He protects you.

The suffering that touches you does not do so at the whim of chaos or at the will of others; it is filtered through His loving hands. Because of this, there is even more to the picture.

Display picture #5.

Meet Christ, the Good Shepherd.

Whenever the Ruler of ALL filters suffering through His all-knowing hands and allows it to touch your life in a personal way, He ensures that the Good Shepherd steps into that experience with you.

What does that mean for us? It means that He increases our strength, both physically and emotionally, beyond what we think we have. Perhaps you have even said to yourself, as I have, "How did I do that? How did I make it through?" That was the result of your Good Shepherd adding His strength to yours, so that you could accomplish the tasks, large and small, that lay beyond your capabilities.

Sometimes He encourages us, through other people or through our awareness of His presence. Other times, He gives discernment when we do not know what decision to make. And at all times, whether walking alongside you or carrying you in His arms, His eyes are on you and His heart is for you.

These images speak clearly: The world is broken. Suffering and evil abound. But you are not at the mercy of chaos, random events, or the evil intent of others. Rather, God protects you from much potential suffering. God filters what will be allowed to touch your life. He draws the boundaries that determine to what extent it can touch you. And then He stands with you in the suffering.

What new truths does this knowledge make clear to us?

> There is no suffering where God is not present.
>
> With God, there is no suffering without purpose.
>
> With God, there is no suffering that can destroy us.
>
> And, finally—with God, there is always the potential for healing.

These may be truths that we already knew about God in our minds. But they will not impact our healing until we embrace them with our hearts. This embrace might not happen all at once, in one big decision, but that's okay—because our perfect Traveling Companion is patient and will remain close, and He will offer us persistent words of assurance.

In the meantime, practice embracing these truths with your heart whenever the past events of your life sweep over you, one after another, and remind you of the devastation. There may be a time when you lift your gaze to the heavens and whisper, "Was that really necessary?" After time, you will hear the simple answer come: "I am ALL. I am good. There has been purpose in your suffering."

This is why Naomi was able to respond as she did. To see God in her suffering did not frighten her. In fact, understanding that her affliction had passed through her Father's hands is what gave her the confidence to launch out again into the unknown. Her awareness of God in her suffering is what kept her in conversation with Him. And it is that awareness that made it possible for her to hear His voice say, "Move forward."

> *Naomi felt suffering to the depth of her being.*
> *But she knew to that same depth that God was there.*
> *God. The Almighty. The LORD. Her LORD.*

Likewise, the conversation that we have with God during our suffering is extremely important. God knows when we say only what we think He wants us to say or what others dictate to us. He also knows when our words to Him are genuine. But it only is our honest conversation with Him that will eventually lead us to a place where we can make peace, both with the suffering and with God.

REFLECTION AND APPLICATION

Let's talk about God's goodness. How is God's goodness different from our own?

What did you learn from Naomi about how to respond to God during suffering?

How can you put into practice what you have learned about God's goodness and presence in your suffering?

Allow the students to share in response to the questions above.

Watch for God's goodness this week. Practice embracing it in your heart by doing one or more of the following things:

- Write it down.
- Tell God that you see His goodness—naming the goodness out loud to Him.
- Speak of God's goodness to someone else.

COURAGE AND PEACE

As we leave today, let's remember to take these truths with us:

There is no suffering where God is not present.

With God, there is no suffering without purpose.

With God, there is no suffering that can destroy us.

With God, there is always potential for healing.

TEACHING TOOL
A VISUAL OF SUFFERING

#1

#2

#3

#4

#5

SESSION 18
HOPE

GOALS FOR PARTICIPANTS
- Have a clear understanding of *a hope* as contrasted with *wishing*
- Recognize that there is only one true source of hope
- Embrace God, I Am, as their worthy and dependable hope

MATERIALS
- This lesson
- Plain paper; pencils and pens

VOCABULARY
- **absolute** (ab-suhl-OOT): complete; perfect
- **despair** (dih-SPAIR): the absence of hope; feeling of hopelessness
- **disappointment** (dis-uh-POINT-muhnt): sadness caused because one's hopes or expectations are not fulfilled
- **hope** (HOPE): the feeling that something can be; to look forward with confidence

GREETING

Each session begins with a greeting. This will be unique and personal to each group.

REVIEW

We have completed a serious and important conversation about suffering. We asked the difficult "why" questions and learned some truth that is helpful to us as we face past, present, and future suffering. What truths were important and helpful to you? In what way can these truths help you move forward in your healing?

The central truth we came away with is that God is with us. We often can't explain how but we know that He is all-knowing, all-present, all-powerful, and good. This is a great assurance to us.

LESSON SCRIPT

Today we are going to talk about hope. What is hope? What do you think hope is? What kinds of things have you heard people say about hope?

> Allow participants to briefly share their thoughts.

Hope is something that people often talk about during hard times. For example, it's not uncommon to hear the advice that we should "have hope" in our suffering. That's because, in general, people tend to think that hope is good—we believe it is something that we *should* have or that will help us. And so, we smile and say, "Yes, I have hope. Isn't it wonderful?" But deep down, we are often not so sure. Because of our pain, we feel conflicted and uncertain. The suffering of our past and present has cast shadows over our thoughts of the future and darkened our view—and in this dimmed light, hope has become hard to see —and even harder to grasp. Our relationship with hope has become a struggle. Here are a few common ways that we can struggle:

> **We feel *incapable* of hope.** To think about hope requires that we think about the future. But sometimes our pain is so great that we can't see past the next few hours, let alone hope in something more distant.
>
> Alternatively, some of us might be able to think about the future, but we may not see any chance that life will get better. In fact, if our crisis event is still ongoing, we may feel that we will never move beyond our current circumstances.
>
> Either way, suffering feels like an oppressive and threatening place where we are trapped, and we see no hope that we will ever find our way out. We are convinced that the way life is now is the way life will always be. Deep inside, we believe that nothing can change.
>
> **We feel *guilty* to have hope.** If our trauma involved harm that was done to others, we might think, *Why should something good happen to me when others were hurt so deeply?* Or if we believe that some part of the trauma was our own fault, we might feel undeserving of the opportunity to hope.
>
> **We feel *unwilling* to hope.** Overwhelmed by the surety of failure and pain, we may simply choose not to hope. We may believe that when we dare to hope, we simply set ourselves up for failure. So, why should we allow ourselves to take a chance on good?

Suffering is not the only reason we struggle with hope, however. We likely feel conflicted for another reason— and that reason lies in the very definition of the word *hope*. With that in mind, let's look closer at what this word really means.

Usually when we use the word *hope*, it comes with a feeling of expectation. In other words, whenever we want to express our expectation or desire for a particular thing—usually a good thing—we often use the word *hope*. For example, we might say the following:

> I *hope* you feel better.
> I *hope* it does not rain today.
> I *hope* I get that job.
> I *hope* I can pay my bills.

Used in this way, the word *hope* expresses the very *real possibility* of good. It also expresses our determination to take a chance on that possibility—maybe even to look forward to it with longing, if not confidence. This is a positive perspective of hope.

But if we look closely, we will see that in the very same word, this positive perspective is packaged together with another idea—the idea that *the outcome is uncertain*. We know this because, if we were sure of the outcome, we would not use the word *hope*. Instead, we would use words like these:

> I *know* you will feel better.
> It *will* not rain today.
> I *have been assured of* that job.
> I *will* have the money to pay my bills.

This part of the word's meaning can even make the use of *hope* feel sad. We sometimes actually hear this sadness in the tone of voice with which hope is expressed, such as in, "Well, I *hope* that works out."

How interesting that the same word used to express the possibility of good is also used to express the potential for failure. No wonder we feel conflicted when we think about hope! The word's very meaning is conflicted—it recognizes that what we want may or may not come to be, and it acknowledges that **disappointment** is just as likely as satisfaction.

When we consider how this conflicted meaning of hope looks under the shadows of our suffering, we gain a deeper appreciation of the struggle we are in. In fact, this struggle is the reason why, for many of us, despair begins to feel like a more realistic option than hope.

What is despair? **Despair** is the very absence of hope. It says that bad always wins over good. And it says that our choices do not matter, because nothing ever changes. When we listen to despair, we begin to wonder how we could ever truly hope for something good, when there is always the possibility that something bad will happen. We wonder why we should hope, when our satisfaction is never assured.

And yet, even as we doubt and wonder, it is hard not to hear the thin whisper of something else deep within us. It is hard to ignore the urge, be it ever so small, to keep our hands outstretched toward something besides despair—and hope seems like the right thing.

And so, we are left with a choice. We must either . . .

- hope (because, although good is not assured, it is still possible)
- or give in to despair (because we see no possibility of good).

Although one of these options might seem slightly more beneficial, choosing one over the other still involves chance and risk. Neither option offers absolute assurance that good will win.

Fortunately, we have a third option—and that is to understand hope from a different perspective. This perspective is just as viable as the others and offers the view that hope is "a sure thing."

To fully understand this new perspective of hope and why it's necessary, let's look a little bit closer at why our old idea of hope is a problem. We already discussed that its meaning is conflicting and can even feel sad. But another problem is that there is *no assurance* that the good we want to happen will actually happen. We can hope all we want, but no amount of hope will change the outcome. It would be great if we could wish more or hope harder to increase our chances that we would get what we want, but it simply does not work that way.

This tells us that surety does not lie *in how strongly we hope*; rather, it lies in *the object of our hope*—or what we put our hope into. In other words, if we want the kind of hope that comes with assurance, we must know with one hundred percent certainty that whatever or whoever we put our hope in will not fail. We must put our desires and expectations into a *sure thing*.

With that in mind, let's think about what we now put our hopes into—the objects of our hope. Think carefully. Is there anyone or anything in your life that you would consider *a sure thing*? Is there anyone or anything that you can place your hope in with *all confidence*? You may think, *Yes!*, but remember, we are not talking about someone or something that you simply "think well of" or "expect the best of" or "wish" will always be there. Rather, we are talking about someone or something that you have a hundred percent assurance will never fail.

There may be someone or something in your life that comes close to meeting this criteria, but in reality, there is always some potential for failure: people can move away or literally be gone in a heartbeat; material objects are subject to decay and damage; even principles or ideas, no matter how fail-proof they may seem, are always prone to error and change.

In fact, one of the reasons we are in pain now is because the objects of our hope failed us. Maybe we are suffering because a loved one betrayed us, our health diminished, our house was taken by a natural disaster, or we endured through any other number of potential tragedies. Regardless of the circumstances, the root of our suffering is the same: reality came to our front door, uninvited, and shattered our desires and expectations—reality shattered our hope. When we think about it this way, it seems that there is *no sure thing* that we can put our hope in—because no person or thing or idea on this earth will ever be immune to failure.

So where does this leave us? Is there any *sure thing* that we can put our hope into? Is there anything or anyone that we know, with one hundred percent certainty, will never fail? And if there is, how would we identify it? What characteristics would we look for?

Here are some ideas:

- To start, if we want assurance that the object of our hope will not fail, then it must be **absolute**—or free from imperfection. This means it must be immune to any kind of failure, even failure caused by the harsh influences of life, such as death or disaster, damage or decay.

- In addition, if we are to have a hundred percent certainty in the object of our hope, we must know that, regardless of circumstances, it will not change or waver. It must also be something or someone we can rely on no matter where we are physically located.

- Finally, if perfection and goodness are to result from our hope, then what we hope in must be good and truthful and just, and it must have our best interests at heart.

It seems impossible for anyone or anything to have all of these characteristics. And yet there is One:

He is absolute—free from imperfection.

He is all-knowing and all-powerful.

He is unchanging and unchangeable.

He is eternal and present everywhere at once.

He is accessible to all people, at all times.

He is good and just.

He is love and truth.

He knows and cares for each one of us intimately.

He is our creator, and He literally holds all things together.

He calls Himself I AM.

Yes, you most often hear Him called God. But in the book of Exodus, when He announces His plan to rescue His people, who are *suffering* and have *lost their hope*, He introduces Himself as I AM.

As the story goes, God instructs a man named Moses to lead the effort to rescue hundreds of thousands of families out of slavery—and Moses has questions. Moses knows that these people, the Israelites, have suffered abuse for decades. Year upon year upon year, they have lived without any hope. And yet now he must go and ask them to put their hope in his leadership. So,

> Moses said to God, "Who am I that I should . . . bring the Israelites out of Egypt?" And God said, "I will be with you. . . . " Moses said to God, "Suppose I go to the Israelites and say to them, 'The God of your fathers has sent me to you,' and they ask me, 'What is his name?' Then what shall I tell them? God said to Moses, "I AM who I AM. This is what you are to say to the Israelites: 'I AM has sent me to you.'" (Exodus 3: 11–14)

I AM. This name for God tells us He is ALL and He is GOOD. And because He is I AM, He is a *sure thing*—we can put our hope in Him.

Every other thing and every other person on our path has fallen short—or has the capability to fall short in due time. There is no person who is worthy of our complete trust. There is no sure thing to which we can attach our hope. But then our Traveling Companion says, *"I AM,"* and suddenly, there is more to the story. In the midst of all the unknowns and uncertainties and disappointments of life, He is the one answer for the longing that is inside all of us for an absolute hope.

I AM is a name full of meaning and value. It holds layer upon layer of truth. When God says, "I AM," He expresses the following:

> I AM absolute—free from imperfection.
>
> I AM all-knowing and all-powerful.
>
> I AM unchanging and unchangeable.
>
> I AM eternal and present everywhere at once.
>
> I AM accessible to all people at all times.
>
> I AM good and just.
>
> I AM love and truth.
>
> I AM the one who knows you and cares for you intimately
>
> I AM your creator, and I literally hold all things together.

And as such, He also says,

> I AM *worthy of your complete trust.*
>
> I AM *a sure thing.*
>
> I AM *your hope.*

Our creator knows that we need hope, or He would not have inspired this writing:

> "Let us hold *unswervingly* to the hope we profess for he who promised is faithful" (Hebrews 10:23; emphasis mine).

What does this verse tell us?

We need not give up hope or choose despair. Neither should we get stuck between the two, unable to move forward from the uncertainty that arises from our old idea of hope, which offers no assurance.

We must not focus on the *act of hope* and be consumed by wishful thinking, which puts us at the mercy of chance and luck. Although this may calm our spirits for a time, because we temporarily push aside the pain of reality, eventually, our luck will run dry and things will not turn out "as we hope."

We must shift our focus to the object of our hope. But rather than entrust ourselves to one undependable wish after another, each one eventually falling short, we are to hold *unswervingly*—to what?—to *the hope Himself.* No other person or thing that we put our hope in will hold us in the storm. There is only One who can say, "*I AM*" and then prove that He Is.

REFLECTIONS AND APPLICATION

What has your experience of hope been? Do you often just "wish" that good things will happen? Which of your hopes have gone unfulfilled and resulted in disappointment?

In the coming days, watch for opportunities to replace your wishes for something good to happen with true hope. For example, if you think, *I hope I get a new position at work,* replace this wishful thinking with a new thought, based on the one sure object of our hope; for example, *Regardless of whether I get that new position, I know that God, my sure hope, will help me in my work.*

COURAGE AND PEACE

Listen to the following reminders from God about His intention and assurance of hope for us.

For those who hope in the LORD will renew their strength. They will soar on wings like eagles; they will run and not grow weary, they will walk and not be faint. (Isaiah 40:31)

May the God of hope fill you with all joy and peace as you trust in him, so that you may overflow with hope. (Romans 15:13)

SESSION 19
OTHERS IN OUR STORY

GOALS FOR PARTICIPANTS
- Recognize others who are a part of our story of suffering
- Understand that these others may respond to the same crisis event differently than we do
- Understand the need to let others take their own journeys of healing
- Release others to their own timelines of healing and their own emotions of pain

MATERIALS
- This lesson
- Plain paper; pencils and pens

VOCABULARY
- **compare** (kuhm-PAIR): to consider or describe two or more things as similar or alike
- **intensity** (in-TEN-sih-tee): strength; power or depth

GREETING

Each session begins with a greeting. This will be unique and personal to each group.

REVIEW

Our previous discussion might have caused you to think carefully about *real hope*. Did it surprise you to discover that much of our hope is actually wishful thinking? And yet there is a true and dependable hope—the God who is ALL. In what ways is God ALL? How do these characteristics give you real hope?

Allow participants to share in response to the questions above.

We will find in this lesson—and in many to come—that the characteristics of God are of great importance to us. We need this God who is ALL to be with us as we respond to our suffering and to those who caused our suffering. He is the one who is our real and true hope when everything and everyone else fails.

LESSON SCRIPT

Thus far, each of us has told our own stories and talked about our own perspectives of suffering. But there are likely additional perspectives to consider, too—those viewpoints of others who are part of our story. These people may have been good to us, or they may have caused harm. They may have even been innocent bystanders affected by the same tragedy we were. But in some way, they were touched by our story of suffering.

Regardless of whether they continue to be a part of our everyday lives or whether we will never see them again, it is important that we take time to recognize these other people and perspectives, along with our reactions to them—especially when our relationships have been impacted. It is not uncommon for the relationships in our lives to change as a result of suffering. Some bonds may break, while others can grow stronger. And some changes may be neither good nor bad; they are just *changes*. Maybe we don't even understand why a particular relationship is not as it once was—we only know that something is different.

All of this is okay. We have learned that "new and different" can be a safe place, especially because the Good Shepherd is in that place with us. We have also learned that it is important to face the reality of the effects of our suffering, which includes the changes—because if we expect everything to be as it was before, this causes trouble and disappointment. And so, we must think about the changes in our relationships. We must also think about the changes in those people that we have—or had—relationships with, as well as our responses to them.

To do this, we must start with a recognition that each person's journey through suffering is unique. No two people who experience a crisis will have the same journey through healing—and that includes those impacted by the exact same event. One person may experience different emotions than the next, for example, or two people who feel a similar emotion will express that emotion differently. In addition, each of us experiences emotions with a different level of **intensity**. And we each have our own timeline of healing.

Think of it this way: Earlier in this study we talked about how it is unhealthy to keep our pain hidden and locked away in a box, and so each of us learned how to take our suffering out of that box. We started by telling our story, and then each of us took steps toward understanding "the way life is now." That initial part of our journey was very personal to us, and it has continued to be that way since. It is so personal that, even if others were touched by the same tragedy we were, we could not expect them to see or recount the events that played out in same way we would; neither could we expect them to feel or express the exact same emotions we do. And if their healing process seemed faster or slower than ours, we could not be surprised.

Even if two people have undergone the same tragedy and live in the same house or belong to the same family, each must walk a personal road through suffering and healing. Consider siblings or neighbors or coworkers who want to heal from a shared crisis. One may respond in anger, while another feels fear and guilt, and a third person pretends that all is fine—because they are not ready to take their suffering out of the box. Each person is at a different place in their journey; each experiences and expresses different emotions; and each will face loss on a different timeline. In fact, as time goes on, they may even "exchange" places on the journey, "swap" emotions, and change their rate of speed! The losses we feel can be different, as well. One person might grieve the absence of a particular thing very deeply, while their friend or family member does not.

In addition to differences in the way individuals process suffering, there are also more generalized variations in the way groups of people respond, due to cultures, values, resources, and other factors. For example, one family may process the loss of a loved one differently than another family, each community or tribe may react to the same natural disaster in its own way, and citizens in war-torn countries may respond variously to the tragic events. Each group will respond in their own way, at a time that seems right to them—and, in turn, each person in that group will also respond individually.

Suffering is not *comparable*. I cannot **compare** my suffering to yours. Our suffering is personal to each of us—in its impact, in the fallout that comes after, in the ways it pushes against our everyday lives. Because of this truth, I cannot become angry with others because they do not share my feelings, even though we share the same crisis event. I cannot force someone to feel "my" anger or share my perspective. Perhaps, I can respond to someone's different perspective by sharing my own or even demonstrating it through my actions, but I cannot insist that their response look like mine or impose my own steps of healing upon them.

So, for example, maybe you discover a new truth—even one from this study—that helps you move forward, but when you share it with someone close to you, they do not give you the response you expected. They do not feel the relief that you felt for yourself. This is because you encountered that truth on your road. It is personal to *you*. Neither of you can become angry with or impose your own viewpoint on the other because they responded differently.

We may find this difficult at times, because our emotions and responses seem so clear to us, and we truly feel that they are the correct emotions and responses. But if we cause someone to feel guilty or ashamed because their response to suffering is different than ours, then we have not only hindered their healing but added to their suffering. We may have also created confrontation, which can lead to hurt feelings, strained relationships, and other problems. And so, we must give each person the freedom to take their own journey through suffering.

Think of your journey like a complicated jigsaw puzzle that you must put together. You have been left with a mess of mixed-up pieces—details, emotions, and responses—that you must sort through, identify, and lay out before you try to piece them together. To go through this process with your own puzzle is difficult enough: you must study your pieces, with their various colors and shapes and designs, and then put them together based on their best fit. But what would happen if you told another person to complete their puzzle in the exact same way as you? That would be an impossible task. They might have pieces that look similar to yours, but in reality, your two sets would not be exactly the same—because you each have pieces unique to your puzzle's design. Even if they wanted to follow your lead, they would need to force-fit together the similar-looking pieces, which would result in a muddled, incomplete picture. And if they were offended at your suggestion, then conflict might ensue.

This is why we cause more problems if we insist that others respond to suffering as we do—or worse, insist that everyone in a group respond in a united way. But if each person can freely and honestly take their own journey of suffering—and allow others to do the same—then we have the opportunity to take *our individual journeys in peace together.*

REFLECTIONS AND APPLICATION

Consider the others in your story of suffering. Is there someone that you must release to their own journey of suffering? What might that look like?

If you are suffering from an event that happened to a group of people, what differences do you see in how people have responded? Has this caused additional trouble between individuals or groups of people?

Let's talk about how we can mourn and heal as a group while still taking our own personal journey through suffering and toward healing.

Invite participants to share in response to the questions above.

COURAGE AND PEACE

God gives everyone the opportunity to heal by coming close to Him in a personal way. He does not expect everyone to suffer in the same way. He does not require particular steps for healing. God meets you personally wherever you are, and He offers you courage, peace, and hope for your own unique journey.

SESSION 20
THOSE WHO CAUSED THE HARM

GOALS FOR PARTICIPANTS
- Express our thoughts and emotions about pain inflicted by others
- Understand the dangers of revenge and vengeance
- Release our desire for revenge and vengeance
- Allow justice

MATERIALS
- This lesson
- Plain paper; pencils and pens

VOCABULARY
- **justice** (JUHS-tis): moral rightness; the provision of a deserved punishment or reward
- **revenge** (ri-VENJ): to pay back harm with more harm
- **vengeance**: (VEN-juhns): the intent to harm another because they have harmed you

GREETING

Each session begins with a greeting. This will be unique and personal to each group.

REVIEW

It can be easy to assume that everyone who suffers—especially when they are involved in the same crisis—will have the same emotions and responses to it; but we learned in our previous lesson that this is not always true. In fact, we add tension to the situation when we expect—or worse, force—others to respond as we do. If each person can freely and honestly take their own journey of suffering, however, and can allow others to do the same, then we have the opportunity to walk together in peace.

Was this lesson helpful to you? How did this advice affect how you see others in your story? How did it affect your relationships?

Allow participants to share in response to the questions above.

LESSON SCRIPT

In this lesson, we will continue to talk about the others in our story, but we will shift our focus to those who may have caused our suffering.

There is a chance that at least some of your suffering has come through the actions of others—whether one person or several. In some stories, it may be immediately clear who fits this role, but in others, the actors may not be obvious. It could be a stranger, an acquaintance, or someone very close to you—maybe even a family member. Or perhaps, there is a combination of people. Regardless, their role in causing your pain means that your relationship with them somehow changed. Here are some examples of what that might look like:

- A stranger, with no previous connection, was pulled into your story because of the crisis.
- A once-trusted person shattered your expectations, so you stopped trusting them—but due to that person's position or relationship with you, you either feel obligated to remain loyal to them or you continue to long for reconciliation.
- A family member broke your trust in a conflict that would have once been unimaginable, but you feel the continued need to protect them because you think that you should be loyal to family at all costs.
- A friend's actions broke your mutual relationship, and you have no desire to repair the friendship or return it to its former status.

These are the types of situations we often want to keep shut away in a box, with the hope that they will take care of themselves. They won't. Because these relationship changes were caused by hurt, they will continue to set up roadblocks on our path to healing unless we address them in a way that leads us to peace—peace within ourselves and with the state of these relationships going forward.

This subject is a difficult one for many reasons. But our Creator God knows this, and so He opens this discussion in His Word. He also knows that we tend to respond to those who hurt us in ways that hinder our healing, so He addresses this directly.

One such unhealthy response to those who cause us pain is to *cover over* evil. There are times when a group of people, even a church, will cover up the evil done by one of their members. They might do this to protect the reputation of someone—either the evildoer or the group—or they might simply want to avoid the confrontation that can come when evil is revealed. Alternatively, they might cover up evil because they underestimate its impact. Regardless of the reason, whenever we cover up intentional abuse against another person, we put ourselves on the opposite side of God. Remember that God's heart is for the victim, the abused, the weak, and the oppressed—and by protecting evil, we add to the abuse of the victim.

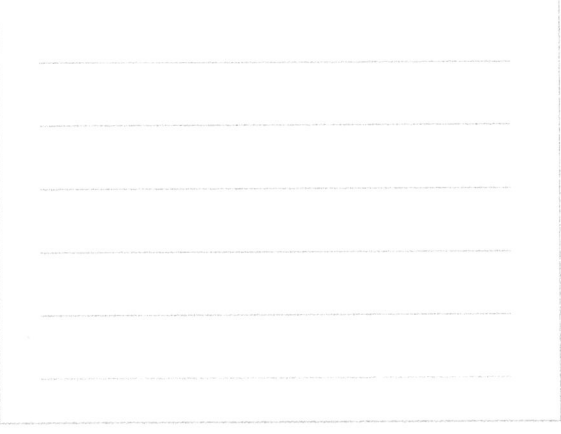

Another unhealthy response is **vengeance**. To take vengeance is to pay back evil for the evil that has been done to us. Vengeance is a common response to hurt. People, tribes, and even countries often take vengeance on others.

A more personal or individual form of vengeance is **revenge.** When someone hurts us, and we begin to think about ways that we can hurt them back, we consider revenge. Wrapped up in the emotions of revenge is the desire for the other person to comprehend the hurt they inflicted on us. With amazement, we look on, as their actions, words, and even facial expressions seem to prove that they lack awareness of the deep pain and destruction they have caused, and we want them to understand our pain. We also tend to feel that we have the right to exact payback, and so we consider ways that we can make them hurt as much as we do.

Yet, God tells us over and over again that we should *not* pay back evil for evil. Consider the following verses:

Make sure that nobody pays back wrong for wrong. (1 Thessalonians 5:15)

Do not take revenge, my dear friends, but leave room for God's wrath. (Romans 12:19)

Do not say, "I'll do to them as they have done to me; I'll pay them back for what they did." (Proverbs 24:29)

You see, there is an inbuilt problem with vengeance and revenge: We are never able to "pay back" the exact amount, with the same emotion and the same results. In fact, the "results" are often that the person who is paid back feels equally if not more wronged, after which they respond with their own revenge—and the cycle continues. So, God knows that if we try to repay evil for evil, the only thing we will accomplish is to move from one difficult situation to another, each escalated above the last, until things sometimes even become dangerous. Imagine what it would be like if every person took revenge—the trouble would never end!

Yet, without repayment for the hurt that was done, the matter can feel unsettled. We may wonder if it is even possible to move forward from the pain caused by others if we do not seek, or at least hope, for vengeance. After all, isn't that the purpose of justice—to "settle the score"?

Justice is "rightness." Justice is a part of God's plan in this world. But justice and vengeance are not the same thing. Although we are to refuse the instinct to intentionally pay back the evil that is done, that does not mean it is wrong for justice to be done. When we refuse to seek vengeance, this does not mean we refuse to allow justice to do its job.

From our close and emotional viewpoint, it can be easy to feel that if we do not immediately settle the score, we might be swallowed up by our pain while the other person gets away with evil. But our God sees the situation from a timeless vantage point—one in which perfect and complete **justice** will happen at His appointed time.

So, if we are not to cover up or seek revenge for evil, then what *do* we do?

The answer to that question is this:

We speak the truth.

And we wait for God to carry out justice in the appropriate and right way.

You see, when we cover over evil or take revenge, we bring only more problems and suffering; but when God exacts His own form of vengeance on those who hurt the weak, He is able to bring perfect justice. Sometimes, He does this through the legal system or other authorities. Sometimes, He uses circumstances to bring discipline upon someone in some way. And in some instances, we may not even see God's justice occur, but we can trust that it will come in the right way and at the appointed time—whether that be in this lifetime or in the next.

God's anger *does* come against those who harm the weak and the oppressed. It *will* come. For the weak and oppressed hold a special place in His heart:

> But if you do wrong, be afraid, for rulers do not bear the sword for no reason. They are God's servants, agents of wrath to bring punishment on the wrongdoer. (Romans 13:4)

It brings great relief and peace when we give up the need to "make someone pay" and place that responsibility into God's hands instead.

REFLECTIONS AND APPLICATION

Let's take some time now to share about these unhealthy responses in our own stories.

Do you ever have the desire to cover over evil? Or do you ever have a deep longing for the person who caused your pain to feel your hurt? If so, do these thoughts or feelings ever impact your actions?

Allow participants time to discuss the questions.

Without giving specific names or events, let's talk about how these unhealthy responses can cause harm in our families, communities, and churches.

Allow participants time to share their ideas in response to this discussion prompt. Be careful to avoid talking about specific people, groups, or churches. The intent is to understand that these unhealthy responses do cause harm rather than bringing resolution.

One way that we can help ourselves with these unhealthy thoughts and feelings is to write a letter to the person or people who wronged us—a letter we will never deliver. This is not an opportunity to be vengeful with accusatory words. This is an opportunity to express how their actions made us feel—for example, how we were hurt or felt betrayed. It can help us to express our pain without actually expressing it to those who hurt us. Putting our words and thoughts onto paper in this way can also help us relieve our minds and hearts of those words and thoughts.

Again, we will not give this letter to the person. We will not even share what we have written with each other because if we did, we would put thoughts in one another's minds and stir up feelings that were not necessary or good.

As you write your letter, know that it might feel and look *ugly*—even though you will not share what you have written, you might be unsure whether you even want to admit some of your emotions to yourself. But to face these ugly emotions is part of the cleansing—the cleansing that opens the wound for healing.

So, let's write our letters. And then, when we're finished, we will give the emotions and hurts that we have expressed on the page to God, because He knows what to do with them. How can we share with Him? We can honestly read the letter to God. We can trust Him with our suffering, and we can trust that He will bring justice. He alone knows best how to defend us, and He will do it at just the right time and in the right manner.

What do we do with the letter? It is best to destroy the letter so that it cannot fall into hands that might carry it to another and add fuel to the fire of hurt or revenge. This conversation is with God, only, because He is the one who expresses perfect compassion and justice.

> Allow participants time to write their letters.

COURAGE AND PEACE

The conversation today focused on some negative experiences and feelings. So, to help you end the session with a more positive spirit, I want to give you some thoughts to take with you: Remember that when you feel weak, God's heart is for you. He sees every instance in which you have been wrongfully hurt—even when no one else is aware. He stands with you. You are not alone.

This verse is for you:

> The LORD is a refuge for the oppressed, a stronghold in times of trouble. (Psalm 9:9)

Let's say it together and insert our name:

The LORD is a refuge for _____, a stronghold in times of trouble

SESSION 21
FORGIVENESS

GOALS FOR PARTICIPANTS
- Understand what forgiveness is
- Understand what forgiveness is not
- Embrace the peace that comes from following God's instructions for forgiveness

MATERIALS
- This lesson
- Participant worksheet: Forgiveness: A Poem
- Plain paper; pencils and pens

VOCABULARY
- **forgiveness** (for-GIVE-ness): an act in which you forgive; to stop feeling angry or resentful in response to an offense
- **misconception** (mis-kuhn-SEP-shuhn): an incorrect idea or conclusion
- **repentance** (rih-PEN-tuhns): deep sorrow over a wrongdoing; a change of heart and mind that causes you to turn away from wrongdoing; a stated commitment to turn away from wrongdoing
- **restore** (rih-STOR): to return something back to its original condition; to return someone to a former position or relationship

GREETING

Each session begins with a greeting. This will be unique and personal to each group.

REVIEW

It is likely that some of the pain you have experienced is due to the intentional or unintentional actions of others—whether one or many. We are often tempted to cover over the evil that has been done to us to take revenge, but what did we learn about those responses in our previous lesson?

Allow participants to briefly share their thoughts in response to the question.

Those unhealthy responses do not solve the problem—nor do they make us feel more at peace. What does make us feel more at peace is when we trust our pain and suffering to God. It brings great relief when we give up the need to make someone pay and place that responsibility into God's hands instead. He knows best how to defend us, and we can trust Him to bring justice at the right time and in the right manner.

Were you able to apply these truths since we last met?

> Allow participants to respond to the question.

LESSON SCRIPT

In this lesson, we will learn about something else we can do to help us with the pain caused by injustice. But before we start, know that our topic today may be sensitive for some. We may have been seriously hurt by another person and the defensiveness is real as we feel the need to protect ourselves. Remember that we are together—even though our journeys are different. You have faced some difficult things during our sessions. As always, you can take courage—you are in a safe space, and your creator walks alongside you, so you will not face this difficult topic alone.

However, we must have this discussion whenever there has been injustice, because no matter who caused the harm, how much time has passed, or how hard we may have tried to push it aside, eventually we will have to encounter and make a decision about this topic: **forgiveness**.

Forgiveness is a word that we use, or hear others use, without full comprehension of its meaning. Just to read the word brings up different definitions, expectations, and even emotions in each of us. For example, some of us may think forgiveness is expected. Others may recall advice or opinions we've received, such as, "It is a sin not to forgive," or "I could never forgive someone who did that." And others still may suggest that forgiveness is valid only as part of a package—such as "forgive and forget" or "forgive when the other person repents."

It is important to understand our perceptions of forgiveness, because *what we do with forgiveness* will be filtered through these ideas. If we view forgiveness as something we must offer without choice, for example, then we will probably offer it begrudgingly; and if we view it as impossible, then we may not forgive at all. To make the best decision about the role that we want forgiveness to play in our stories, then, we must know exactly what forgiveness means.

> Each point below is followed by a verse that supports it. In other words, these concepts are not simply ideas from the author but are grounded in God's Word—they are truths we can trust and apply.

So, what is forgiveness? Let's start with what forgiveness *is*:

1. Forgiveness is to remove our focus from the source of the pain and replace it with our awareness of the goodness of God.

    I remain confident of this: I will see the goodness of the LORD in the land of the living. Wait for the LORD; be strong and take heart and wait for the LORD (Psalm 27:13–14).

2. Forgiveness is to give up our right to pay back, or seek vengeance for, the harm done to us.

    Do not say, "I'll do to them as they have done to me; I'll pay them back for what they did" (Proverbs 24:29).

3. Forgiveness is to release the desire that bad—in general and from any source—will happen to the offender(s) and to accept—in time and without bitterness—any good that comes to them.

    "But to you who are listening I say: Love your enemies, do good to those who hate you, bless those who curse you, pray for those who mistreat you" (Luke 6:27–28).

4. Forgiveness is to think of our offenders as fellow image-bearers of God, responsible for their actions but broken by sin just as we are.

    There is no one righteous, not even one . . . for all have sinned and fall short of the glory of God (Romans 3:10, 23).

5. Finally, forgiveness is something that happens *inside us*—for our good and for God's glory. God instructs us to forgive because He knows what it will mean to our healing process. When we forgive, we can, in turn, more fully experience God's forgiveness, which allows us to have spiritual healing.

    Bear with each other and forgive one another if any of you has a grievance against someone. Forgive as the Lord forgave you (Colossians 3:13).

Now that we have considered what forgiveness is, let's think about what forgiveness is *not*:

1. Forgiveness is *not* something we should offer out of loyalty or because we feel someone deserves or demands it. (Side note: If you feel obligated to forgive for any of these reasons, it may be that the offender has told you these things to manipulate you. If so, and if you offer them forgiveness in response, this will only lead to further pain. It will not lead to healing.)
2. Forgiveness is *not* to say that what the offender did was okay or that we deserved the harm done to us. We might feel that forgiveness minimizes or makes light of our suffering, but this is not true: God never takes the suffering of the oppressed lightly.
3. Forgiveness is *not* something that requires us to stay loyal to or under the control of someone who repeatedly harms us.
4. Forgiveness is *not* the same as protecting the offender from justice or due discipline. It is also not the same as hiding their evil. We do not seek vengeance; however, we do allow God's justice.
5. Forgiveness is *not* to take responsibility for the offender's healing.
6. Forgiveness does *not* require us to restore our former relationship with the offender to its previous status, especially when that relationship is harmful to us.

Some of these statements about what forgiveness is and is not may surprise you or run contrary to what you have been taught. If so, then you have probably come to believe one of the common **misconceptions** about forgiveness. We will address some of those misconceptions now and replace them with their corresponding truths.

TRUTH #1: FORGIVENESS DOES NOT REQUIRE RESTORATION

People often avoid forgiveness because they believe that when they forgive, they must restore their relationship with the offender. This is not true. To **restore** is to return something back to its original condition.

In some instances, it may be possible to restore our relationship with an offender after we forgive them, but restoration is in no way required—and to think otherwise is a dangerous misconception. This misconception not only skews the definition of forgiveness; it also twists the very purpose of forgiveness, which is to lead us further on the path of healing.

Suppose you discover a negative balance in your bank account that you did not cause. You speak to someone at the bank and learn that the deficit happened because of a bookkeeping error by the bank's president. A couple of days later, the money is returned to your account and you receive a formal written apology from the bank's president, who promises that he will never make the same errors again. But the following month, your account suddenly falls negative again. When you speak to the bank this time, you discover that the president has been fired because he has been stealing from the bank all along. In fact, he had been doing this for years. The very person who had promised to protect and care for what you had entrusted to him had been taking that privilege for granted. He took what was not his and used it for himself.

Over time, you might forgive the man for the harm he did, but if you are wise, you will probably not ask that he be rehired at the bank or recommend him for a financial position at your own company! He lost the privilege of that position when he broke the trust in his relationship with you and all of the other customers.

It is the same in life. You can forgive someone who has harmed you and still choose *not* to restore their privilege of position in your life. You can even choose not to put your trust in them again.

This truth is particularly important to understand wherever there has been physical, emotional, or sexual assault or abuse. In these cases, a very clear boundary of trust has been broken that has almost certainly changed your relationship forever. In fact, scenarios like this most likely require your separation from the offender. Such change and separation do not prevent you from moving toward an attitude of forgiveness; rather, they release you from any obligation you feel to return to a place of harm—and this gives you freedom to choose true forgiveness.

Sadly, many who have suffered abuse avoid forgiveness altogether because they have been told that, if they forgive, they must restore the relationship—they must return to the abuse. So, in their *correct sense of self-protection,* they assume forgiveness is not an option for them, and the results of this assumption can be harmful.

In some instances, people may misinterpret the unforgiveness as a spiritual shortcoming—an *unwillingness* to forgive. As a result, the victim tends to turn inward, experiencing a deep sense of personal defeat and shame, or—due to incredible social pressure—they return to an environment of harm.

In other instances, the abuser may use the requirement to forgive as a tool to manipulate the abused. "Say you forgive me," the abuser says. "You must. It is what God says to do." And so, the victim, falsely believing that forgiveness requires restoration, allows the relationship to be "put back together," and the abuse continues. In this scenario, the victim tends to become stuck in a devastating cycle of further abuse, followed by further such requirements for forgiveness.

When forgiveness is evidenced in these ways, it not only perpetuates a dangerously false idea of what forgiveness looks like but also invites the potential for more serious harm—emotionally, physically, and spiritually. In addition, even if the abused eventually severs the relationship, they are likely to continue to avoid the idea of forgiveness at all costs, which sadly impedes their own healing.

That said, there are many instances when restoring a relationship *is* possible and healthful—and in those instances, we want to be careful not to withhold restoration merely *for the sake of vengeance or bitterness.* For example, restoration can be especially promising when all parties involved feel the relationship has value and strive to build a new relationship on a new foundation, rather than attempt to restore the old one.

Each situation is different. The nature of the original relationship you held with your offender, combined with your level of trust and the severity and type of their offense, all contribute to how possible it is to find restoration. But in those times when restoration is not the best option, or even healthy, it is important to remember this truth: *even without restoration, the obedient act of forgiveness is still possible.*

TRUTH #2: FORGIVENESS DOES NOT REQUIRE REPENTANCE

Sometimes, restoration comes after **repentance.** Maybe the offender apologizes, for example, and in response, we forgive them. This kind of restoration can be also appropriate and right. We should not run from the possibility that relationships can be restored this way, whether out of fear or bitterness; after all, God has written beautiful stories of healed relationships as only He can. However, repentance *is not required* for forgiveness to happen—and this leads us to our next misconception: the belief that one must repent before we can forgive them.

What does it mean to repent? Does it mean that we feel remorse? That we express regret? Do we have a change of heart? To *repent* is to change one's mind—even one's direction. If we are going one direction and we repent, then we will turn and go the opposite direction. In that sense, repentance is more than words and promises; when there is true repentance, there is *evidence of change.*

But change usually takes time. Depending on the offense, we may not see change for days or even months. So, while we wait, we are caught in an internal struggle: we wonder, *Is the person truly repentant? Or is he just pretending in order to convince me? Does he really even understand how he hurt me?* We struggle this way, because we do not truly know the offender's heart.

When we understand the truth that repentance is not required for forgiveness to happen, however, we realize that we do not need to know our offender's heart in order to forgive them. We see that *forgiveness is possible even if that person never repents.*

To better understand this truth, it might help to remember that the act of forgiveness is something that happens in *me*—for *my* good—independent of another person's heart, actions, or expectations. This means that I can forgive that person even if they never say the words I want to hear.

So, what's the big deal with forgiveness? Why should we even be concerned with the idea, let alone consider it so carefully?

The answer is this: Forgiveness is a critical part of our ability to come to peace with suffering. Without it, we remain at the mercy of our pain.

Let me give you an example. There are probably moments on your journey when you feel that you are really making progress. Maybe you even see a glimmer of peace or hope. But then something makes you think about the person who caused you harm, and your disposition suddenly changes. Another mood takes its place, and it seems to hover over you—even encompass you. It is a vague feeling—something you can't quite define—but if you had to label the emotion, you might call it "unresolved" or "unsettled." It is as if, suddenly, there is no sense of peace to found.

Some may describe it as a sense of anticipation. But for what? What are we waiting for? What do we want to occur? We have already discovered that we cannot change what happened. Life is as it is now.

Perhaps, we are still waiting for the offender to take initiative—to do something that would truly bring resolution and peace to our pain. But what would that "something" be?

The "something" that we anticipate that we long to have happen, is forgiveness. Only forgiveness can bring the kind of resolution and peace that we seek. But forgiveness is dependent on one person alone—and that person is us. The resolution, the invitation for peace, will come from us . . . and go back to us. And so, we must give ourselves permission to release our hold on bitterness. Because when we do, our bitterness will also release its hold on us.

You see, when we cling to our anger to prove the intensity of our pain, we allow ourselves to be bound together with it. We are bound to the anger and the pain and the ones who caused it—and the chain that binds us is our own unforgiveness. Unforgiveness holds us in the grip of suffering. And so, forgiveness becomes a powerful motivator for our healing:

- We forgive so that our anger and fear do not lead to bitterness that overtakes our lives.
- We forgive so that we can be released from the negative control of suffering.

We might also feel motivated by the spiritual healing that comes with forgiveness. Because when we forgive, we . . .

- nurture our relationship with God
- open ourselves up to receive His forgiveness
- keep a correct perspective of our own need for forgiveness
- know the peace of obedience to the One who forgives us
- fully express the image of God in us

It is amazing how much mental time and emotional strength become available to us once we release our anger and put justice in God's hands.

To understand and personalize these layers of *forgiveness*—what forgiveness is, what it is not, and what it requires—takes time. It is almost as if we "grow into" the ability to forgive. In fact, in most cases, there is no one single "I forgive" moment; rather, to say, "I forgive" is often just a place to start. It is a statement that really means "I have begun the process of forgiveness." And that is a good place to be.

Throughout this process, we will probably need to revisit forgiveness from time to time. It is not uncommon to sometimes find that we have slid back into a desire for vengeance or allowed bitterness to hold us in an unhealthy place. But each time we find ourselves in this position, we can revisit the truths of this lesson: we can remember what forgiveness is and what it is not. Then, strengthened by this clarity, we can intentionally reclaim our peace and well-being.

It's interesting how peace sometimes comes from the most unexpected places.

REFLECTIONS AND APPLICATION

Distribute copies of the Forgiveness worksheet.

This worksheet will help us think about where we are in the process of forgiveness. You may follow along as I read the poem, and then we will give everyone time to fill in the blanks. *Be careful* not to complete the statement if it is not how you feel. Each truth of forgiveness will come in its own time. There is no shame in being honest that you are not ready to truthfully make a particular statement. On the other hand, you might discover that you are closer to forgiveness than you think. When everyone is finished, we will talk about what forgiveness means to us in our own situations.

Read the poem and give participants time to complete the worksheet. When they are finished, invite them to discuss any reactions and questions they have to the concepts discussed in the lesson.

COURAGE AND PEACE

God's direction toward forgiveness is for our good. What a wonderful gift He gives—to surrender our resentment into His hands and rest into His peace. This is an important part of our journey—release from the control of the past and freedom to move toward healing.

FORGIVENESS: A POEM

Read the poem and then consider the statements of forgiveness. These statements will help us see ourselves honestly and determine where we are in the process of forgiveness.

Forgiveness is not identified by forgetfulness,
but it is evidenced by release.

Forgiveness is not proven by restoration,
but it is felt by peace.

Forgiveness is not something I give.
Forgiveness is a mystery that I embrace.

It is an invitation to untangle myself from the grip of
bitterness, shame, and fear
that brutally holds me to the past.

By embracing forgiveness,
I am able to fully express the image of God in me.

By embracing forgiveness,
I am released—truly free to move forward with peace.

Forgiveness is a gift to me from God—for my good and for His glory.

STATEMENTS OF FORGIVENESS

I am in the process to forgive _____.

I will not seek vengeance on _____.

I know that _____ and I are both created in the image of God and in need of Jesus as Savior.

I will not be angry if positive things happen to _____.

I desire to embrace forgiveness and release bitterness, shame, and fear.

SESSION 22
MOVE FORWARD

GOALS FOR PARTICIPANTS
- Be aware of the temptation to stay in the familiar place of pain
- Make the choice to press on and toward healing

MATERIALS
- This lesson
- Participant worksheet: Trauma's Lies that Trap Us: Familiarity, Fear, Guilt, and Ease
- Plain paper; pencils and pens

VOCABULARY
- **endure** (en-DOOR): to suffer patiently through something painful or difficult; to tolerate
- **purpose** (pur-PUHS): the reason for something

GREETING

Each session begins with a greeting. This will be unique and personal to each group.

REVIEW

Our previous discussion about forgiveness was important in our healing process. We brought clarity to what forgiveness is and what it is not. Perhaps, what we learned opened the door for you to consider forgiveness in your own life. Did you have an opportunity this week to think about forgiveness on a more personal level? Do you feel that you may be more open to the possibility of forgiveness, now that you understand it more clearly?

Allow participants to respond to the question.

LESSON SCRIPT

Let's take a minute to look back at what we have done to this point. At the start of this course, we shared our stories, which was difficult and uncomfortable for some, but became easier as we spent more time together.

Our first major lesson was about trauma, which includes all of the after-effects of a crisis. We learned that trauma can take on a life of its own—that despite our attempts to hide, ignore, or even deny its existence, trauma will not only torment us but also take control of our lives, influencing our emotions and actions.

We also realized that trauma is like a wound: we must tend to it, or it will get worse, causing infection and even illness. Because many of us already had this type of emotional infection, we made the difficult but brave decision to reopen and cleanse the wound, so that it would not continue to poison us: we described the trauma, we drew pictures of the pain, and we poured out our hearts to God.

Then we set boundaries on the trauma: we gave it a beginning and an end. We also named our losses and sorted through our tangled emotions. None of this work was easy, but it allowed us to begin to take back the control that trauma had stolen from us. It also taught us that it is good to face our suffering, as hard as that might be.

Then more recently, our lessons showed us common obstacles that we can face on our path: the *whys* that can easily distract us; the skewed definition of hope that can prevent us from accepting good; and the unforgiveness that can hold us in bondage to our anger. In these discussions, we received reassurance as we became more familiar with the role of our creator on this journey. We also discussed concepts like hope, healing, and release.

Now we are at a place in our journey where, although we know the crisis will always be a part of our story, we can put it in its place and give it proper perspective. Our pain is still real. Our problems are not all solved. Our emotions are not all controlled. Our hurts are not all healed. But look how far we have come! We have worked hard. We have been courageous. We have showed trust in each other as we shared, cried, and laughed together. We have taken each step and followed it with another step—and then another and another—until, in time, we arrived at where we are today.

This is what it looks like to move forward. We make steps. Some steps are smaller than others. Some are harder. Sometimes, we make two steps forward only to take a step back. Still, when we look at where we have been, we can see that we are further on the path than when we started. And so, overall, we know we have moved in a *forward direction*.

Yet, even as our direction on the path has been forward, up to this point, our eyes have been focused mostly on what lay behind. This backward gaze has been necessary—it has allowed us to see the parts of our stories that brought us to this path of suffering, and it has helped us become aware of the wounds that so badly needed cleansed. But we cannot spend our entire journey this way. If we want to continue with our progress, we will eventually need to turn our gazes forward. We will need to look at what lies on the path ahead.

At the same time, it is as if we have reached a bend in the road, because what lies ahead seems out of our sights in some way. As if, perhaps, it has disappeared around a curve. This part of the journey can be exciting, but it can also be unsettling. Because the road ahead is unknown and unfamiliar, we can feel trepidation. And this trepidation can make us more vulnerable to the criticisms and temptations of trauma, which does everything in its power to keep or regain control.

So, it is at this point in our journey when we must become familiar with a few of trauma's most common lies. These lies can be like traps in the road—they grab hold of us and keep us from moving toward healing:

The first and most common lie of trauma is that suffering is comfortable and familiar. Suffering can become a comfortable place for us. How can something so horrible become "comfortable?" This happens because we have lived with it a long time. We have adjusted our lives to it. We have learned to walk in a particular way.

Think about a pair of shoes that do not fit your feet well. They pinch and cause pain on your little toe and your heel. But you need to keep moving. So, you begin to adjust how your feet hit the ground. You roll them a bit to one side so that the shoes won't rub painfully across your little toe. You put less of your weight on your heel. You might not even realize you are making these adjustments; you just do it subconsciously in order *to avoid the pain.*

After walking this way for some time, your adjusted stride begins to feel familiar, almost comfortable. In fact, when you finally buy a new pair of shoes that fit you well, they feel strange at first. You had become so familiar with the way you needed to walk in the ill-fitting shoes to avoid pain that walking correctly almost feels uncomfortable now.

The same thing happens when we learn to "walk" a certain way through suffering. We attempt to keep going. We adjust our stride in whatever way necessary to elude the dull aches, the sharp twinges, or the ever-present tenderness. We adapt. We avoid. And we never give ourselves fully to life, because the weight of doing so increases the pain. After a while, this adjusted way of life becomes familiar.

So, in the same way that we might feel uncomfortable in new shoes after we adjusted to the old ones, we might also feel discomfort as we attempt to walk a new pathway—even one that leads us beyond the control of trauma and toward healing.

Guilt is another trap that trauma can use to keep us from moving forward. Guilt tells us that our willingness to "walk away from the pain" means that we don't really understand the seriousness of the event—that our desire to bring joy and hope back to life means that we are in denial of suffering or that we believe everything is now resolved.

Another trap of trauma is the lie that it is easier to stay where we are. Think of a dramatic play or a musical that is performed by actors. These actors do not create their own words and actions; rather, they follow a script. No matter how they feel that day, they must express the actions, words, and emotions described in the script.

Now, think of yourself like an actor in a play about your life. Who has written the script? It can be easy—or, at least, comfortable—to allow *trauma* to become the writer of the script we follow. We allow our words, emotions, and actions to be dictated by the script of suffering, regardless of how we really feel. In the short term, this feels easier because it does not require us to think about or spend energy on our own emotions and action and choices. But in the long term, it is detrimental to our healing to follow the script of trauma. We become stuck under trauma's negative control and never get the chance to experience the joy that lay on the other side. We cannot move forward.

Finally, trauma can tell us to listen to our fear. Fear can have a strong influence on our direction. And so many at this point in the journey are tempted to turn back. But when we change the direction of our feet from forward to backward, we only become more vulnerable to the influence of trauma. We may even give trauma back some of the control that we worked so hard to regain.

We are going to begin our reflection time here so that we can apply what we just learned about our fear to move forward. Now is the safe time and place to express the comfortableness and fear that hold us in place. Our worksheet will help us do this.

Distribute copies of the worksheet for this lesson. Read over the worksheet together and discuss any questions or thoughts.

What about you? What has become comfortable about your story of suffering? What has threatened you or convinced you to fear, or even avoid, moving forward? Guilt? Ease? Familiarity?

If you have time, the participants may complete the worksheet in class—or you may encourage the participants to complete the worksheet at home.

LESSON SCRIPT (CONTINUED)

Yet, despite these traps of trauma—comfort, ease, guilt, and fear—most of us continue to feel a stirring inside to move forward. Most of us don't want to remain stuck under its control. And so, as we face this crossroads where we are ready to turn our gazes forward and where our future path seems to disappear around a bend, we must make a choice. Either . . .

- **We continue to adjust and avoid in order to survive.** We believe the lies of trauma, take on its identity, and give in to the fear of further disappointment. When we choose this route, we choose to live life in pain. Or . . .

- **We consider the possibility of moving forward.** We courageously acknowledge our pain, accept suffering as part of our story, then open our souls to the remainder of our journey and the possibilities it brings.

It is not as easy as it sounds to choose the second option. In fact, the second option usually requires that we continue to make the intentional choice to move forward, over and over again. It is a challenge that often takes courage and determination. It requires us to recognize these lies of trauma, to be honest with ourselves when they have us trapped, and to make the intentional decision to remove ourselves from their grasp so that we can continue toward healing. It is not an easy one-time decision. Rather, it is a process by which we maintain our forward movement.

So let's look at Hebrews 12:1-2 for some inspiration and instruction for how to do this.

> "Let us throw off everything that hinders and the sin that so easily entangles. And let us run with perseverance the race marked out for us, fixing our eyes on Jesus, the pioneer and perfecter of faith. For the joy set before him he endured the cross, scorning its shame, and sat down at the right hand of the throne of God."

Let's break the words of this passage down and see what it asks us to do:

First, we are to "throw off what hinders." In this case, what hinders is the grasp of trauma's lies. So we must identify the lie that we have fallen prey to and make an intentional choice to remove ourselves from it. The worksheet we do today will help us with this process.

Second, we are to "run with perseverance the race marked out for us." This means that we continue to put one foot in front of the other. We take the steps we know are good and right for our healing. If we feel winded, we take a break, but then we get back to it. We do our best and don't give up.

Third, we fix "our eyes on Jesus, the pioneer and perfecter of faith, who for the joy set before him endured the cross, scorning its shame, and sat down at the right hand of the throne of God." Paul says that as we run our race, or take our path, we should fix our eyes on the perfect example of endurance. And why did Jesus endure? He endured "for the joy set before him."

In other words, just as Jesus did, we have a purpose for this life and for our movement toward healing. Our very lives have purpose simply because God gave them to us! And when these lives are over, God will take us home to heaven, where we will see a reward for our perseverance: we will sit down "at the right hand of the throne of God." Think of that. Think of sitting at the right hand of God's throne. Is that a place of suffering and pain? Is that a place of defeat and hopelessness? No! The right hand of the throne of God is a place of victory! As our example, Jesus shows us that if we keep moving forward on this path, even when it is hard or when we feel trapped, we will eventually fulfill our purpose and reach a place of joy and victory.

But until that day when we receive our reward, we are to follow the lead of Jesus and also of Paul—the man we talked about earlier who endured a lot of suffering. Paul put it this way: "I press on toward the goal to win the prize for which God has called me heavenward in Christ Jesus" (Philippians 3:14). Paul's goal was to receive the "prize" of heaven. And to reach that goal, he was determined to "press on."

To "press on" means to *continue to make choices* that move us toward our goal. But to press on takes effort. Sometimes, it takes a lot of effort. But we continue to press on because God calls us forward—heavenward.

REFLECTION AND APPLICATION

This week, watch for moments when you are tempted to withdraw from moving forward, moments when you may actually encourage the pain and refuse to see blessing and hope. Write about those moments. Remind yourself that the temptation to remain in the comfort of the pain is holding you back from the peace of moving forward to a new place.

Be sure to remember the encouragement to press on—to make choices that move us toward healing. Insert your name in the blank below to remind yourself of what you can do when you feel trapped by the lies of trauma:

My commitment to move forward toward healing:

So then I, _____ who suffered according to God's will, now commit to:

> throw off what hinders,
>
> run with perserverance,
>
> and fix my eyes on Jesus.

COURAGE AND PEACE

As we turn our gaze forward, the path ahead disappears around a bend in the road. Where is our Traveling Companion? He is next to us and He is already there, around the bend. He calls us forward to experience new hope and new joy and new peace.

> "The LORD will guide you always; he will satisfy your needs in a sun-scorched land and will strengthen your frame. You will be like a well-watered garden, like a spring whose waters never fail" (Isaiah 58:11).

TRAUMA'S LIES THAT TRAP US: FAMILIARITY, FEAR, GUILT, AND EASE

The question below can help us discover if there is any comfortableness or fear that keep us from moving forward. Now is the safe time and place to express the truth—even when it is difficult.

Do any of the responses that follow this question ring true for you, even a little?

How does my suffering feel familiar, even *comfortable*? **In what ways does a life** *outside* **my trauma seem** *un*comfortable?

- In some odd way, my suffering feels comfortable because I know what to expect from it. I know the emotions it will bring, and the ache has become familiar.
- I find some level of comfort in my pain because of the fact that I have been wronged.
- If I begin to move away from my trauma, people will think that I am healed. As a result, they will expect more from me. They will move on and expect me to do the same.
- My trauma somehow validates my negative responses to others. I am not accountable for how I treat others because I was hurt.
- If I begin to live outside my trauma, the one who harmed me will think I have forgiven or passed beyond the suffering.
- If I do not make trauma my identity, whomever I enter new relationships with will not know my pain; they will not know my struggle and my story.
- If I begin to release my trauma, it will minimize the severity of the initial event.
- I feel guilty when I step forward beyond my trauma, because others were hurt, too. Joy and hope in my life might cause others to think that I don't remember or care about their pain.

These concerns are real—but we do not want to give them the power to hold us back from healing.

My commitment to move forward toward healing:

So then I, _____, who suffered according to God's will, now commit to:

    throw off what hinders,
        run with perserverance,
            and fix my eyes on Jesus.

SESSION 23
TRUTH AND UNTRUTH

GOALS FOR PARTICIPANTS
- Identify untruth, then remove it
- Identify truth, then establish it and feed it

MATERIALS
- This lesson
- Participant worksheet: Truth and Untruth
- Plain paper; pencils and pens

VOCABULARY
- **establish** (ih-STAB-lish): to set something on a firm foundation in a way that it remains stable and permanent
- **identify** (ih-DEN-tuh-fy): to recognize something; to call something by its name and bring it to light
- **maintenance** (MAYN-tuh-nuhns): care or upkeep; the act of keeping something in good order

GREETING

Each session begins with a greeting. This will be unique and personal to each group.

REVIEW

Last time, we talked about how we long to move forward, and yet it often seems more comfortable to stay in a place of pain and suffering . . . either because it feels easier or more familiar than moving on or because we have guilt about moving on. To address this challenge, we must be honest with ourselves as we move forward into the unknown. So, now is a good time for us to talk about truth and truth.

LESSON SCRIPT

Throughout this journey we have taken together, we have been faced with *truth and untruth*.

Untruth is the language of trauma. It often sounds like sympathy or help—as if trauma is on our side. But when we observe more carefully, we find that it is either an attempt to hold us in captivity or to lead us away from the path of healing and down a path of destruction.

On the other hand, *truth challenges trauma*. It opens the door to release us from trauma's captivity and shows us a way forward. But this often leads us into unfamiliar territory. It challenges our status quo and prompts us to move away from that place we have lived in for so long. Whether that place is fear, anger, or guilt, it has seemed a logical, unavoidable, and even somewhat comfortable place to stay. Until now.

Often, it is a challenge to discern between truth and untruth. But once we identify untruth, we can remove it—and, in its place, plant truth. We use the word *plant*, because we want to **establish** truth. When we establish something, we put it on a firm foundation, so that it will remain stable and permanent.

Imagine that you have been given a small garden plot. The plot has been left alone for several years, so it is full of weeds. You decide that you want to plant flowers in your plot. Do you simply add new flower seeds to the ground? No. You must first clear out the weeds. If you don't, the weeds will quickly choke out any new flowers that start to grow. The flowers will be consumed by the weeds, and the ground will return to its former state. After all, the weeds have been there for quite some time. They have taken ownership of the ground—and they are tenacious!

Our journey of suffering is like that too. It is like a garden plot that we have been given to tend. We want our garden to be a place of peace and beauty and productivity, but the negative effects of suffering—the untruths—have already taken root there and grown prolifically into weeds.

At this stage, if we simply plant new seeds, the trauma will attempt to choke out any new growth we may see.

So, first, we must uproot the weeds.

In other words, we cannot simply plant the truths we learn among all of the untruths that are already there. Those untruths have been around for some time, and they have become strong and familiar, controlling our reasoning and lives. So, we must pull them out as we discern them, or they will eventually choke out any new growth we may see.

We dare not allow both to coexist in our garden; we have come too far to have our growth undone.

REFLECTION AND APPLICATION

> Distribute copies of the worksheet for this lesson. Tell the participants that there are arrows on the page but they will not use those until the next session. They should just follow the guidance for this session.

With all that in mind, let's work on our gardens.

This worksheet will help us to . . .

- *identify untruth* and remove it, then
- *identify truth* and provide what it needs to grow strong.

When we look at our gardens on the worksheet, we can see that the flowers and weeds have grown together and are sometimes even intertwined. If we want our flowers to survive and thrive, we cannot simply leave the garden this way and hope for the best. So, today, we will work to identify and label the weeds that we want to uproot—these are the untruths in our particular story. We will also identify and label the flowers of truth that we want to nurture—to ensure they not only survive but thrive.

To start, we must think carefully about the truths and untruths we have discovered on our journey. Here are some ideas to keep in mind as you consider what is true:

- First, you might need to use scientific logic or "If-then" statements, such as "If *this*, then *that*." We have a tendency to collect ideas from various places—from this person, that book, or this new program—that we assume are true. But when we look more closely, we find that many of these "truths" contradict. So, we must reason that "If *this* is true, then *that* cannot be true," or "If *this* is truth, then *that* must be untruth."

- Another idea that can help you to come up with truth is to think about the concepts that have helped you on this journey—discoveries that have given you strength, for example, or have helped you stand strong when you felt insecure—things that are "tried and *true*."

- Finally, make sure that the truths you add are honest, practical, and specific. Stay away from statements that are overly generalized and, instead, write truths that relate to your unique situation—truths that you can realistically apply to your own life for your own healing. Then, whenever you identify a truth, you can try to think of the untruth that it needs to displace.

Now, here are a few things to keep in mind as you try to come up with untruths that have impacted your life:

- Untruth can be tricky. Sometimes it starts from one small root of truth—but that truth is fed with lies so that its outgrowth becomes poisoned and twisted and it can no longer be trusted to guide our actions. In other words, the truth is bent and tainted until it becomes untruth.

- Examples of untruth that might come from your own mind include . . .

    "I got myself into this mess, I am going to have to learn to live with it."

    "It's my responsibility to keep my family together and happy."

    "If I would have done things differently, this would not have happened."

- Untruth might also include words from others, like . . .

    "You are suffering because you are guilty."

    "If you love me, then you should not care about justice."

    "You are making too big of a deal about this."

    "If you would have done things the way I told you to, this would not have happened."

So, think carefully. Test the words and ideas that begin to float inside your head and discern where they lead you. Follow each assumption to its logical conclusion. Ask yourself, *Is this a truth that strengthens me or an untruth that debilitates? Does this idea steer me toward healing or toward defeat? Do these words sound like words from my Perfect Creator and Savior, the I AM—or not?*

Then, whenever you think of an untruth, write it on one of the weeds in your garden. When you think of a truth, write it on a flower. Use words and phrases that are clear and specific. And remember that, to become established, truth must be planted with conviction, so label each flower with confidence.

As you begin to label the weeds and flowers, you might find that some labels help you to think of other labels. For example, to identify truth, sometimes you simply need to speak the reverse of untruth. This means you might be able to look at one of your labeled weeds and write down its opposite on a flower. So, if a weed is labeled "It is my responsibility to keep everyone happy," you would label a flower with "It *is not* my responsibility to keep everyone happy." This might not always be possible, however. Many truths present themselves as new thoughts, unrelated to the weeds that hold us back; for example, "My life is not at the mercy of the suffering."

Take time now to write words and phrases of truth and untruth in your garden.

Allow time for participants to ponder and to label their gardens. When you feel it is about time to bring the activity to a close, simply resume with the script below.

Truth. Untruth. The two cannot grow together agreeably in our garden. One must be uprooted. The other must be planted and tended with care. So, let's get our clippers and shovel and do some clean-up.

We know which way this must go. Truth must win. And so, untruth must be removed. Yes, some untruth is deep and difficult to get rid of—it is familiar to us, even though it has caused harm—but we are stronger now. We can do this.

Go back to the weeds that you labeled and place an X next to one or two that you want to uproot first.

> Give participants a minute or two to follow the instruction above.

When you are finished, just be prepared keep the clippers and shovel handy, because weeds grow back! Yes, even after we have uprooted some weeds, we may find ourselves feeling anxious—and when we take the time to understand why, we realize that it is because we are once again listening to the same old untruth that used to plague us, time and again.

As long as we are in this fallen world, our garden will require routine **maintenance**—but the more we identify and root out the weeds, the more we will be able to maintain our new growth. The truth will spread its roots and become established. It will take greater ownership of our lives and set us free to grow. And as it does, the untruth, which is a proven deceiver and threat to our well-being, will begin to wilt away—and its grip that has held us for so long will loosen.

As you move forward on this journey, continue to watch for any weeds of untruth that come to your attention. If an untruth comes to mind that you do not already have written down, write it off to the *side of your worksheet*—rather than on a weed—to show that you stopped the untruth before it even had a chance to take root. To gain this ability will be a powerful step forward in your journey.

In the meantime, return to this worksheet as often as you need to identify newly revealed truths and untruths on your continued journey. And, in turn, use this visual expression to help you tend to your actual life garden. Eventually, you will sense the overall growth of peace.

COURAGE AND PEACE

Some words of encouragement for you before you go: Remember that our Good Shepherd only speaks truth, and that truth is being planted in you. As you grow stronger in this truth, you will gain wisdom to see even more clearly, so that it will become increasingly easier to discern untruth from truth. The work you do now, to establish and nurture a healthy garden, will gain momentum and continue to grow a garden full of hope and renewed life long into the future.

TRUTH AND UNTRUTH

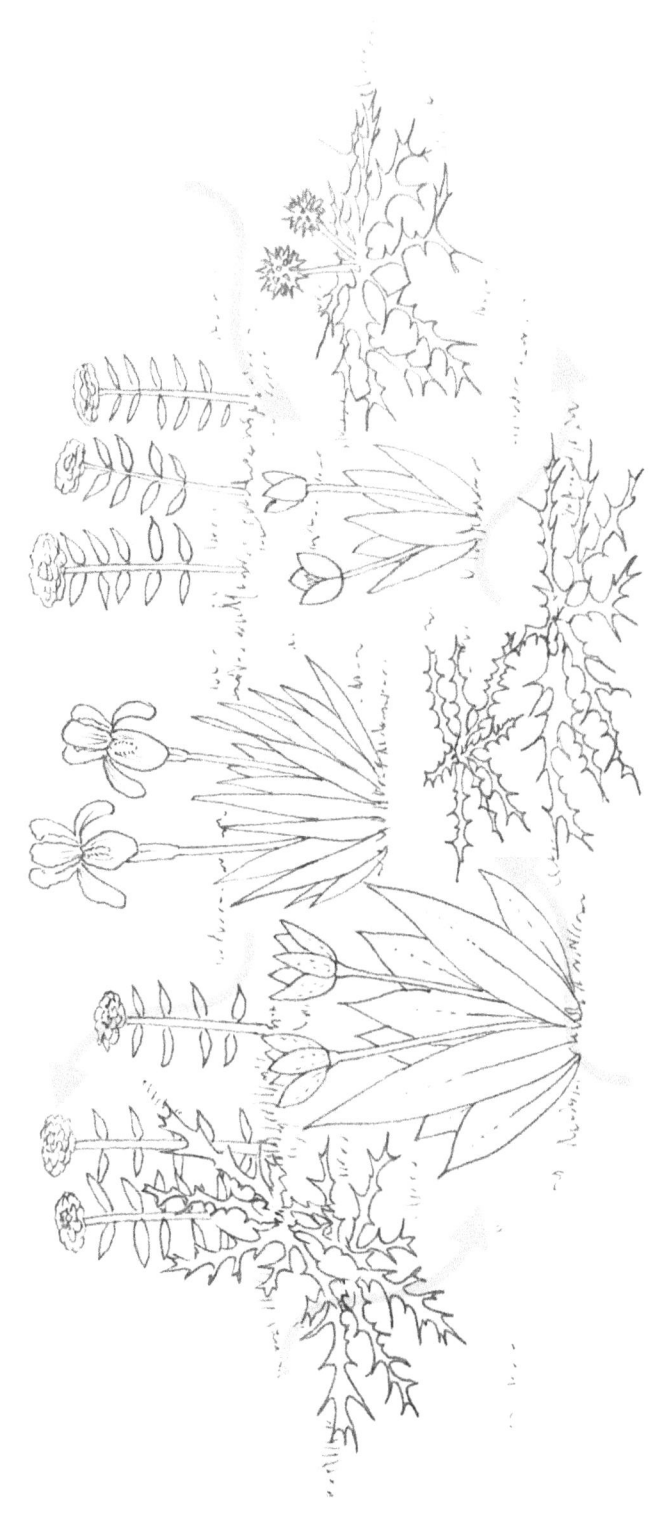

SESSION 24
DISCOVER THE NEED FOR PROTECTION

GOALS FOR PARTICIPANTS
- Identify threats to our well-being
- Identify weak areas where good things might slip away
- Learn about triggers
- Recognize that we need protection, if we want to stay in a place of health and well-being

MATERIALS
- This lesson
- Completed Truth and Untruth worksheet (from the previous lesson)
- Participant worksheet: Discover the Need for Protection
- Plain paper; pencils and pens

VOCABULARY
- **boundary** (BOUN-duh-ree): a border or limit where one thing ends and another begins
- **diligent** (DIL-ih-juhnt): careful in work and action; persistent
- **manipulative** (muh-NIP-yuh-lay-tiv): a way of acting in which one tries to influence others' behaviors or emotions, often in an unfair or selfish way
- **perceive** (per-SEEVE): to regard or understand in a particular way
- **trigger** (TRIG-er): something that brings up the memory of a traumatic experience in a way that sets off an intense negative emotional reaction

GREETING
Each session begins with a greeting. This will be unique and personal to each group.

REVIEW
In our previous lesson, we learned that truth and untruth do not grow well together. And so, we must identify untruth and remove it and identify truth and strengthen it. But this process is not always as easy as it might sound. What did you discover about truth and untruth in your own life?

LESSON SCRIPT

One of the most important steps on our journey so far has been to acknowledge suffering—to see it, feel it, and become familiar with it—but also to *set boundaries* on it. A boundary is a like a border or an endpoint to something; it is a marker that shows where one thing ends and another begins. The boundary that we put up allowed us to look at suffering on our own terms and within our own timetables, so that we no longer felt we had to hide from it out of fear that we'd be overwhelmed.

That boundary enabled us to became familiar with trauma and its tactics. This familiarity did not make us more fearful of suffering, as some might expect; rather, it only strengthened our boundary against the negative effects of trauma.

These two steps—putting a boundary on the negative effects of suffering and becoming familiar with trauma —helped us to resume some control over our lives, but it did not completely stop trauma's potential for destruction. After all, trauma, left to its own devices, would gladly consume us. So, at this point in our journey, as we do the **diligent** work that is necessary to identify and uproot untruth and plant truth in its place, we must not only continue to be aware of trauma's tactics—we must also continue to actively set up boundaries against it. The new boundaries we put up will help us to protect the growth, productivity, well-being, and beauty of our gardens that we have worked so hard to establish.

To make these new boundaries as effective as possible, let's look at the tactics that trauma uses most often to harm our gardens:

- **Trauma will feed our fear of attack at times when that fear is *unnecessary*.** This occurs when we **perceive** a threat from someone or something that neither intends or desires to hurt us. We *feel* threatened but nothing is actually trying to harm us.

- **Trauma will calm our concern over a potential harm at times when that concern is *necessary*.** This happens when we talk ourselves out of the uneasiness we feel in response to a perceived threat; we might tell ourselves, for example, that "this person," "that event," or "that action" would never hurt us and, therefore, the threat must be in our imagination. We *should* take the feeling of unease seriously but we ignore it.

Now, let's return to the image of our gardens from the previous lesson.

REFLECTION AND APPLICATION

Let's begin with a careful walk-about in the garden.

1. First, let's revisit our flowers and weeds—our truths and untruths. As you read the labels, think once again about the role of these truths and untruths in your life and how you plan to tend to them. Remember the healthful environment that you want to create for yourself as you maintain your garden.

2. Next, consider any potential threats to your garden. Keep in mind that threats can be multidirectional—harm will try to come *into* your garden, while good and beauty will try to go *out*. Threats can also take on various appearances—sometimes, they enter boldly; other times, they sneak quietly or ride in on the back of something good.

    One particular type of threat to be aware of is called a **trigger.** *Triggers* are those places, people, events, or sensory inputs that can bring up painful memories connected to our suffering and cause us to have powerful emotional and behavioral responses. Triggers can happen unexpectedly and are often the result of common, everyday experiences—a certain sound or smell, a particular situation, or even a momentary "look" from someone can pull us suddenly and definitively back into our time of suffering. So, as you consider potential threats to your garden, don't forget to think about triggers. Consider whether there are certain places, events, or even people that may "trigger you" to go back to an unhealthy place.

3. Finally, think about any areas of weakness in and around your garden. Perhaps, there are areas where courage and peace are getting out, for example; or maybe there is a spot where confidence is being overwhelmed by the weeds of guilt and fear.

As you ponder these potential threats and weak areas, I will distribute our worksheet for today, which will help you further with this process.

Distribute copies of the worksheet for this lesson.

Read through the questions on the worksheet and do your best to write honest and thoughtful answers in response. Your responses will be important, because through them, the threats and weak areas will reveal themselves. As always, be gentle, yet honest. Be open about your fears and uneasiness. Accept the emotions that come.

Be sure to write down *all* of the threats you feel—whether real or simply perceived—because each one will influence your ability to move forward on this path. Some of the threats to your sense of well-being might surprise you. They might come from unlikely places, even places you thought were safe or trustworthy.

Do not talk yourself out of the uneasy feelings that come. Honestly identify the threats and bring them to light; otherwise, they will continue to lurk in the shadows, where they will cause you distress and block your path to resolution. Identify your weak areas so that, later, you can build protective borders around them.

Know that our goal right now is just to identify areas where we might need protection. The act of building this protection will come later; that will be another part of the journey.

Allow participants sufficient time to respond to the questions. When you feel it is about time to move on to the next application, ask the participants to take out the worksheet from the previous lesson—the garden worksheet. Then continue with the script below.

Now we can use the arrows on the worksheet from the previous session. Notice that some of the arrows point into the garden and some point outward.

It is time to place your responses into the garden image on your worksheet. On the arrows that point into the garden, identify the dangers, threats, and untruths that you feel might intrude on or threaten your place of well-being. On the arrows that point away from the garden, write down the things of beauty, good, and truth that you feel are at risk of slipping away.

Allow participants more time to complete the second part of the exercise. When you feel it is about time to bring the meeting to a close, gently continue with the script below.

You may need to come back to this conversation often. As you go through the days, and even weeks or months, of your journey, you will likely recognize threats that you did not see before. Whenever you become aware of a new threat or area of weakness, write it down on this worksheet. As you do, perhaps it would be good to speak these words:

> "These threats are forceful and **manipulative**.
> If my garden is to grow strong and healthy,
> I will definitely need protection against them."

As you continue on this path, you will face intruders in your garden, and you will find areas of weakness where good things are at risk of slipping away. But you now have the tools to detect and combat these threats to your well-being. *This is a profound step in moving forward.*

COURAGE AND PEACE

God uses the visual of a garden to encourage us as we move forward. Yes, we make good choices to protect our garden—but it is God who satisfies and strengthens so that we become a well-watered garden, like a spring whose waters never fail. He cares for us with abundance.

> "The LORD will guide you always; he will satisfy your needs in a sun-scorched land and will strengthen your frame. You will be like a well-watered garden, like a spring whose waters never fail" (Isaiah 58:11).

DISCOVER THE NEED FOR PROTECTION

Use the questions below to help reveal potential threats to your garden as well as weak areas in and around your garden. As always, be gentle, yet honest with your answers.

- What threatens you?
- What triggers the desire to run, to hide, to stand paralyzed?
- What causes your body and spirit to prepare to fight?
- Where is trauma encroaching on your ability to live in peace?
- Who or what makes you uneasy?
- How does suffering affect your daily activities?
- How has suffering affected your future plans?
- Where and when do you feel your courage slip away from you?
- What overwhelms or buries your confidence and your strength?
- What are the threats to your healing?
- Where is trauma encroaching on your ability to live in peace?
- What effects do you feel in your body? In your spirit? In your emotions?
- Where do you need protection?

Now place key words and phrases from your responses into the garden image.

Task #1: Identify intruders that threaten to come *into* your garden. Write them on the arrows that point into the garden. These arrows will help you to visualize the dangers, threats, and untruths that you feel want to intrude on your place of well-being. Add more arrows as needed.

Task #2: Identify the positive influences that you feel are at risk of slipping away. Write on the arrows that point away from the garden. These arrows will help you to visualize the things of beauty, good, and truth that you feel are at risk of slipping away. Add more arrows as needed.

As you continue on your journey of healing, you may need to come back to this worksheet often, either to revisit the potential intruders and weaknesses that you have noted or to add new ones. Whenever you write down a new threat or area of weakness on this worksheet, perhaps it would be good to speak these words: "These threats are forceful and manipulative. If my garden is to grow strong and healthy, *I will definitely need protection against them."*

SESSION 25
SET BOUNDARIES

GOALS FOR PARTICIPANTS
- Identify triggers that can lead us to an unhealthy place
- Identify behaviors that we can use to help us cope
- Identify particular boundaries that we need to put into place to protect our physical, emotional, and spiritual health
- Set relevant boundaries

MATERIALS
- This lesson
- Participant worksheet: Set Boundaries
- Plain paper; pencils and pens

VOCABULARY
- **abusive** (uh-BYOO-siv): intentionally harmful
- **addiction** (uh-DIK-shun): a state in which you feel a need or strong inclination to continue a habit that is physically or psychologically harmful
- **indulge** (in-DUHLJ): to yield to a desire to a degree that it becomes comfortable

GREETING

Each session begins with a greeting. This will be unique and personal to each group.

REVIEW

In our previous lesson, we identified areas in our garden of well-being where untruth may sneak in and truth may leak out. These threats and weak areas showed us that we have a great need for protection. In this lesson, we will learn to build boundaries that can preserve the truth, goodness, and beauty that we have worked so hard to establish.

LESSON SCRIPT

In the previous lesson, we learned that a *boundary* is defined as a border or a limit—it is a point where one thing ends and another begins. In general, all boundaries have two purposes: to keep harmful influences out and to keep good in. But what does a boundary *look like* in our lives—and in this journey that we are on?

Although we may not realize it, all of us set boundaries in our everyday lives; these boundaries are simply limits that we put on certain behaviors for our own benefit. For example, we might have boundaries that determine what time we go to bed, what foods we eat, who we spend time with, or how much effort we spend on certain activities. These boundaries can protect our well-being physically, mentally, emotionally, and spiritually.

In terms of our healing journey, the boundaries that we use can look very similar to those in everyday life—they protect our well-being by putting limits on behaviors (including thoughts, actions, responses, and feelings) that will harm us or limit our growth.

In the previous lesson—by using the arrows—we recognized that boundaries are needed to limit the control of trauma in our lives. But now we will consider exactly how boundaries can help us do this.

You might be surprised to realize that we have already started to set those boundaries:

- *We limited* the amount of time that we looked at portions of our suffering. This boundary protected us from being swept away by the intensity of the pain.
- We put limits on the control that suffering had over every part of our life. This boundary was enacted when *we allowed* ourselves to see the legitimate good that exists in the world.
- *We recognized* that our crisis event already had natural boundaries, as it was limited to a specific timeframe that had a beginning and an end. This limitation protected us from constant illogical fear.

The key phrases here show how we put boundaries on our trauma: *we limited, we allowed,* and *we recognized.* In other words, to set boundaries, we can *limit* some things and *allow* other things. We can also make an effort to *recognize* any natural boundaries that may already exist.

Because trauma is a common trait in all of our stories, we were able to set up these boundaries together. But now we are at a point in our journey where we need to consider more individualized boundaries, so that we can offer the type of protection that is necessary to our specific gardens.

You see, each of our gardens has unique truths and untruths as well as specific threats and weaknesses that need protection. In addition, there are various types of boundaries that we can put in place based on our garden's specific needs.

We need boundaries, but if those boundaries are not durable—if they do not have a lasting impact—they will eventually fail. So, let's look at two basic guidelines that will help us to put up boundaries that can last.

<u>First, make sure to set your boundary with truth.</u> If a boundary is not established in truth, then it is not strong enough to withstand the lies of trauma. So, as always, be honest with yourself and draw from the truths that you have established on this journey.

<u>Second, make sure to set your boundary in reality.</u> The boundaries we set are not intended to keep us from *all* pain or discomfort. That would be wishful thinking! Rather, boundaries are meant to protect us from those attacks that will overwhelm us or take us to a point of despair.

REFLECTION AND APPLICATION

Our worksheet is going to help us as we consider three boundary types and our individual need for each. We will look at the worksheet together and we will stop at particular times to work individually.

Distribute copies of the worksheet for this lesson. As you read through the worksheet together, you will stop at particular times for reflection.

1. The first type of boundary that we would do well to consider is a boundary on our emotions and "mind time."

   Mind time is simply the amount of time we spend in conscious thought. We have limited amounts of mind time and emotional energy, and when they are depleted, we feel stressed and exhausted. So, how do we spend these precious resources wisely?

   The questions on our worksheet will help us to consider whether we might need boundaries in these areas. Let's read through the questions together.

Do I Need Boundaries to Protect My Emotional Energy and Mind Time?

- How much time do I spend each day thinking about my suffering? Do I often have pretend conversations, dwell on the *what-ifs*, ponder the details, and play out scenarios in my mind?
- Do I feel emotionally exhausted?
- When I make decisions, how large a part does my suffering play in the reasoning process?
- Is my suffering always in the forefront of my thoughts? Is it draining my emotions or physical energy?
- How many of my conversations with others eventually come back to the suffering? For example . . .
    Can I converse with others without bringing "it" to attention?
    When I am asked about myself, is "it" the first thing I want to tell?
    When someone else shares a painful experience, do I feel the need to share my story too?

As you read these questions, you might think, *But I need to think about it! It is important for me to process.*

The truth is, it is natural for the topic of suffering to consume us in the beginning. But a large part of our journey has been to learn to express our suffering in a way that is healthful—we no longer try to hide it, and we are no longer shamed by it. Once we learn to speak about our suffering with others in this way, we often find less *need* to refer to it in our everyday conversations. This does not happen because of fear or shame, but because the suffering has loosened its grip on us. It does not consume us as it once did.

This means that in the later stages of our journey, although it is healthy to talk about our suffering at appropriate times, if our thoughts and conversations continue to be consumed by it, this can be unhealthy.

Remember, *trauma consumes*. It will always demand more from our minds and emotions if we let it. So, if we follow the natural path, we will always find ourselves stressed and emotionally exhausted.

Let's take some time to reflect on these questions. Write your answers on your worksheet.

> Give participants time to write on the worksheet.

2. The second type of boundary that we might consider is a boundary on the behaviors that we use to cope with our suffering.

We all have things that we do to help us through difficult times—to help us cope. Some coping behaviors can be healthy—perhaps, we like to work or read or exercise, for example. Others are unhealthy and often used to numb our feelings—overeating, undereating, alcoholism, drug abuse, or pornography. But all of these behaviors—even the healthy ones—can begin to consume time, energy, and resources to the extent that they become detrimental to our healing. Sometimes, they even become addictions, which means that we believe we cannot function without them. This hinders our healing and only causes more problems.

So, let's go over some questions we can use to consider whether we might need boundaries in this area.

Do I Need Boundaries to Protect the Way That I Cope?

- How often and how quickly do I return to this behavior of escape? Do I tend to hide and escape more often than I live in the real world?
- When I use this behavior to cope, does it take me toward a greater sense of well-being? Or has it begun to cause harm to my health, body, mind, relationships, or emotions?

These are important questions to think about. Our actions—especially the way we tend to run away from our pain—reveal unhealthy habits. Think carefully and then write your answers on your worksheet.

> Give participants time to write on the worksheet.

3. The third type of boundary that we might need is on our relationships.

In a previous lesson, we discussed the role of others in our crisis and suffering. Some of those others might have relationships with us, and some relationships might have changed after the moment of impact. The list of relationships and problematic scenarios can sometimes seem endless, which can overwhelm us when we consider the necessary boundaries.

And so, before we discuss this particular boundary type, let's remind ourselves that our boundaries must be realistic. It is not realistic to protect ourselves from *all* hurt and every negative interaction, and we cannot run from *all* confrontation. This means that, in this discussion, we will focus on those relationships directly related to our trauma. Protection in those relationships is a necessary priority if we are to move forward. Otherwise, we remain stuck, mired in the conflict.

In particular, there is a real and healthy place for boundaries in the following types of relationships:

- Relationships that are a strong trigger for unhealthy responses, including panic
- Relationships in which abuse, negative influence, and manipulation continue

For these relationships, clear boundaries are a necessary part of our healing. The exact boundaries needed, as well as the degree of severity of those boundaries, will vary based on the details of each relationship; however, here are a few examples of boundaries that you might consider:

Example 1: A boundary of interaction. This is a limit on the frequency or depth in which you interact with another person. Interactions might include anything from basic conversations to joint activities.

Example 2: A boundary of communication. This is a limit on the type of communication that can happen between you and another person. The severity of this boundary will vary based on the details of the relationship, but it might take one of the following forms:

- Only voice contact is allowed; in-person communication is not permissible.
- In-person contact is allowed, but phone calls and texts are not permissible.
- Not even voice contact is allowed.

Some boundaries of interaction and communication can be temporary, while others might need to be permanent. You might also choose to change a boundary over time. For example, you could adjust the length, severity, or extent of a boundary based on the other person's response: if they respect your boundary, you might lessen its severity over time; but if they push back, you might make it stronger.

You may also find that a boundary in one area clears a path to greater interaction in another. In this way, as we grow stronger in our healing and peace with the way life is now, we also may grow stronger in our ability to welcome *new kinds of relationships* with those connected to our story. We don't want to miss out on reclaimed relationships for those doors that open in a healthy way.

A special note about parental and other family relationships. What about relationships with our parents? Do we not have instructions to honor and respect parents in all things? As adult children, we learn that to honor and respect is not the same as "to remain under the control of." Yes, we honor. Yes, we respect. But sin and suffering have impacted how we express these attitudes toward our family members.

So, how do we honor abusive parents?

- To honor them, we do not respond to their abuse with more abuse—either toward them or others.
- To honor them, we do not enable their bad behavior—this means that we do not allow them to continue their abusive ways with us or with others under our protection.
- To honor them, we set clear boundaries with consequences when they are not repentant or willing to work toward ending their abusive ways.

We can also choose actions that honor the *position* of parent:

- We can discontinue the cycle of abuse by not abusing our own children.
- We can protect ourselves from relationships with others who continue the cycle of abuse into the next generation.

When we set these kinds of strong boundaries, we not only help ourselves heal; often, we prevent future generations from suffering, as well.

What about kindness, love, and grace? you may ask. Kindness, love, and grace are necessary in our relationships—and they are still possible to show even as we set boundaries. Remember the story about the banker in our lesson on forgiveness and reconciliation? That story taught us that whenever a family member or other loved one becomes a source of danger, they give up the privilege of position in the relationship—because trust and intimacy are not given "on demand"; neither are they owed simply because of a family title. You may struggle to set boundaries with family members and other close loved ones. Even though it is difficult, it is an important step to protect your healing process.

The truth that I want you to hear is that you have permission to set boundaries in many types of relationships. I also want you to realize that boundaries are not only for your good—often, they are also for the good of others and for the good of your relationships with them. Clear boundaries actually plant the seeds for more peaceful interactions.

So, let's consider the questions on our worksheet, which will help us to observe any signs that boundaries are needed in this area.

Do I Need Boundaries in My Relationships?

- Am I engaged in relationships that are a source of ongoing abuse?
- Do I experience trauma-related symptoms that are detrimental to my well-being in some situations?

Again, it is time to apply these questions personally. Let's take some time to reflect and write our answers on the worksheet.

Give participants time to write on the worksheet.

We have covered a lot of information, and perhaps, your mind is reeling. You might wonder, *Where do I need boundaries? Where do they need to be firm and strong? And where do I leave open a small gate? How can I make sure that the boundaries I set are from a place of wisdom and not from a place of fear or overreaction?*

These are all good, valid questions. They indicate that you should expect to take time, because as with most other things on this journey, setting boundaries is a process.

We are well into the process and consideration of what boundaries we may need. We see ourselves more clearly and understand some of the thoughts and actions that have hindered our healing.

You have probably noticed that the garden on your worksheet now has a fence around it. You might think of each slat on the fence as a boundary that you will put into place.

Perhaps through our discussion, you found that you overwhelmingly need boundaries in one of the three categories, or you may have discovered that your needs fall more evenly among two or three of the boundary types. Either way, your answers should bring to light which boundary types are most necessary for your garden's protection.

Maybe you are now asking, "How do I set a boundary?"

The questions on the worksheet helped us see where we spend too much emotional or mind time, where we are coping in unhealthy ways, and what relationships are causing trouble. Now it is necessary to *set limits*.

Consider the following:

- I find I am thinking again of the event—the time passes—I continue to relive the details over and over. My thoughts are distracted from other things and I become more anxious.
- I have conversations with myself—and others—in my mind. I create conversations that give me the opportunity to say what I want to say. It goes on and I become more upset.
- I am feeling anxious and turn to food, alcohol, drugs, shopping, movies and other things to distract me or dull the ache that consumes me. I begin to want those things more than things that are good for me. I depend on them to help me survive.
- I realize that I feel anxious or depressed after spending time with certain people who lead me down a harmful path or who continue to abuse or manipulate me.

BOUNDARY: I STOP. I CHANGE my activity. I say: NO MORE.

The purpose of the boundary is to protect you—for your good. We cannot always take control of the things that try to harm us. We cannot stop them from being the way they are. But at times, we can take control of how far we let those things come into our life and disturb us. And so, you will learn what helps you and what hurts you. To set a boundary is to say No to the things that make you anxious and confused.

Go for a walk. Read God's Word. Do something creative. Visit someone who leads in a good way.

We may need to take these actions multiple times but eventually we will begin to change the course of our thoughts or our actions.

You now have a better idea of where you need physical, emotional, or spiritual protection. This is personal for each of us. Take some time to write specific boundaries on the slats of the garden fence. These are defenses that you need to put in place for the health of your garden. These are reminders for when to say stop, of when to change direction, of when to choose a new activity.

Give participants time to write on the worksheet.

Now that you see some areas that may be harmful to you, I'd like to ask you to stop and contemplate one final question: Which of your boundaries do you feel will be most difficult to put into place? Choose one or two, and speak to God about them over the next several days.

You will not think of all the boundaries that you need from this one lesson and worksheet. Often, we are not made aware of a necessary boundary until we find ourselves in a bad situation. We suddenly realize that we need a boundary in that place! When that happens, come back to this worksheet and write it down.

Neither will the boundaries that we set today keep us from all pain or discomfort. Some onslaughts will get past, and we will feel them deeply. However, even then, we have permission to set a further boundary—one that limits how much or how long we will **indulge** that particular experience of pain. We can say No to the conversation in our mind that encourages the hurt. And, as mentioned, we can adjust our boundaries as we go.

But eventually, we will discover the boundaries that are necessary, we will defend those boundaries with confidence, and we will be encouraged when we begin to see our gardens thrive.

COURAGE AND PEACE

We need some encouragment—assurance that we are not alone as we make hard choices, as we consider how to protect ourselves. The following passage reminds us that our Good Shepherd is with us in our healing process.

The LORD is my shepherd, I lack nothing. He makes me lie down in green pastures,
he leads me beside quiet waters, he refreshes my soul.
He guides me along the right paths for his name's sake.

Even though I walk through the darkest valley,
I will fear no evil, for you are with me;
your rod and your staff, they comfort me.

You prepare a table before me in the presence of my enemies.
You anoint my head with oil; my cup overflows.

Surely your goodness and love will follow me all the days of my life,
and I will dwell in the house of the LORD forever. (Psalm 23)

SET BOUNDARIES

Your garden now has a fence. Answer the three sets of questions below. Be open and honest. When you are finished, use your responses to help determine specific boundaries to put up around your garden of well-being.

Do I Need Boundaries to Protect My Emotional Energy and Mind Time?

How much time do I spend each day thinking about my suffering? Do I often have pretend conversations, dwell on the *what-ifs*, ponder the details, and play out scenarios in my mind?

Do I feel emotionally exhausted?

When I make decisions, how large a part does my suffering play in the reasoning process?

Is my suffering always in the forefront of my thoughts? Is it draining my emotions or physical energy?

How many of my conversations with others eventually come back to the suffering? For example . . .

> Can I converse with others without bringing "it" to attention?
> When I am asked about myself, is "it" the first thing I want to tell?
> When someone else shares a painful experience, do I feel the need to share my story too?

Do I Need Boundaries to Protect the Way That I Cope?

What activities or actions do I use as an escape from my pain? How often and how quickly do I return to this behavior of escape? Do I tend to hide and escape more often than I live in the real world?

When I use this behavior to cope, does it take me toward a greater sense of well-being? Or has it begun to cause harm to my health, body, mind, relationships, or emotions?

Do I Need Boundaries in My Relationships?

Am I engaged in relationships that are a source of ongoing abuse?

Do I experience trauma-related symptoms that are detrimental to my well-being in some situations?

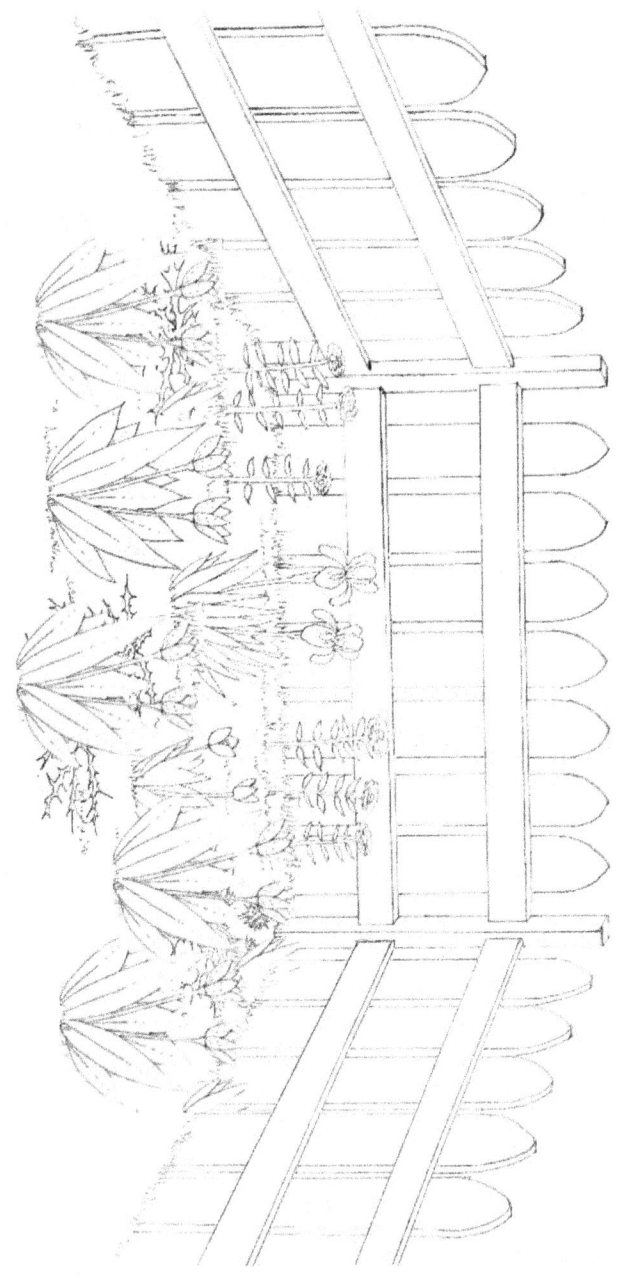

SESSION 26
A STRONG PROTECTION: IDENTITY

GOALS FOR PARTICIPANTS
- Become aware that we are all unique and purposeful creations of God
- Become aware that we are all created in the image of God
- Understand that it is important to have an identity that never changes
- Discover the idea of beauty and how it expresses and connects to God

MATERIALS
- This lesson
- Plain paper; pencils and pens

VOCABULARY
- **beauty** (BYOO-tee): A quality present in a thing or person that gives intense pleasure and satisfaction to the mind
- **identity** (i-DEN-ti-tee): who a person is, including their qualities and what sets them apart from others
- **image** (IM-ij): the mental picture of something; the representation of something
- **likeness** (LIKE-ness): a representation of something; the state of being similar to or "like" something
- **purposeful** (PER-puhs-full): full of purpose; intentional

GREETING

Each session begins with a greeting. This will be unique and personal to each group.

REVIEW

In the previous few lessons, we recognized our need for protection and we set boundaries to protect our well-being. These boundaries, which are meant to keep evil threats out of our garden and peaceful assurances in, were unique to our individual stories. But there is another form of protection that we all have in common—and that protection is our identity.

LESSON SCRIPT

You may wonder why we would even consider the need for additional protection, after we spent so much time setting up boundaries in our last session. It is true that our boundaries will be tremendously helpful to our progress on this journey, but they will not be fail-proof. There will still be times when threats and triggers and untruthful thinking get through and even seem to overwhelm our gardens of peace—and during those times, we will need reinforcement.

But how could reinforcement come through **identity?** Let us take a look.

Our *identity*—which includes who we are and how we see ourselves—is something that most of us spend a lot of mind time and energy on, although we may not realize it. It has a huge impact on the decisions we make, how we respond to others, how we care for ourselves, and what we expect from ourselves.

The problem is that much of our identity begins with what others think about us and expect from us. We tend to live up to and define ourselves by these expectations and viewpoints unconsciously, without even trying. For example, when asked to describe ourselves, we often list who we are in relation to other people. We might say, "I am a wife and mother," or "I am a father and business owner," or "I am a student."

Our identity is also largely based on what we think about and expect from ourselves. This can be seen when we name our accomplishments to describe who we are—for instance, "I graduate from college next month," "I am a tailor," or "I work with wood"—or when we share our plans and goals: "I am going to be a nurse," "I plan to have a family," or "I am studying to be a businessman."

For those of us on this journey of suffering, we might even list *negative events* that we think identify us—because the event we experienced, along with the resulting trauma, now seems to define who we are.

However, this type of identity—one based on the unsteadiness of events and circumstances, what others think about us, and what we think about ourselves—is at constant risk. It can easily be harmed or compromised, because it is dependent on factors that might change at any moment. This means that whenever those factors do change, the way we see ourselves will suddenly crumble. We will feel lost and vulnerable and unsure of who we are. This is *not* the type of identity that will defend us against outside threats. In fact, quite the opposite, this type of identity will fall apart when our boundaries fail to protect us from trauma's attacks.

The good news is, we don't have to base our identity on shifting events and expectations. We can base our identity on truth.

And the truth is this:

- You are so much more than what someone else expects of you or even what you expect of yourself.

- You are so much more than your circumstances.

- You have another identity. This identity is not dependent on what you do or how you feel. It is not based on what others think about you. And so, this identity will never change. In fact, it is an identity that has always been uniquely yours. And it comes from the very first person who ever knew you. Listen:

> For you created my inmost being; you knit me together in my mother's womb. I praise you because I am fearfully and wonderfully made; your works are wonderful; I know that full well. My frame was not hidden from you when I was made in the secret place, when I was woven together in the depths of the earth. Your eyes saw my unformed body; all the days ordained for me were written in your book before one of them came to be. (Psalm 139:13–16)

God, the Creator, was the first one to know you. He created you. Although, your mother's womb carried you, it was God who put you there when He *knitted you together*.

Some of you have done knitting. You understand that, before you even begin, you must choose the colors and textures of the yarn that you want. Then you must choose just the right kind of stitch that will be needed to create the final product. Some of these choices are creative, based on how you want the finished product to look; other choices are practical, based on what purpose this product will serve.

That is exactly how God created you. He carefully chose each of your physical and emotional and intellectual traits—your identity—and then with great detail, He wove together His precious creation: *you*. Therefore, this is the first truth about your identity:

You are a unique and purposeful creation of God, the Perfect Creator.

Before anyone else saw you or knew you, before you were even aware of yourself, God thought of you and planned you. He gave each detail of you careful attention. And then He purposely knitted everything together to fashion you as a unique creation.

So, you see, nothing about you happened by chance; instead, God was **purposeful** in His creation of you. And He made no one else exactly like you. You are His unique creation, created for a particular purpose.

Sometimes we might feel that we are simply born and then left to disappear among all of the other people on this earth. And we might feel that our stories are unimportant, or, at least, that they are unseen and unheard. But listen carefully: regardless of whether anyone else has even heard your story, God has it written down. He not only has seen and heard your story; He also knew that story before your days even began.

You are a unique and purposeful creation of God, the Perfect Creator.

Hold fast to this truth and keep it planted deep down inside of you. When untruths such as "all is lost" or "you have no purpose" try to take root in your garden, this truth will act as a protective boundary that limits their growth.

This is a strong truth, but it is not the only truth about our identity that we have to rely on. There is a second truth as well. To discuss this truth, we will begin at the beginning—with the creation of the world and all that is in it. This is an amazing story, and God does not give us all the details, but He does tell us that He accomplished something that no one else could: He created everything "out of nothing." Light and dark, water and heavenly bodies, plants and vegetation, fish and birds and animals of all kinds—*everything* He created came out of nothing! But God did not stop there. Because in Genesis 1:26–27, we read what He created next: "Then God said, 'Let us make mankind in our image, in our likeness. . . .' So God created mankind in his own image, in the image of God he created them."

Wait, did we just hear that correctly? Not only did God create humans out of nothing, but He also created us in a way that was unlike anything else He had created before. How? He made us in His **image** and **likeness**. These two words—*image* and *likeness*—have a common meaning. They both refer to something that "is similar" or "has a resemblance" to something else.

Think about members of a family. If we say, "Little Mary is the image of her mother," we do *not* mean that Mary

- looks exactly like her mother,
- can do everything her mother can do,
- has all the characteristics of her mother, or
- could take her mother's place in responsibility and authority.

What we *do* mean is that Mary

- reminds us of her mother,
- has some of her mother's characteristics, and
- resembles her mother.

The same is true for us. When the Bible says that we are made in the image and likeness of God, it does not mean we look exactly like God or have all His characteristics. It also does not mean that we are "little gods." What it does mean, however, is that we resemble Him in certain ways. We bear His likeness.

One way to understand this is to compare some of the characteristics of God, as described in the Bible, with human characteristics. Such a comparison shows that, as humans, we have many of God's characteristics, but we do not have them to the same extent that He does. For example,

- we can love, but we cannot love perfectly;
- we are creative, but we cannot create something out of nothing;
- we long for justice, but we cannot judge men's hearts or intentions.

God chose to identify us with Himself. And so, the second truth about your identity is this:

Because God created you in His image, you can find your true identity in Him.

To find our identity in God is much like using Him as our mirror—a way to see ourselves honestly. Rather than looking at others and attempting to reflect *their* expectation of us, we look to God and simply reflect His assurance that we are made in His image—we are connected to Him. And as we look to Him, we will attempt to reflect His image in us more and more. In fact, this is the only way we will become satisfied. As we become more like Him, we become more fully ourselves—and this makes us content, confident, and strong so that we are better equipped to withstand the untruths that threaten to invade.

The evil one knows this and will try to lead us away from God and our identity in Him. He will take advantage of our human tendency to look at ourselves through the lenses of others who are less important—family, friends, cultural icons, media, or even people at church—and lead us down paths that will get us into trouble and eventually even destroy us. And so, it is important that we plant this truth deep within us.

That being said, take some time to think about this amazing truth. Take time to recognize that the Creator God could have made you in any image, but He chose to create you in a way that would remind others of Him. And so, your true identity is founded by and centered in God Himself.

Now, let's combine these two truths:

You are a unique and purposeful creation of God, the Perfect Creator

and

Because God created you in His image, you can find your true identity in Him.

When we put these truths together, we form a strong protective boundary against the threats of trauma—we create a new identity. The thing about this "new" identity, however, is that it is not really new. We are who God made us to be from the very beginning—and so, this identity has always been ours. This means it is our *true* identity.

Our true identity is not something that we design or work on; rather, it is something that we simply recognize and embrace—but the moment we do is the moment it can begin to actively protect us against the triggers, untruths, and other threats to our well-being brought on by trauma. And it is in this same moment that our God-given identity becomes *new to us*.

This new-to-us identity differs from the previous identity we held in five main ways:

1. **This identity never changes.** Every minute of every day of every year, this truth remains: You have always been and will always be a unique and purposeful creation of God, the Perfect Creator.

2. **This identity is not dependent on you.** Your unique identity is yours simply because you exist! It will not change based on how you think or feel or act. Neither will it change based on anything you do, whether for God or anyone else.

3. **This identity is not dependent on others.** Because your identity was given to you by God and is in God, no one can take it from you. Some might not believe this or might not treat you as if this is true, but that does not change the reality.

4. **This identity is not dependent on events or circumstances.** Neither the harmful events that put you on this journey of suffering, nor any current or future events and circumstances can change your true identity. These events and circumstances are part of your story, but they are not your identity. Even the pain that you have experienced is not your identity—it is only a part of your story.

5. **This identity is an expression of God's own beauty.** Beauty is named in the Bible as one of the characteristics of God. *From Zion, perfect in beauty, God shines forth.* (Psalm 50:2)

It is also a description that we often use when we talk about His creation. When we witness a sunset or a mountain range, for example, we might say, "How beautiful!"

The beauty we recognize in the sunset or the mountains is an expression of God's own beauty. Our minds connect with this outward expression, and the connection brings satisfaction. It is this satisfaction that we call beauty. In fact, the very definition of the word *beauty* is "a certain quality in a thing or person that gives intense pleasure and *satisfaction to the mind.*"

Not all beauty lies in the *outward* appearance, as it does in a mountain range, and beauty will not always be as obvious as it is in a sunset; however, all of God's creations contain unique expressions of His beauty—and that includes us.

REFLECTION AND APPLICATION

A new identity. This is big news, isn't it? This can actually take some time to really sink down inside you and change your way of thinking.

But, whenever we learn something new, we tend to absorb it better when we express it or process it in several different ways—and so, that is what we will do today. We have already heard these truths. Now we will write and speak them.

The first truth was this:

> *You are a unique and purposeful creation of God, the Perfect Creator.*

Words come to life when we write them ourselves, so go ahead and write these words on your paper:

> *I am a unique and purposeful creation of God, the Perfect Creator.*

Now, take some time to read and think on these words. How does this make you feel? Do you believe that it is true?

> Give participants a few moments to contemplate.

Next, speak the words to yourself. You may do this quietly, but speak the words out loud:

> *I am a unique and purposeful creation of God, the Perfect Creator.*

> Give participants a moment to speak the words quietly, or invite everyone to read the words out loud together.

Now, I will repeat the second truth from today:

> *Because God created you in His image, you can find your true identity in Him.*

Write this down on your paper, and then contemplate on these words:

> *Because God created me in His image, I can find my true identity in Him.*

> Give participants a few moments to write and contemplate.

Now, speak these words out loud to yourself as you did before.

> Give participants a moment to speak the words quietly, or invite everyone to read the words out loud together.

Finally, write the following words on your paper:

As God's creation, made in His image, I connect to and express His beauty.

> Give participants a few moments to write.

How does it make you feel to know that you are made in the image of God? Does it give you a sense of family connection with God that you had not considered before? Does this give you courage? Does this provide confidence that you lacked?

> Give participants a few moments to contemplate in response to the questions.

These truths will help you to know your true identity. They will help you make choices that are wise. They will give you courage and hope when others reject you or are displeased with "who you are." And they will protect you as you move forward and toward healing.

Finally, I want you to write the following words on your paper:

Thank you for the identity you have given to me.
I embrace it.
I see value in it.

> Give participants a few moments to write.

Over the next several days, find some time to sit alone with God. Open your hands, palms up, and speak these final words that you wrote down.

COURAGE AND PEACE

Weeks ago, you were uncertain about how this journey would unfold. Even now, not everything is known or resolved. Yet, here you are, identifying threats, considering boundaries, speaking truth to yourself. You have shown courage. You have confronted difficult choices. By taking back control from trauma, you have become more capable of moving forward with hope. And by removing untruth and speaking to yourself in a language of encouragement, compassion, and truth, you are sowing peace.

SESSION 27
VALUE: WHERE DO I FIND IT?

GOALS FOR PARTICIPANTS
- Know that we have value because we are created in the image of God
- Know that our value as God's creation will last for eternity—this value cannot be lost, stolen, or destroyed by suffering

MATERIALS
- This lesson
- Plain paper; pencils and pens

VOCABULARY
- **value** (VAL-yoo): (noun) the worth or usefulness of something; (verb/action word) to see the good or advantage in a thing or person
- **perceived** (per-SEEVED): (adjective/descriptive word) regarded or understood a certain way

GREETING

Each session begins with a greeting. This will be unique and personal to each group.

REVIEW

You might not have understood the influence of identity on your life until our last conversation. But then we learned that much of the way we think and many of the decisions we make are actually based on our identity. As such, an identity that relies on changing expectations and circumstances can lead us to ruin, especially when trauma enters the story. Fortunately, we discovered a strong new identity that will defend us against any threats to our peace.

What were the two truths that made up this new-to-us identity?

What does it mean to you that God created you in His image and gave some of His identity to you?

Give participants a few moments to respond after each question.

LESSON SCRIPT

Today we will discover another strong form of protection that God gives us—and that protection is **value**. *Value* is "importance or worth." When someone or something is *valuable* to us, we believe that it has a lot of worth.

Let's share briefly about some things that we think are valuable. For now, we are just going to talk about objects—not people.

> Give participants a few moments to respond. Examples might be a home, car, education, church, etc.

Now, let's think about why these items have value to us.

> Give participants a few moments to contemplate and share in response.

Often, we judge the value of a thing by how much money it costs, how useful it is, how rare it is, or what it represents to us. These criteria can be helpful in some ways, but the reality is that, over time, our standards can change. This means that how much we value certain items will likely change as well.

Here is an example. Think of an item that you value because it is useful to you. If that item broke tomorrow and became unusable, how would you value it differently? You would very likely value it less—or not at all.

Another example is when we value objects based on what influential people have said about them. For instance, we might put more value on a particular shoe style after it has been endorsed by a celebrity. In this case, nothing about the object itself has changed—all that has changed is its professed value.

These examples demonstrate how easily we can change our minds about the value of an object. They also show that the value of something is largely based on viewpoint. For this reason, we are going to learn about a special term that we can use whenever we refer to an item's worth: this term is *perceived value*. Remember that perceive means "to regard or see in a certain way." So, the **perceived** value of something is the value that *we see in it*.

But, what about the value of *people*? It is interesting that many of the standards we use to determine the worth of objects also seem to apply when we assess people. We might consider someone valuable if they have a lot of money, for example, or if their title or position represents something we think is important. Most of us also value people who mean something special to us. And, out of necessity, we all value people based on what they can offer.

In fact, it is a natural tendency—and not necessarily bad—to value others for what they can do for us. For instance, I value my doctor because she can help me stay healthy and give me advice when I am ill; and many others find her valuable for the same reason. Likewise, my car mechanic is valuable to those whose vehicles he repairs.

You and I are perceived as being valuable to others because of what we offer too. It can actually bring us joy and self-worth when we feel useful to others, especially when we receive praise for what we do. All of this is good and right.

However, it becomes harmful when we value people—whether ourselves or others—based *only* on what they can do. Consider these scenarios:

- We have such a longing to prove our value that we make unwise choices about what or how much to do for another person.
- Someone tells us that if we do not meet their demands—some of which may be immoral, harmful to us, and displeasing to God—then we are "worthless."

In situations like these, our natural tendency to want to help others and feel valued by them is abused or manipulated—by them. As a result, our desire to do right and good can be overpowered by our longing to feel valuable—and when this happens, we tend to act unwisely. Our decisions and behaviors become harmful—to ourselves, to others, and to our relationships—and although we may feel needed and valuable for a time, any sense of self-worth that we gain is usually quickly followed by the sense that we have been used. This leads us to feel even less valuable than before, which makes us more likely to continue our harmful behavior. In turn, our self-worth diminishes more, and the cycle continues.

Why is this so important? The fact that we can feel more or less valuable based on situations and actions—whether our own actions or the actions of another—tells us that people, just like objects, also have "perceived value." Another reason we know that people have perceived value is because we tend to gauge others' importance based on certain criteria.

It is important that we understand this idea of perceived value, because it shows us that, as humans, our own value is largely based on perception—whether that perception is ours or others'. One reason this is a problem is because perception changes. As with the celebrity-endorsed shoes, we might be seen as worthless one day and important the next—or vice-versa!—simply because someone changed their mind.

A second problem with perceived value is that perception is often different than reality. This means that the perceived value of something or someone is usually not the same as their true value. To understand this difference, let's go back to the example of shoes:

Suppose I am walking down a busy sidewalk and I am not wearing the style of shoes that has been endorsed by the celebrity. In fact, these shoes are not even the latest fashion. They are warm and sturdy, but they are an odd color, and they do not fit my feet exactly the way they should. A woman walks by me and looks disapprovingly at my shoes. She apparently judges them to be of little value. When she passes, I suddenly feel embarrassed. I ask myself why I would wear such low-quality footwear.

I continue to walk, and not even a minute later, it begins to pour rain. Puddles form on the sidewalk, and the pavement becomes muddy and slippery. A man in flip-flops walks by me and looks longingly at my shoes. Suddenly, the remorse I felt over my choice of shoes turns to relief. Now, the true value of my shoes has become quite clear! They cover my feet, keep my toes warm and dry, and give me traction on the slippery sidewalk. These are not low-quality shoes! They are well-made shoes that have served their purpose well.

Do you see how the disapproving woman's perceived value of the shoes was different from their real value? The woman perceived that the shoes were of low value simply because of their outward appearance. But when the rain came, they provided warmth, protection, and safety, and the true value of the shoes became clear.

It is the same for us. The value that others see in us is often skewed, because they only see what's on the outside. Their judgment is based on an incomplete picture of who we are. In many instances, people do not realize that they have judged our value based on only a small portion of the picture. However, there is another type of perceived value in which an individual deliberately judges the worth of another based on one single aspect. This is called *assigned value*. Assigned value occurs when someone connects the worth of a person to a particular personal characteristic. The more the person demonstrates that particular characteristic, the more value they are perceived to have.

Here is a simple example of assigned value:

> A man who has brown eyes states that all people with brown eyes can learn more easily than people with other eye colors. His statement assigns worth to brown eyes, which adds value to brown-eyed people and removes value from people with other eye colors.

Now, here is a more complicated example:

> Two people are in a relationship. One begins to physically abuse the other. The person being abused is seen as valuable as long as they remain in the relationship and allow their abuser's mistreatment. But when that person takes steps to stop the abuse, the abuser no longer considers them of value and leaves the relationship to find another.

What these different meanings of *value* ultimately show us is that perception is an unreliable way to measure worth—especially the perceptions of others. We will never get an accurate portrayal of our value if we look at it through the viewpoints of those who cannot see the whole picture.

The sad reality, though, is that so many of us—women, men, children—suffer tremendously because of this very thing. Our true value has been distorted by someone else's perceived value of us. Or our longing to be important has been manipulated by someone who assigned us their version of worth for selfish reasons.

You may be experiencing this now, or you may have endured it in the past. Either way, I want you to listen to this truth, because it will be essential for your healing on this journey:

> *You have value just because you are you.*

Deep down, this is what we all long for. Yet, because so many others do not see our true value, we feel the need to prove it is there. We work hard, we improve ourselves, we meet expectations—and it might work for a time, but eventually, something always goes wrong.

So, we grow tired of being valued for what we do . . . for how we look . . . for how we make others feel, because eventually, those things will falter—and when they do, our perceived value will falter with them.

But is it possible to have value simply because we *are*? Yes! To understand this truth, let's revisit what we have discovered about our identity so far:

- *I am a unique and purposeful creation of God, the Perfect Creator.*
- *Because God created me in His image, I can find my true identity in Him.*

These two truths alone give us great value—true value. They tell us that we are valuable simply because we *are*! We do not need to earn this value. And because we can do nothing to earn it, we also can do nothing lose it. This worth is ours because God gave it to us when He created us—and nothing and no one can change that.

This brings us to a third truth about our value:

> *You are valuable because God has declared you to be valuable.*

From the very beginning of time, when God created human life, He proclaimed it "very good."

> And God looked upon all that He had made, and indeed, it was very good. (Genesis 1:31)

That is a proclamation that we, as God's creation, have value. He has declared it!

Jesus also made it clear that we have value in God's eyes. In Matthew 6:26, Jesus said, "Look at the birds of the air; they do not sow or reap or store away in barns, and yet your heavenly Father feeds them. Are you not much more valuable than they?" This teaching of Jesus shows us that God, the Perfect Creator, places more value on us than He does on even the beautiful, soaring birds of the air.

You may wonder, however, *If our value is based on God's perception, isn't that perceived value—not true value?* God's perception is different than human perception. Humans perceive the value of others based on an incomplete picture, selfish motives, fickle opinions, and criteria that constantly change. But with God, there is no incomplete picture or selfishness or changing criteria, because He is all-knowing, all-present, and all-powerful—and He is good. So, when God proclaims, with authority, that something or someone has value—which He has—we know that this proclamation is truth. Therefore . . .

> *You are valuable because God has declared you to be valuable.*

As you absorb this truth over the coming days, remember that there is nothing you can do to earn or lose this value. Neither is there anything you can do to earn or lose God's love. In 1 John 4:19, we see that "We love Him… because He first loved us."

This means that God loved you before you were even capable of doing anything for Him. As your creator, He was the first to set His heart on you and love you just because of you. Then He proved that love not only in words, but in action.

He does not say,
> *If you do this thing for me, I will love you.*
> *If you do that thing, I will be with you.*
> *If you show me love, I will value you.*

You may face such expectations, spoken or unspoken, by others. The type of conditional love and value they express might even be the root of your crisis event or your suffering. But these expressions do not convey the heart of God, who values and loves you simply because of who you are: created by Him.

It is nice to be valued by others—but not necessary. You do not need to prove your worth. You do not need to meet the demands of others in an attempt to be valuable. Because now you know the truth: your value is not dependent on others.

From eternity past to eternity future, in every day and every circumstance, your value is yours just because you are you. This is God's declared truth.

REFLECTION AND APPLICATION

Find something to write with and use it to put these words on your paper:

> *I am valuable because God declares me to be valuable.*

> Give participants a few moments to write down this new truth.

It is not enough for us to write this down and remember the words. This truth must become a part of us. It must settle and live in our very souls—because only then will it begin to influence our choices and actions and actually protect us from harm. You see, we protect the things we value, and that includes ourselves.

So, when you long to feel valued, turn to the Creator of the Universe. He has proclaimed you as valuable, and He will never turn away. You do not need to look in other places or at other people for your worth. Instead, you need only to look to Him.

How might this awareness of your own value change your life? Let's talk about it.

> Give participants time to share in response to the question above.

Watch for times this week when you are tempted to speak poorly of yourself, put yourself down, or be discouraged about your situation, and instead speak the truth about your value. Say to yourself, "I am valuable because God declared me to be valuable." Repeat these words as often as you need to let them soak into your heart and mind.

COURAGE AND PEACE

This week, watch for the birds of the air. When you see them, let your heart remember God's message to you as He speaks of your value. Matthew 6:26: "Look at the birds of the air; they do not sow or reap or store away in barns, and yet your heavenly Father feeds them. Are you not much more valuable than they?"

SESSION 28
TETHERS

GOALS FOR PARTICIPANTS
- Understand the meaning of a tether
- Memorize the tethers that God holds out to us
- Choose a tether to hold onto when the fear threatens

MATERIALS
- This lesson
- Participant worksheet: Tethers
- Plain paper; pencils and pens

VOCABULARY
- **abandon** (uh-BAN-duhn): to leave behind; to forsake or withdraw from
- **tether** (TETH-er): something used to hold an object closely to a particular location

GREETING

Each session begins with a greeting. This will be unique and personal to each group.

REVIEW

Before we start the main lesson, let's briefly review the three most recent truths that we learned to protect us on our journey of healing:

- *I am a unique and purposeful creation of God, the Perfect Creator.*
- *Because God created me in His image, I can find my true identity in Him.*
- *I am valuable because God has declared me to be valuable.*

How have these truths impacted you over the past week? Which truth or truths have been most helpful to you?

LESSON SCRIPT

Let's take a moment to look at where we are on the path. Behind us, the grips of trauma probably look smaller now. Some of its tendrils may be within reach, and a few might even grip us weakly, but they are few and far between compared with earlier points on the road.

This is amazing, isn't it? For so long, we felt tethered to our suffering—a **tether** is something that holds an object close to a particular location, keeping it within certain bounds—but now, we have moved farther from that captivity and feel more freedom. This is a welcome breath of fresh air.

To walk in freedom, however, does not mean that we wander aimlessly. We must continue to walk with healthy boundaries and a sense of direction, because many other things on the road will continue to distract and tug at us. We do not want to get consumed by fear and emotion or be easily entangled by the expectations of others. And we do not want to wander off the path altogether and end up someplace we do not want to be—a place of confusion or perhaps even re-traumatization.

So, we need something to keep us within certain bounds of safety. We need new tethers—safety tethers. *These tethers are gentle, firm, truthful, dependable, and unaffected by our emotions and others' expectations. These tethers are for our protection, for our good. We welcome them.*

Like a strong rope that holds a boat to the dock in harsh wind, these seven tenacious, unbreakable tethers will hold us during unexpected storms, times of confusion, and even renewed threats of destruction.

> Distribute the worksheets so the participants can follow along with the next part of the lesson.

1. **God's love:** We may be suspicious of love as a tether because, in truth, many of us do not trust it. We have found it untrustworthy in some situations. But as we discussed in our previous lesson, God's love is different from the love of all others. He loved you before you ever knew of Him. He set His heart on you. You can do nothing to earn His love or to make Him stop loving you. God's love is pure, good, and just. God's love is a perfect tether, because it began with Him, and it is eternal.

2. **God's presence:** One of our heart's desires is for someone to be with us—really *with* us. In our pain, in our suffering, in our longings, and in the depths of our souls. God's presence is different from any other. He never runs out of time or interest. He never runs low on patience. In His presence, we are not at the mercy of chaos or human will. God is with us in our suffering. Even when we push Him away, He remains. God's sure presence with us is a tether that holds us when we feel **abandoned** and unseen.

3. God's goodness: *Good* is a term that, for most of us, lost much of its meaning as we scrambled for answers in our suffering. For many of us, what we thought was good exploded into evil. But there is *true* goodness in our lives. This is a unique goodness that we can learn to trust even when we do *not* see it. It is God's pure and right goodness, and it is a tether that holds us, even in the chaos of doubt and despair.

4. Identity in God: Although trauma is a part of our story, it is not our identity. Further, when we attempt to restore or reestablish our identity as we imagined it before our crisis, we make unwise decisions. The truth is that our *true* identity is not what we imagined it to be. Our true identity cannot be destroyed by abuse and pain. This true identity, as a unique and intentional creation of God, tethers us. It holds us when uncertainty calls us to run after other assurances.

5. Value from God: The ability to make good choices is jeopardized when we do not consider our personal value in the equation. Fortunately, we have value that is not diminished by the events that happen to us. The value given to us by God is a tether that holds us safely whenever we are tempted to seek value in harmful ways.

6. The truth about suffering: We have become familiar with the negative effects of suffering—trauma—we can recognize many of its threats, lies, and accusations, and we know that it wants to consume us. We have also realized that suffering is temporary and that there is good that comes *in* it and *from* it. Knowing these truths is a tether that keeps us from being carried away by the tactics of trauma.

7. A sure hope: We have discovered that when hope is actually wishful thinking, we can be swept away by suffering and disappointment. Therefore, the one and only sure hope is the great I Am. This hope cannot be destroyed, will never fail, and will not disappoint. This sure hope is a tether that keeps us from wandering off after unrealistic wishes go unfulfilled.

These truths are good, powerful, and capable tethers; they never change, they never lose strength, and their truth is eternal. As long as we keep them in focus, we stay connected to them. And this connection is what keeps us within the bounds of clarity and safety whenever a trigger threatens to send us off-course. If we find ourselves outside of the bounds of their safety, it is not because the tethers broke under stress; it is because we did not keep our connection and focus.

To stay connected to our tethers is easier said than done, however—because in the moment when we are triggered, we are often not able to think clearly. Our gaze is easily distracted and often wanders away from the truth. And it is then that we lose our connection to these safety tethers.

In those instances, it can be helpful to have a tangible object that will capture your attention and refocus your gaze on the truth. This might be a particular bracelet, a string of prayer beads, a piece of needlework, a printed picture, or a verse. Whatever item you choose is not to be worshiped and is not strong enough in itself to tether you to safety; however, it can help you to reconnect mentally to your tethers by reminding you of the powerful truths that hold you.

It can also help to look to the perfect example and mentor, Jesus. Because Jesus lived in this world, He experienced His own journey of suffering, and He was often tempted in the same ways we are—tempted to abandon His true purpose and embrace false promises and enticements. But He fixed His eyes on the joy that would come with the completion of His work—the joy of obedience. This enabled Him to endure with perfection. We see this in Hebrews 12:1–2:

> Let us throw off everything that hinders and the sin that so easily entangles. And let us run with perseverance . . . fixing our eyes on Jesus, the pioneer and perfecter of faith. For the joy set before him he endured the cross, scorning its shame, and sat down at the right hand of the throne of God.

This passage reminds us that, even when we forget or feel disconnected from these truths, we can fix our eyes on Jesus. As the "pioneer" of our faith, Jesus set the course that we are to follow, and He is the one to whom all other truths are tethered.

REFLECTION AND APPLICATION

To stay connected to these seven tethers of truth, you must first remember them. So, before our next lesson, commit these tethers to memory:

1. God's love
2. God's presence
3. God's goodness
4. My identity in God
5. My value in God
6. The truth about suffering
7. A sure hope

Which of these tethers feels the strongest to you personally?

> Allow students time to respond to the question above.

Watch for a moment this week when you feel that you need a safety tether and write about the experience in your journal or on today's worksheet. Describe the challenge that threatened to push you back under the control of trauma, share about the emotions that came, and explain what tether you chose to hold onto to keep you in a place of clarity and peace. Your written testimony will help you to remember this success when another challenge comes—or when the same challenge comes again.

COURAGE AND PEACE

As we prepare to go our separate ways, let's remember that the tethers that we hold onto are attached to God in a loving way, different from any other attachment we have experienced. They will give us stability, so that we are not easily thrown off-balance by the winds and storms on our path.

As we turn our gaze forward, the path ahead disappears around a bend in the road. Where is our Traveling Companion? He is next to us and He is already there, around the bend. He calls us forward to experience new hope and new joy and new peace.

TETHERS

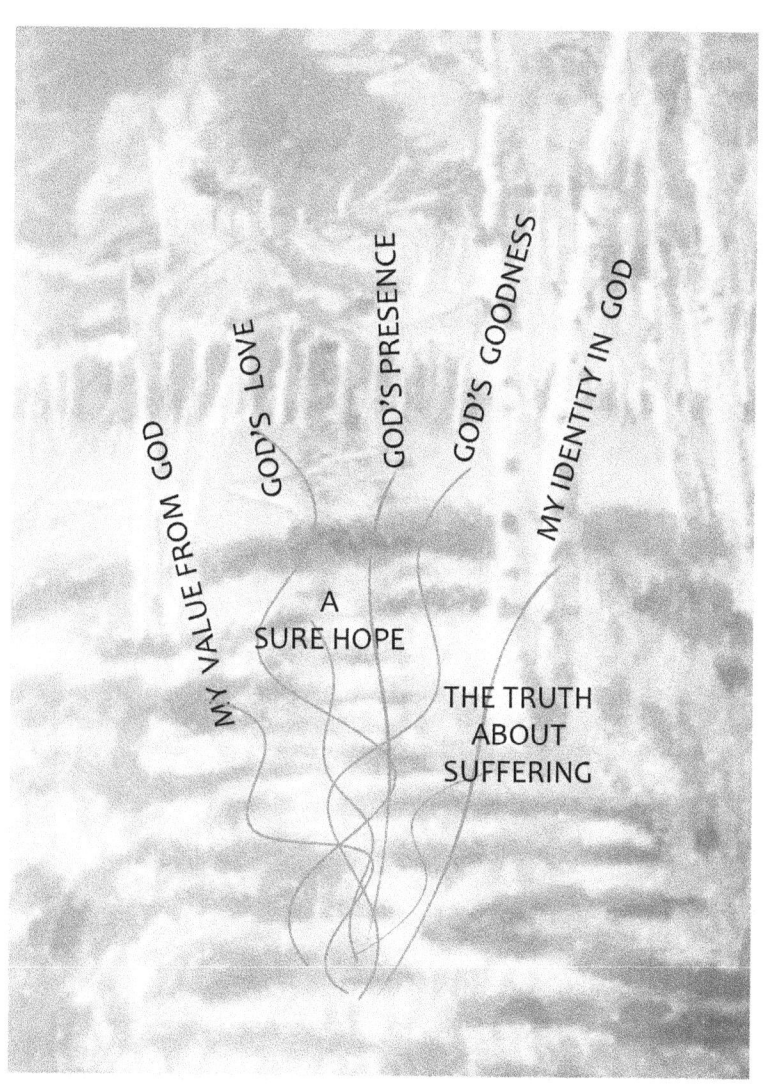

SESSION 29
THE REALITY OF FEAR

GOALS FOR PARTICIPANTS
- Acknowledge the presence of fear
- Identify those thoughts or experiences that feed fear
- Choose a tether to hold onto when the fear threatens

MATERIALS
- This lesson
- Plain paper; pencils and pens

VOCABULARY
- **fear** (FEER): a feeling of concern or anxiety
- **hollow** (HOL-oh): empty; meaningless
- **radiance** (RAY-dee-uhns): light, warm, cheerful brightness

GREETING

> Each session begins with a greeting. This will be unique and personal to each group.

REVIEW

In our previous session, we discovered that we need tethers to hold us to the truths that God gives us. These tethers are good tethers. They keep us in a place of clarity, protected from the impacts of triggers and other threats that cross our paths.

What did you learn in that previous lesson? Since we last met, were you able to hold onto any of the particular tethers that we discussed to help you through a rough time? If so, which ones?

> Give participants a few minutes to share in response to the questions.

LESSON SCRIPT

This session, we will learn how tethers can help with a particular threat—the threat of fear.

Fear is a distressing emotion. It can feel like anxiety or worry or a sense of impending danger, evil, or pain.

At one point in your life, you might not have used the word *fear* to describe yourself. But then there was that moment of impact and things changed. Now, **fear** might grasp with such suddenness and strength that, at times, you feel afraid to live forward into the next few minutes.

Sometimes, fear comes as an unexpected assault, pressing on you and instantly taking your breath away. Other times, it is stealthier. It seeps slowly into the soil of your life garden, completely undetected, until the choices and perspectives that push through the earth make it clear: fear is at the root. Most of the time, though, fear starts with *what-ifs* that take hold of the imagination. These *what-ifs* instill anxiety as they taunt your mind with every potential scenario for disaster.

The emotion of fear itself is difficult to deal with, but this difficulty is compounded by the fact that sometimes fear is a reasonable response. When there is a real threat—for example, a physical threat to your health or life—fear serves a noble purpose: it alerts you to the danger so that you can remove yourself from it. In these situations, fear is good, because it motivates you to find safety. But other times, fear is *not* reasonable. It is our reaction to a threat that we imagined, and there is no real danger.

And so, we have uncertainty.

Before trauma entered our story, we probably felt more confident in our judgement about whether a threat was real or merely perceived. But when crisis came, that changed. Because what usually happens with crisis is that . . .

- something unknown becomes known,
- something unexpected is revealed, or
- something once perceived as safe is now dangerous.

So now, we wonder, *If one unimaginable thing has become reality, then what else is possible?* And this uncertainty can produce even more fear.

But unnecessary fear can hinder our forward movement. It can keep us from hope and possibility and healing. So, what do we do?

The reality is, we cannot always stop fear. Sometimes, fear just comes. It takes over before we even notice. And in those times, it seems impossible *not to fear*.

So, we must find a tether that will hold us close whenever that fear comes. This tether must not only keep us within the bounds of clarity and security; it must also pull us away from—even talk us out of—fear.

But how? What could someone possibly say that would remove us from the sudden, strong pull of fear? Who could actually speak to us in a way that would impart peace? Is there anyone even trustworthy and powerful enough who could overwhelm the fear that overwhelms us?

Maybe you know where this is leading.

The truth is, our fear is not a surprise to our perfect Traveling Companion. In fact, the reality of fear is the foundation of one of I AM's most frequent promises to us:

> I AM *with you.*

This is where our conversation about tethers comes *to life.* Because this tether is not simply a truth to hold onto. This tether is God Himself.

His profound words speak this powerful reality:

> So do not fear, for I am with you; do not be dismayed, for I am your God. I will strengthen you and help you; I will uphold you with my righteous right hand. (Isaiah 41:10)

> For I am the LORD your God who takes hold of your right hand and says to you, Do not fear; I will help you. (Isaiah 41:13)

Many assurances are hollow. Many promises are broken. But not this one. With this tether, God *holds us to Himself.* "It is I," He says. "I hold your hand."

This assurance, this promise, this tether to God's presence is strong, because it comes from the LORD, who knows no fear. Everything and everyone answers to His call. Nothing can overwhelm Him. There are no unknowns for Him, no uncertainty. And yet He is near. He is present. He chooses to be by your side.

In fact, He promised you His presence even before your moments of fear. Before your anxiety came, He reached out to uphold you. Before you knew suffering, He was your God. He knows. He sees. He feels. He hears. And He is stronger than your fear.

In the Bible, this idea of God as our safety tether is explained in these words:

> God is our refuge and strength, an ever-present help in trouble. Therefore we will not fear, though the earth give way and the mountains fall into the heart of the sea, though its waters roar and foam and the mountains quake with their surging. (Psalm 46:1–3)

This passage tells you that God Himself is your refuge. Even when everything else in life gives way, He is your safe place. Whenever you call on Him, He will hear your call. And you will have this assurance:

> *I see you. I know you feel fear.*
> *Do not give in to the fear. For it is I.*
> *I hold your hand.*
> I AM *with you.*

We see the author of Lamentations recount his own experience with this, when he says to God,

> You came near when I called you, and you said, "Do not fear." (Lamentations 3:57)

The author of this passage in Psalm tells a similar story when he says,

> I sought the LORD, and he answered me; he delivered me from all my fears. Those who look to him are **radiant**; their faces are never covered with shame. (Psalm 34:4–5, emphasis mine)

Radiant? Amid aggressive, destructive, palpable fear? But how could that be possible?

You see, whenever we turn our face to the LORD—whenever we grasp the tether that He uses to hold us to Him—fear, in turn, releases its grasp on us; and in that release, a new expression flows from us. The presence of the LORD shines through our countenance, replacing the gray desperation of fear with brightness. The dependable promise of His place at our side breaks through our expression of fear and shame.

Fear is a reality.

But even while we are in that fear, even before we feel that fear, God holds us with the strong tether of His presence and goodness. For this reason, we can follow the advice of Proverbs 3:25-26, which tells us not to give in to sudden fear, because the Lord is at our side.

REFLECTION AND APPLICATION

So, now that we have talked about the tether that can hold us in the midst of fear, let's look at how this might work in our own lives.

Take a moment to think about the questions I am about to ask you and write down any thoughts you have in response.

What fear is threatening your peace? What anxieties threaten your everyday choices and activities? No one else needs to understand these fears—they need only be real to you.

> Give participants a few minutes to contemplate and write down their thoughts.

Now that you have some of your fears in focus, think about what assurance from God you can use as a tether to hold you in a safe and peaceful place whenever you encounter this fear. What verse or promise can you hold in your heart and even speak out loud that will help you to keep your focus on your Good Shepherd rather than on your fear?

Write these promises below the fears on your paper.

> Give participants a few minutes to contemplate and write down their responses. You may need to repeat some of the passages from the lesson to help them with this part of the activity.

It is often not enough to have these promises in our minds; we need a visual to hold and see and read and hear—this makes the tether even stronger. So, keep your paper with you over the next few weeks and refer to it whenever fear comes.

Remind yourself of the presence and promises of God that tether you to Him in the face of that fear. And then hold tight to that tether by calling out to Him. Choose one or more of your fears and talk to God about them. Know that He is by your side and hears your call. Accept His reassurance. And in time, you will experience release.

Conversation with our Good Shepherd is a tether that can hold us safe in many situations. By Him, we are delivered from the stronghold of fear. And from Him, our radiance becomes a reality.

COURAGE AND PEACE

As you go into the next week, take this passage with you to remind you that there is peace and strength —even when fear threatens:

> God is our refuge and strength, an ever-present help in trouble. Therefore we will not fear, though the earth give way and the mountains fall into the heart of the sea, though its waters roar and foam and the mountains quake with their surging. (Psalm 46:1–3)

SESSION 30
ALONG THE WAY

GOALS FOR PARTICIPANTS
- Identify with the emotions or expression of the picture figures
- Tell a part of their story with the picture figures
- Use the picture figures to help identify their emotional state at any particular time

MATERIALS
- This lesson
- Participant worksheet: Along The Way (Before the session, cut the figures apart so that each participant can use them during the lesson.)
- Plain paper; pencils and pens

VOCABULARY
- **confused** (kuhn-FYOOZD): unclear in your thoughts; perplexed
- **emotional state** (ee-MO-shun-nuhl STAYT): the way a person feels at a particular time

GREETING

Each session begins with a greeting. This will be unique and personal to each group.

REVIEW

In our previous lesson, we talked about the reality of fear in our lives and how it sometimes comes when we least expect it. But when we grab hold of the tether that God uses to hold us to Himself, when we set our eyes on the LORD who is at our side, we are not consumed by that fear. It is even possible for radiance to replace the fear in our eyes!

What particular promise did you choose that tethers you to God when fear threatens to overwhelm you?

Give participants a few minutes to share in response to the questions.

LESSON SCRIPT

What a journey we are on! Even this far along the path, we have discovered that we can still move in and out of emotions like fear and sadness and insecurity. One minute, we might feel content, with our heads held high, and then suddenly, we are triggered—and we find ourselves in a puddle of tears.

We have known from the beginning that coming to peace would not be a straight road. But it is the road we chose and committed to move forward on—and now we are!

To get to where we are today, we have had to let go of incorrect expectations and unrealistic ideas at various points along our journey. For example . . .
- We have acknowledged that the crisis happened and have not tried to deny or forget about it.
- We have accepted the reality that not all relationships can be restored.
- We have realized that we cannot attempt to put life back together the way it was. We also know that we cannot create a new life that does not include an awareness of the past.

Now we are at a place in the road where we must accept these realities:
- We may still have tears to shed and emotions to be expressed.
- We cannot assume that our movement on this path will always be forward.

This is the reality of our journey. There will still be challenging and painful moments. There will still be memories, triggers, emotions, decisions, and—dare I say even *new* events of suffering. New fears. New pain.

But we are stronger and wiser than we once were. And now we can be proactive and prepare ourselves for when these moments arise. Our worksheet today will help us do this.

> Provide each participant with a set of figure cards from the worksheet provided.

Every once in a while on this journey, it helps to pause and look around—to see where we are now and reflect on where we have been.

Each of you now has a set of cards that depicts human figures. We will use these little figures to help us understand and express our *emotional states and perspectives*, both now and along the way. This visual task is meant to help us honestly "see ourselves," both where we are and where we have been, to ensure that we don't get stuck and that we keep moving in the right direction.

Let's talk about the figures before we begin our own application.

> Hold up the picture of each figure **in the order shown below** and instruct participants to hold the card with the same figure.
>
> One by one, use discussion prompts by each figure to engage the participants in conversation about the emotions represented. Use the script to guide them, but allow them to participate fully. In other words, avoid just telling them about the figure—allow them to tell you. This may mean that you adjust the script to include and follow their train of thought. Their participation in this discussion is crucial because their understanding of these figures' emotions will help them tell their own stories in the next part of the lesson. **That said, do NOT engage in conversation about the participants' stories at this time**. Right now, you simply want them to have a correct understanding of the pictures and the emotions they represent. This will help them when they begin to share about their own journeys.

 Tell me what you see in this picture. (Allow discussion.) This person is in a defensive place, possibly to protect or shield themselves from further harm. Maybe the person is even desperate.

 This person is down and cannot seem to get up. Maybe the person feels it is best to just lie still, so that more harm will not come. Notice that the face is to the ground, which suggests they need help.

 What can we say about this person? What emotions might they have in this moment? There are many possibilities! Fear. Pain. Perhaps, great loss. To shed tears is not a sign of weakness. Tears release emotion; they are helpful and healthy.

 This person is confused. Maybe they are having difficulty with a decision. Maybe they just want to stay in bed or hide from all that is happening around them. Maybe they cannot remember clearly what really happened. This is a hard place to be.

 This person is standing, but let's notice some other details. The person is standing still. There is no movement. It is almost like they are paralyzed or frozen. Their eyes are not faced forward, toward the future. They are faced back, toward the crisis that must have happened. What emotions do you think this person has?

 This person is much like the previous person, except for one thing. What is it? Yes, they face the opposite direction, toward the future—although they still seem unable to move.

 What is different about this person? Their feet show movement, as if they are on a walk. But they look discouraged, as if they carry a heavy burden. The eyes are down. It is as if they are only existing—or as if they are moving forward but with much effort.

 How would you describe this person? This person shows movement, as if on a walk, but their posture is straight and tall. Their head is up and their eyes are faced toward the future. Even their arms show movement. This person is moving forward with purpose.

REFLECTION AND APPLICATION

Perhaps, as we talked about these pictures, you saw yourself in one or more of them. It is very likely that we have all felt these emotions at one time or another.

So, let's use these figures to tell one more story. This story begins at the time of the crisis and ends *today*—as you look toward the future.

We will start with how we have felt at a moment of pain—crisis. Then we will reflect on the feelings that followed as we continued in our lives. And, finally, we will express how we feel now, as we look to the future.

You may use as many of the figures as you like. And here is something important to remember: we might feel these emotions more than once.

For example, I might begin my story with this figure.

> Hold up a figure as an example.

And later down the road, when I feel that I have moved forward, I might feel more like this.

> Hold up a figure as an example.

But then, I have a bad dream or see something that causes me to feel this way again.

> Hold up a figure as an example.

And then I wake up one morning and feel like this:

> Hold up a figure as an example.

There is something powerful about holding these images in your hands and connecting your own experiences to them visually. We might even think of them as little friends who can help us tell our story.

With that in mind, I will give you a few minutes to think about how you might connect these figures to the emotions you felt on your own journey, and then I will open up some time for sharing.

> Give the participants a few minutes to contemplate and then invite them to a time of sharing. As participants share, do not respond with advice or guidance. Each participant must feel free to share how they actually feel and not how they "should" feel.

Who wants to share first? Use a figure to tell us about a portion of your story—either at the beginning or somewhere in the middle—and then show us the figure that expresses how you feel today, or how you feel as you think about the future. Use as many of figures as you need.

After the sharing time, bring the time to a close with the following.

We will continue to have lots of emotions as we move forward on this journey. We will have difficult times in the midst of the good. We will have times when we remember the pain. We will shed tears. We will feel many of the emotions we talked about today. But, through all of these emotions, our goal is to continue to move forward.

Do you remember this verse that was written by a man who suffered much?

> But we have this treasure in jars of clay to show that this all-surpassing power is from God and not from us. We are hard pressed on every side, but not crushed; perplexed, but not in despair; persecuted, but not abandoned; struck down, but not destroyed. (2 Corinthians 4:7–9)

In our physical bodies, these "jars of clay," we experience many things. Some of those experiences leave scars, cracks, bruises, even broken pieces. But remember that there is a *valuable treasure* inside.

That valuable treasure is what can move you forward—not because of your own strength, but because God is with you and upholds you.

> Are we hard-pressed? Yes, but we are not crushed.
>
> Are we perplexed? Yes, but we are not in despair.
>
> Are we persecuted? Yes, but we are not abandoned.
>
> Are we struck down? Yes, but we are not destroyed.
>
> With God, we are moving away from our trauma.
>
> With God, we are moving forward.

On your paper, I want you to write about a particular time in your life that you feel could be described by one or more of the following words:

> Hard-pressed
>
> Perplexed
>
> Persecuted
>
> Struck down

Give participants time to write in response to the prompt.

Now that you have connected an emotional experience to one or more of these words, reflect on how this journey of healing has helped you see that God can protect you from being crushed, in despair, abandoned, and destroyed? I will give you a few more minutes to write these thoughts down.

Give participants time to write in response to the prompt.

As long as you continue on this journey, you can periodically return to these figures—these sweet little friends. Take some time with them to check on your "position." You might do this whenever you have a hard day or just when you sense that you may be stuck or headed in the wrong direction. Or you might schedule a routine "check-in" time on your calendar.

Either way, look at the figures and ask yourself, *Where am I right now? Am I still looking back? Am I faced forward, even though my head is down? Am I in a heap on the floor?* As long as you are directionally correct—with your face toward the future—you are moving away from the control of trauma and toward healing.

If you find that you have been stuck or not faced forward for an extended period, then further time and attention is needed. Ask yourself, *What is happening in my life that would trigger this response?* Revisit your notes and worksheets from this course to remind yourself of the truths you have learned, the boundaries you have set, and the tethers that can hold you in safety. And, if necessary, reach out to someone you trust.

There is something helpful in seeing your mental and emotional states in this simple way: it helps us to see the possibilities.

COURAGE AND PEACE

I want to remind you of a verse we shared in a previous session. Listen carefully:

Let us throw off everything that hinders and the sin that so easily entangles. And let us run with perseverance . . . fixing our eyes on Jesus, the pioneer and perfecter of faith. For the joy set before him he endured the cross, scorning its shame, and sat down at the right hand of the throne of God. (Hebrews 12:1–2)

Hold the little figures and think about these words and how these actions help us move forward:

- throw off everything that hinders or entangles
- run with perseverance
- fix our eyes on Jesus

ALONG THE WAY

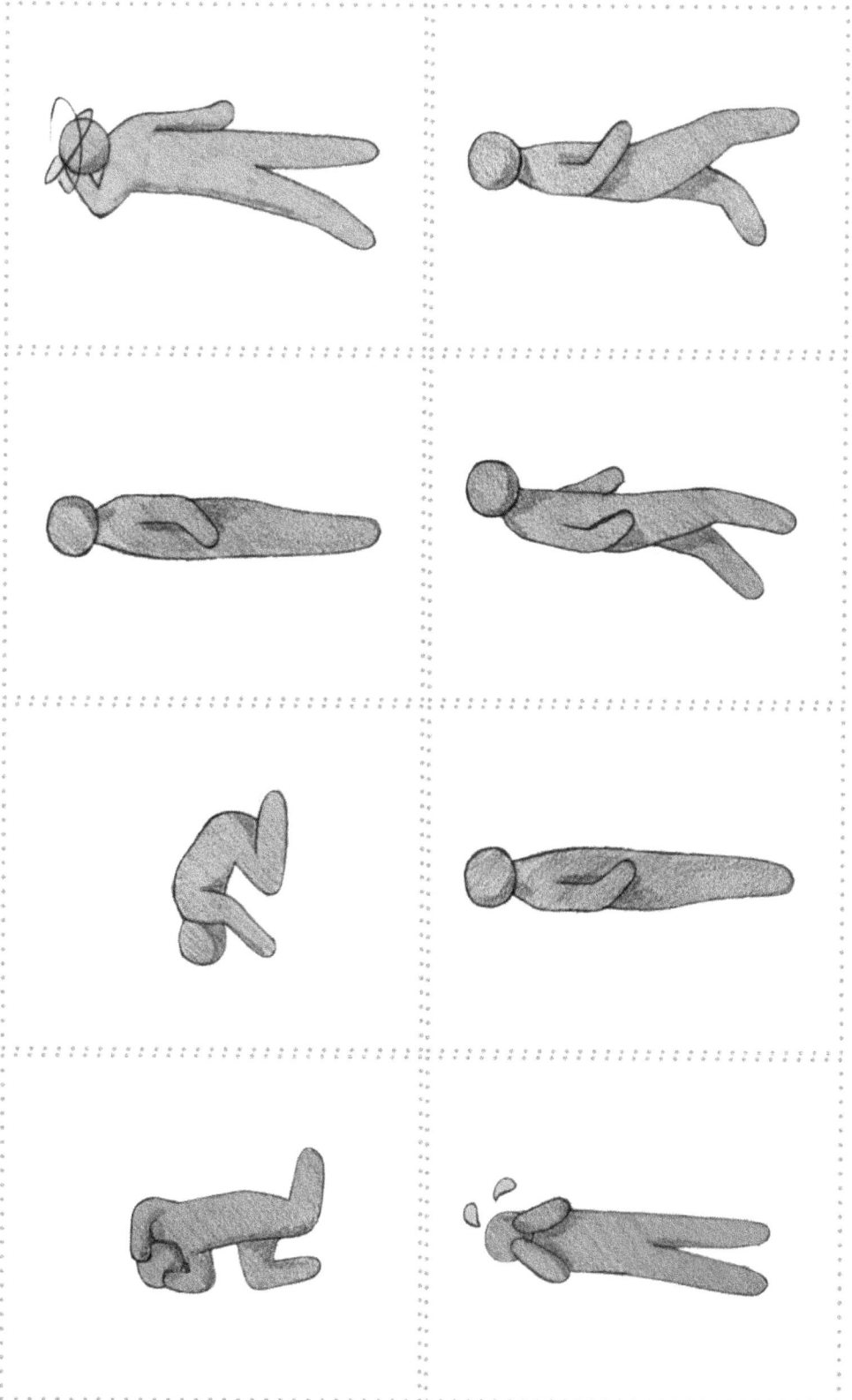

SESSION 31
REDEEMED

GOALS FOR PARTICIPANTS
- To understand what it means to renew and redeem
- To understand the impact of a renewed vocabulary
- To identify things in our life that God has redeemed and still needs to redeem

MATERIALS
- This lesson
- Plain paper; pencils and pens

VOCABULARY
- **renew** (ri-NYOO): to restore or revive; to bring to life in a new way
- **subtle** (SUHT-l): difficult to recognize or see
- **redeem** (ri-DEEM): to exchange for something of value; to recover or rescue
- **redemption** (ree-DEMP-shun): the act or state of being rescued

GREETING

Each session begins with a greeting. This will be unique and personal to each group.

REVIEW

Last time, our little figures helped us tell our story in a new way. We also learned how they can help us determine whether we are moving forward at any given time in our journey. Have you looked at them or thought about them since our last meeting? How have you found them helpful?

Give participants a few moments to respond to the questions.

Remember that you can use these figures to help you check in with yourself periodically, even after this course is over. The goal is to make sure that you are in a direction that is forward, despite the emotions, triggers, and even new hardships that you may face.

As we learned, it may not always be easy to maintain this forward movement on our journey, with all of its ups and downs, but with God at our side, we will not be crushed, abandoned, destroyed, or given to despair. God gives us the strength we need to move toward the future—and as our next lesson will show, He also gives new value to the things of our past.

LESSON SCRIPT

Wasted. Spoiled. Ruined.

Many of us have probably used these or similar words to describe parts of our story. Whether we have expressed them or just thought them, they are words that trauma tends to whisper into our lives. They enter our vocabulary after our moment of crisis and change the conversations we have with ourselves—and as a result, our inner voice begins to sound something like this:

All is lost.

Nothing good ever happens to me.

I am to blame.

I can never trust anyone again.

I can't get this out of my mind.

I am not valuable to anyone.

Why me?

No one understands.

This is who I am; nothing good can come of it.

Nothing will ever change.

I will never be able to fix this.

I always make wrong choices.

Do any of these phrases sound familiar?

The problem with words and conversations like these is that they only add to our destruction. The emotions and ideas they carry not only feed our pain but also leak into every other part of our lives, eventually showing up in the form of disappointment, bitterness, and apprehension about the future.

One way to address this problem is to **renew** our vocabulary—to think about and use words and the ideas they express in a way that is *for our good*. We have already done this at various points on our journey, whether we realized it or not. For example, we have tried to change the words and ideas we speak to ourselves . . .

- from untruth to truth,
- from fear to courage, and
- from despair to hope.

Some of these changes have settled into our minds already. Some are **subtle**, while others are monumental—but all have a profound impact, as they keep us away from those words and thoughts that lead us deeper into the despair and control of suffering.

So, whenever despair challenges hope, whenever untruth whispers in our ear, whenever unreasonable fear disturbs our peace—we speak these new words to ourselves. Whenever we think, *Nothing will ever change,* we replace this idea with words of truth.

When we renew our vocabulary in this way, we **redeem** it. *Redeem* means "to exchange for something of value." We replace negative words with positive ones. We exchange truth for untruth. We replace the idea of waste with blessing. This is **redemption.**

Similarly, we can experience redemption in other areas of our lives that we feel have been spoiled or ruined by suffering. For example...

- Places that we no longer return to
- Seasons or holidays that we avoid
- Songs that are difficult to hear

It is not uncommon to see God redeem these more specific and unique parts of our stories through experiences, lessons, and encounters that change the way we view things. Somehow, we come to understand that the particular place, time, or song that we want to avoid did not directly cause the suffering but is only one detail of that painful time. I have seen God redeem something as simple as a piece of clothing and something as complex as a relationship. He can redeem things, places, and even people in a way that they can be woven into our story anew.

Here is an example. Perhaps, your suffering came through the actions of certain family members. So now, the very idea of *family* brings you pain. As a result, you avoid contact with all your family members—even those who were not involved in your crisis. You also reject the idea of ever forming a new family. The good news is that God can redeem the idea of family in your mind. He can help you replace the idea that family brings pain with the idea that joy is possible through family.

God specializes in the exchange of destruction and hurt with value and purpose. He replaces negative with positive, waste with blessing, lies with truth, and fear with peace. There are countless testimonies of God's redemption, both in the Bible and throughout history, but let's look at one example from the author of Lamentations:

> I called on your name, LORD, from the depths of the pit. You heard my plea.... You came near when I called you, and you said, "Do not fear." You, LORD, took up my case; you redeemed my life (Lamentations 3:55–58).

When God speaks the possibility of value and joy into those moments, ideas, people, and things that we once associated with pain, these parts of our lives are redeemed. And all we must do is receive it. We embrace the potential of hope, we open ourselves to the possibility of joy and blessing in areas that now hold pain, and we focus our eyes on I Am. Then we lift our open hands and let Him do His mysterious and powerful work.

REFLECTION AND APPLICATON

Redemption is a precious gift from God on this journey of healing. So, let's think about some of the areas in our life that have been redeemed even after suffering threatened to hold them hostage. On your paper, describe at least one area of your life that you used to connect with pain. Then share how that painful connection was replaced by, or exchanged with, something more positive.

Give participants time to write in response to the prompt.

Now think about areas in your life that you still connect to your pain—areas that could still possibly be redeemed. What potential joy have you set aside in that area because it reminds you too much of the suffering?

Give participants time to write in response to the prompt.

COURAGE AND PEACE

When we began our journey, we probably wondered if there was truly any way forward. Then, as we made our way along the path, we found ourselves encountering truth and beauty and hope. At times, we still feel weak, but we have continuous reassurance from God. Here is one such reassurance that we can take with us as we leave today: "Those who hope in the LORD will renew their strength. They will soar on wings like eagles; they will run and not grow weary, they will walk and not be faint" (Isaiah 40:31).

SESSION 32
IS THERE PEACE?

GOALS FOR PARTICIPANTS
- To have a correct understanding of peace
- To identify the true source of peace
- To determine to seek a path of peace whenever possible

MATERIALS
- This lesson
- Participant worksheet: Choose a Path of Peace
- Plain paper; pencils and pens

VOCABULARY
- **absolute** (ab-suh-LOOT): complete; perfect
- **embrace** (emBRAYS): to take or receive gladly and take hold of
- **nurture** (NUR-cher): to feed or support; to encourage

GREETING

Each session begins with a greeting. This will be unique and personal to each group.

REVIEW

Last time we discussed the importance of the words we use to talk to ourselves. What are some ways that you renewed your vocabulary so that your words would lead to your good rather than to more destruction?

Give participants time to share in response to the questions.

In a sense, when we switched out destructive words for words of value, we redeemed our vocabulary. Then we talked about how God can redeem other areas of life—areas that we associate with suffering. This week did you discover any new areas in your life that you feel God already redeemed? Are there other areas that might still benefit from His redemption?

Give participants time to share in response to the questions.

As we ended our last session, I mentioned that the only thing left for us to do was to focus on God and to open ourselves to the possibility of redemption. This means that we embrace the potential for joy and blessing in areas that now hold pain. In this lesson, we will take that idea further as we think about another possibility in our lives—the possibility of peace.

LESSON SCRIPT

You might have heard someone say, "Peace is not the absence of conflict." This statement is rarely used alone and is most often followed by one of the many varying descriptions of what peace actually *is*.

But the fact that there are so many different ideas of peace can make us wonder: What is peace *really*? This question is important because, if we are to be open to the possibility of peace in our lives, then we would be wise to understand exactly what we will be open to. So, let's see if we can come to a realistic conclusion about what peace is.

As with the other parts of our journey, we want to make sure that what we are reaching for is realistic and attainable, so that we do not set ourselves up for disappointment and frustration. For example, wouldn't it be lovely if peace was something that hovered around us like a bubble and protected us from every little disturbance? Yes. But that definition of peace is not realistic. This is probably why the opening statement of this chapter is so well-known and so often used—because "the absence of conflict"—or the absence of any kind of disturbance to our lives—is unattainable, at least on any long-term basis.

So, as we consider what it means to have true, lasting peace, we must consider the reality: We live in a fallen world, where there is no absence of pain and problems. Conflict is here. Disturbances are here. Suffering—and the possibility of more suffering—are here. These things are unavoidable. However, given this reality, we have to wonder: Is true, lasting peace even attainable?

To help answer this question, let's look at a story about some men in the Bible who needed peace of mind amid a literal storm (Matthew 8:23-27; Mark 4:38-40):

> Jesus and a few of his closest friends were in a boat. The water was calm, and Jesus was asleep on a cushion in the stern. The journey was peaceful—until suddenly, it wasn't. A violent storm began, a squall stirred the water, and waves rose over them, filling the boat.
>
> Jesus's friends were experienced fishermen, so they had likely been in storms on the water before. Yet even they apparently felt the situation was dangerous. We can only imagine that the what-ifs began—what if the boat capsizes? what if we fall in? what if we die!—because they woke up Jesus and pleaded for help. When He awoke, they summarized the situation this way: "Save us! We are going to drown!"

Jesus asked, "Why are you so afraid?" and "Where is your faith?" Then He spoke with **absolute** authority and stilled the waves and wind. At His words, every immediate threat ceased, destruction was halted, and the crisis was over.

These men had already lived with and followed Jesus for some time and had even seen Him perform miracles. And yet, when they experienced this, they were amazed, and asked, "Who is this? Even the wind and the waves obey him!"

It is good that the men knew where to go when they were afraid. But Jesus's response—"Why are you so afraid?"—showed them that, even in the midst of the storm, their fear was unnecessary. He was telling them that they *could have had* peace—if only they had fully understood who was with them in the boat.

But the reality was that they did not fully understand. Even after all their time with Jesus, they still had not truly grasped the extent of who He was. If they had, they would not have been surprised at His power over the wind and waves. If they had, Jesus would not have needed to ask them, "Where is your faith?"

But because their understanding of who Jesus was fell short, so did their opportunity for peace.

It is the same with us. True peace is only possible when we rest in the ALL of our Traveling Companion, who is with us in every storm. We can rest in His . . .

- ALL *power,*
- ALL *presence,*
- ALL *knowledge, and*
- ALL *goodness*

Yes, there are times when we can claim peace without Him, but that is usually because we feel some portion of control during those times; for example, maybe we have a back-up plan. But true peace—peace that remains even when we have no control over the situation—can only exist when two conditions are in place:

- Our minds are filled with the full awareness of who God is.
- Our hearts are filled with confidence in His ability to take us safely through the disturbances of this life.

As Isaiah 26:3 says, "You will keep in perfect peace those whose minds are steadfast, because they trust in You."

This leads us to a realistic conclusion about what peace *is:*

Peace is not the *absence of conflict . . .*
rather, peace is absolute trust in the God who is with us *in conflict.*

Oh, if only Jesus's friends could have had that absolute trust! If only they could have remembered who He really was and set their minds on Him—then they would have had peace even while they were being threatened by the fiercest storm.

And we, too, should remember. We should remember how He has proven Himself so many times. We should notice that *He is in the boat with us*—peacefully at rest—as we should be. And we should know that He is powerful enough to speak with authority to the storm in a way that sets boundaries for our protection.

Yet, even when we are being tossed around by the waves of panic, we are welcome to run to Him. We can jostle Him for attention and say, "Save me! I am drowning!" At those times, Jesus will do as He did with His friends in the boat: He will reaffirm the truth that we need not fear and remind us of His authority over the storm.

To live in the reality of peace, however, we must make the intentional decision to do so. What does such a decision look like? Do we simply proclaim, "I *will* have peace!" That may be a bit optimistic. A simple declaration that something is true does not necessarily make it true. At the same time, there is value in such a declaration—by it, we express intention about how we want to live.

In Psalm 4:8, David, while he was in the midst of great danger, made this kind of definitive statement of intention. He said:

In peace I *will* lie down and sleep, for you alone, LORD, make me dwell in safety. (emphasis mine)

But this strong statement of determination did not come without reason. In other words, David did not just declare, "I will lie down and sleep in peace" and end it there. Rather, he made it clear that this decision was only possible because he trusted the LORD who was with him. His ability to say, "I will . . . sleep in peace" was built on the conviction that "for You alone, O LORD, make me dwell in safety."

David's statement of intention was interwoven with the truths he **embraced** about God, *the object of his peace.* Remember our conversation about hope? We discovered that hope was built not on how strongly we hope but in whom we hope. It is the same with peace. Our peace is not based on how passionately we may proclaim it in our spirit; rather, it is based on the one from whom we receive it. As with David, it is the LORD alone who makes it possible for us to intentionally declare our decision to pursue peace. It is God who makes the presence of peace in our lives realistic and attainable.

But although God puts the possibility of peace within our reach, we must still do the necessary work to take hold of it. We must make a decision to have peace—not to create it, but to pursue it.

Think of it this way: God has made the path of peace available to us, but we must choose to take that path and to follow it, despite all the emotions and circumstances that try to distract us and pull us away. We did not create this path, but we can make the decision to put our feet on it—and when we do, we open ourselves up to the peace that it offers.

Let's consider a real-life example. I have noticed that I struggle with anxiety—or a lack of peace—whenever *what-ifs* enter my mind:

- What if this happens?
- What if that person misunderstood my meaning?
- What if I can't do this?
- What if I was not supposed to do that?

These *what-ifs* not only disrupt my ability to take hold of the peace available to me now; they also threaten the possibility of peace in my future. Sometimes, they can even make it seem as if peace is no longer attainable.

In that sense, these *what-ifs* threaten to pull me off of the path of peace that God has provided. They cause me to focus on all the potential disasters rather than on the only One who can give me peace. And so, I must intentionally choose to redirect my gaze—away from the squall of *what-ifs* that seem to rise above me and put me in danger—and toward Jesus, who is at rest in the boat with me.

To do this, I set up a boundary to the *what-ifs*. I give attention to them only long enough to notice that they are there—and then I cast them onto God. In this way, I follow the instruction given in Philippians 4:6:

> Do not be anxious about anything, but in every situation, by prayer and petition, with thanksgiving, present your requests to God.

This is the choice that all of us must make:

- We can choose to shoulder the burden of anxiety alone.
- Or we can choose to share it with "the LORD your God [who] is with [us], the Mighty Warrior who saves" (Zephaniah 3:17), expressing gratitude for the evidence of His care in our past and present and wrapping ourselves in His assurances for our present and future.

The more we choose the latter, the more we will sense the peace of God, which is mysterious and unexplainable. It will settle on us, calm our spirits and souls, and then flow outward into our choices and responses. This is how we live out the reality of peace.

REFLECTION AND APPLICATON

It is time to think about the possibility of peace.

God has laid out a path of peace for each of us, but every moment carries the potential for distractions away from that path—away from Him—and toward fear and anxiousness. So, we must intentionally choose to keep ourselves focused in the right direction.

Let's start this process by thinking about specific moments when we feel drawn *away from peace* and toward fear and anxiousness. When you think of one or two such moments, write them down on your paper.

Give participants time to contemplate and write in response to the prompt. When they appear to be finished with this part of the activity, hand out copies of the worksheet.

This worksheet contains a list of actions you can choose that can help keep you on the path of peace—emotionally, physically, and spiritually. These actions can help to **nurture,** or feed, the peace that God has for us, whenever emotions and circumstances threaten to pull us toward anxiousness.

Take a minute to read through each one, and then connect them to the situations you wrote down on your paper—those situations where you find yourself easily pulled away from peace. Consider how these actions might help you to welcome peace into these moments rather than drawing you away, toward fear and anxiousness.

When you are finished, we will take time to share our thoughts.

Give participants time to complete the worksheet. When they are finished, gather their attention and ask the questions below. Allow the class enough time to share in response to each question.

Which of these actions do you feel might be hard for you?

Which of these actions do you think you could work on now?

Did you think of any other ways that you might choose a path of peace that are not listed here?

This week, watch for opportunities to intentionally choose peace, and write down how you handled it. Did you immediately recognize the distraction, or pull away from peace? Was the choice to nurture peace difficult? How did your choice impact the stress you felt? Did your choice impact a relationship or another situation later on?

COURAGE AND PEACE

As we close, I want to bring your attention to the Hebrew word *shalom*. In Jewish tradition, *shalom* is used as a greeting, and the direct English translation of this word is "peace." However, the type of peace expressed by *shalom* is one of deeply layered meanings. Among these meanings is the wish that someone will experience a sense of wholeness or completeness.

That is peace—when there is a feeling deep within that, in spite of everything that is happening around me, I am complete, and I am whole; even while there is chaos in the circumstances of life, I am okay.

And so, *shalom* is my parting word to you. As you go through each day, my hope is that you will reach for this sense of well-being, safety, and completeness that God has for you.

> May the God of hope
>
> fill you with all joy and peace
>
> as you trust in him.
>
> (Romans 15:13)

CHOOSE A PATH OF PEACE

How can I choose a path of peace?

- I can see conflict around me but not take on responsibility to solve that conflict. Not *every* battle is mine to fight.

- I can have contentment and refuse to grasp for "what is not."

- I can set aside the attempt to control others, including their actions and responses. I will not spend my energy trying to coerce others to make choices and take actions that I think are best.

- I can remind myself often of God's provision for me—even in difficult circumstances. I can speak it out loud as a prayer of gratitude. I can write it on paper as a reminder of the peace that is possible.

- I can accept responsibility for my own actions and responses. I will avoid looking for a place to set my *baggage (the consequences of pain that I carry)*.

- I can respond to the threat of anxiousness from a true awareness of God's love and goodness to me personally. I will speak out of the truth of His assurance. I will not speak out of accusation or the feeling that He is trying to harm me.

- I can set up a boundary to the *what-ifs*. I will give attention to them only long enough to write them on paper—and then dispose of them. In a sense, I will cast them on God.

- I can refuse to feed fear so that it grows into panic.

- I can put boundaries on things that stir up anxiousness in me. I will avoid movies, television programs, books, computer research, and anything else that ignites fear and anxiety and leads me away from peace.

- I can nurture—or feed—those things that instill in me and draw me toward a peaceful spirit.

SESSION 33
MY GUARDED HEART

GOALS FOR PARTICIPANTS
- Understand the need to guard our hearts
- Understand that peace is a key to guarding the heart
- Embrace and choose a path of peace

MATERIALS
- This lesson
- Plain paper; pencils and pens

VOCABULARY
- **guard** (GARD): to keep safe from danger; protect; watch over
- **recklessly** (REK-lis-lee): with no concern for the consequences of one's actions
- **vigilant** (VIJ-uh-luhnt): watchful

GREETING

Each session begins with a greeting. This will be unique and personal to each group.

REVIEW

Peace is not always the absence of conflict or suffering. We learned from the story of Jesus' friends in the boat that we can have peace even in the middle of a storm! What makes it possible for us to rest peacefully even when the waves threaten to overtake us?

LESSON SCRIPT

Proverbs 4:23 says, "Above all else, guard your heart, for everything you do flows from it."

"Above all else." When we put something "above all else," we give priority to it and pursue it with the utmost determination.

So, what this Godly advice is telling us is that, even above all of the other things we have learned to do on this journey—above facing truth, planting seeds, building boundaries—we are to give priority to this one action: we are to guard our hearts.

To *guard* something means to "stay **vigilant** or keep watch over" it, with an "intent to protect." And God's word says that this is exactly what we should do with our hearts. Why? Because *everything* we do "flows from it." Everything!

Take some time to think about what flows from your heart. Loyalty? Love? Mercy? Trust? Or hurt? Bitterness? Revenge? Most human hearts have a mix of both. It is the heart that most often creates defenses and excuses. It is the heart that most often sees with "rose-colored glasses." It is the heart that allows our wishes to overpower reality. **Recklessly**, things enter and then pour out of our hearts without careful consideration of the consequences. And so God, who always thinks of our good, says, *"More than anything else, keep watch over that—and protect it!"*

To guard the heart does not mean that we shut it off, determined not to feel or love. It means that we protect it by setting up boundaries—the kind of boundaries that we discovered earlier, which protect against harm and prevent good from escaping.

But how do we do this with our hearts? What boundary, stronghold, or protective hedge can be effective, above all else, to guard the one source from which everything else in life flows?

In our previous conversation about peace, we nudged open the door that reveals the answer to this question. Do you remember Philippians 4:6?

> Do not be anxious about anything, but in every situation, by prayer and petition, with thanksgiving, present your requests to God.

In the very next verse, Philippians 4:7, we see what happens when we follow those instructions:

> And the peace of God, which transcends all understanding,
> will *guard your hearts* and your minds in Christ Jesus (emphasis mine).

What does this verse tell us will guard our hearts? "The peace of God, which passes all understanding."

This is the very same peace that we discovered in our last conversation. The peace that flows mysteriously from God's heart to ours, even amidst the chaos, when we choose to focus on Him. We knew this peace was good for us and was necessary to our healing. But now we see that it is also the highest form of protection—a guard for our hearts!

How? As we discovered, true peace is more than just a sense of calm; it is also a sense of fulfillment, completeness, and contentment. This contentment satisfies our constant urge to search for something to "fill the void" in our hearts. But without it, we continue to search for fulfillment in everything else but God. This makes our hearts vulnerable to all of the other things and people and philosophies in life that promise us peace but that always, eventually fall short.

The fact that peace from God can satisfy us in a way that nothing else can is, perhaps, the reason it is described in this verse as "beyond our understanding." But there are other reasons, as well:

- First, we might find that there are times in our life when we cannot find words to adequately express the peace we feel—especially because these are usually moments when peace is completely unexpected.
- Second, in situations where frustration, stress, or fear is expected but we show outward signs of God's peace instead, others cannot understand it.

This peace—God's peace beyond understanding—*is what is needed to protect our hearts.*

When we choose to trust the perfect provider of peace—and embrace and nurture that peace—it then guards our heart, for our good. It keeps us from turmoil. It prevents us from looking for fulfillment in all the wrong places. And it keeps us focused on God alone, who is with us and protects us from dangers seen and unseen.

When His peace settles around our heart, we are protected and strengthened.

REFLECTION AND APPLICATION

Let's discuss some questions:

Introduce the questions below one at a time and allow participants to share in response to each one. When the discussion comes to a close, continue with the script below the questions.

- What tendencies of your heart are weak and often get you into harmful situations?
- How could the peace of God protect you from wandering into dangerous situations?
- What keeps you from embracing this "peace beyond understanding?"

Keep your responses to these questions in mind this week. Note those moments when your heart feels tempted to find fulfillment outside of God, and then reach for God and His peace instead. Then note how, when you shifted your focus and nurtured your peace, this protected your heart and changed your situation for good.

COURAGE AND PEACE

The peace that guards your heart is from God. No one else can offer you such assurance. I AM is with you at all times, in all places. It is His peace alone that can protect you perfectly. So, trust in Him.

SESSION 34
HOW SHOULD WE NOW LIVE?

GOALS FOR PARTICIPANTS
- Understand the eternal reality of existence
- Understand the temporariness of suffering and the promise of hope and joy
- Use this new eternal perspective to look toward the future

MATERIALS
- This lesson
- Plain paper; pencils and pens
- Teaching tool: A New Perspective, parts 1 and 2

VOCABULARY
- **eternal** (ih-TUR-nl): without beginning or end; always in existence
- **integral** (IN-tih-gruhl): a necessary part of the whole
- **opportunity** (op-er-TOO-nih-tee): a situation favorable for a task; a good chance
- **temporary** (TEM-puh-rer-ee): passing; existing for only a time; not permanent

GREETING

Each session begins with a greeting. This will be unique and personal to each group.

REVIEW

Last time, we talked about how we need to guard our hearts "above all else," and the way we guard them is to embrace the peace that God gives. That peace is a mystery, and yet there are practical things we can do to make it a part of our lives. As we embrace the path of peace, we are protected from fear and anxiousness and from the consequences of seeking fulfillment outside of God.

Do you remember some of the ways we pursue a path of peace? How can those actions guard our hearts?

Give participants time to respond to the questions.

LESSON SCRIPT

When we began this journey, the focus of our discussion was on suffering. Little by little, we faced our suffering, became familiar with it, and learned that it need not consume us. This probably felt like a long, difficult process at the time, but if we think about our most recent lessons, where words such as *joy*, *hope*, and *peace* entered our discussion, we get a sense of just how far we have come!

Now, we have reached the point in our journey where we can look at the path beyond. We have already discussed some of what to expect on this future path and have prepared accordingly: we saw the likelihood that we would face threats and even stumble, so we created healthy boundaries and renewed our vocabulary and embraced the real possibility that peace may come to guard our hearts. And yet, from this spot on the road, as we courageously raise our eyes from the ground to more distant points on our journey, it's as if something else appears in our periphery and gives us pause. This "something" subtly breaks our forward line of sight and makes us wonder whether we are actually ready to step into the future. What is it?

If we retraced our steps to the first time we noticed it, we'd probably find that it was there, lurking in the shadows, from the moment pain entered our awareness. Since then, it might have been more or less noticeable at different points along the road—but now, it may have even grown in our previous lesson, as we opened our hearts, our minds, and our very souls to peace.

But why? Why would the very thought of welcoming the treasure of peace suddenly make this potential intruder more obvious? Could it be that the thought of peace brought with it the reminder of how easily peace could be taken away? It was stolen by suffering before. Why wouldn't it happen again?

And there it is. This "something else" that we have sensed in the shadows all along is the likelihood that we will meet more suffering down the road. And then what?

As we've done with all of our other challenges on this road, let's address this one head-on by adding it to our discussion. To do this, we will go back to the outset of our journey, when the likelihood of future suffering first entered our awareness. At that point in our journey, our goal was just to find our way *out of* the negative effects of suffering—and we accomplished that very thing! But to reach that point, we first had to think and talk about our pain, which made us *aware of the reality of suffering*. And when we became aware of the pain in our past and present, we also became aware of the *likelihood of suffering to come*.

So, as strange as it may seem, our arrival at this place where we can now see the potential for peace came only through our awareness of suffering:

> suffering in our past,
> suffering in the present, and
> suffering yet to come.

This awareness of pain is unavoidable; it comes from our *knowledge of good and evil.* It harkens back to the story of our very creation—back to the beautiful, perfect garden where humans first lived, full of newness and goodness, until they ate from the forbidden tree. That's when sin entered the story, and as a natural consequence of humans' newfound knowledge, suffering entered too.

And so now, suffering is a natural part of the human story—an **integral** part of our path here on earth. Suffering creates muddy roads, potholes, and threats of crisis—and it gives us uncertainty. This uncertainty is what gives us pause at this place on our path. We want to courageously look outward, but the very real threat of pain hovers over our hope for any potential peace.

Given this reality, *how do we now live?*

- How do we live in a way that we will not be blindly vulnerable to future suffering?
- How do we live in a way that we will not give in to despair when more pain crosses our path?
- Knowing all that we now know about suffering and ourselves, *how do we now live?*

There is no formula we can follow to answer that question; however, there is a perspective that we can take that might nudge us closer to a reply that we can be at peace with.

Let me introduce you to this perspective by showing you an image.

Display the visual aid in part 1 of the teaching tool (also shown below), and use the script that follows.

Perhaps, you have always envisioned your life in this way:
According to this image, life begins when you are born and ends when you die. However, this is not an accurate depiction of life; this is only part of a larger picture.

To understand this larger picture, let's go back for a moment to that beautiful garden at the beginning of time—that place where everything was perfect, just as God intended; there was no fear and no sorrow. What a delightful place to spend our days!

Now, fast-forward to the end of our days. You may or may not know that there is coming a time when God will once again make all things new and perfect and beautiful.

He tells us this in his Word:

> See, I will create new heavens and a new earth. The former things will not be remembered, nor will they come to mind. (Isaiah 65:17)

> He will wipe every tear from their eyes. There will be no more death or mourning or crying or pain, for the old order of things has passed away. He who was seated on the throne said, "I am making everything new!" (Revelation 21:4–5)

These verses describe a time of newness, when fear and sorrow will be wiped away and no longer threaten our peace. What a wonderful promise for the future.

Until that time, however, we physically live in this broken world "between" the perfection of earth's beginning and the perfection that is yet to come. Many others have come before us in this "between" time, and many others will likely go after. And yet, to God, each of our lives has significance in this bigger picture. In other words, your life and mine, along with all of its suffering, are part of this larger story. Our lives connect to God's larger plan for eternity. As such, life begins even *before we are born*, when God conceived each of us in His mind, and it will continue even *after our physical bodies fail and leave this earth.*

And so, a more accurate image of life is this:

Display the visual aid in part 2 of the teaching tool (also shown below) and use the script that follows.

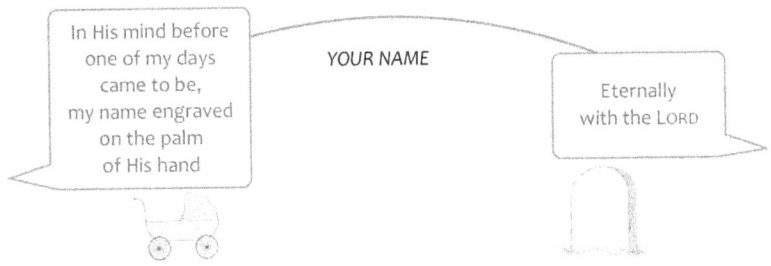

This image shows us the truth that we do not exist *only* in this place between. Rather, there is *more* to this life. There was a time *before*, and there will be a time *after*, when we can live forever with the One who created us and will love us for all eternity.

This **eternal perspective** changes the way that we see and relate to suffering—not only the suffering of our past and present but also any suffering to come. How? Let's break down this perspective into the "before" time, the "after" time, and the "between" time, to get a closer look at how it impacts the way we think about pain.

1. Here is what the eternal perspective tells us about *the time before we were born:*
   - God conceived us in thought before we ever came to be.
   - He created us in His image.
   - Our lives are a part of His overall plan.

   All of this reminds us that we have value and purpose from the Creator of the Universe, who loves us and calls us by name. Because of this, we can have the confidence and courage to move forward, despite any suffering that may lie ahead.

2. Here is what the eternal perspective tells us about *our life here in between:*
   - **This life, with its suffering, is temporary.** Suffering exists only on earth, in this "between" part of our lives. And because this part of our lives is **temporary**, so, too, is suffering.
   - **We can trust God with this "between" life because He sees the bigger picture.** Always beside us in this broken world, with its mud and grime, is our Traveling Companion. He already sees what is on the road ahead, and He is more powerful than any type of suffering we will ever encounter.
   - **Suffering will continue to exist in this current life.** Eventually, we will live in a time without suffering—but as long as we are here in this "between" time, suffering will continue. That may not sound like encouragement; however, it releases us from the grip of those unrealistic expectations that try to convince us we can attain the unattainable. When we let go of those expectations, we feel less disappointed and more prepared for the eventual return of suffering.
   - **We can embrace this life, suffering included, because it has a greater purpose.** When we realize that our life connects to God's larger plan for eternity and that it is significant in this bigger picture, we gain the sense that we are here for a purpose that is bigger than all of us. This sense of purpose helps us to put our life and suffering in proper perspective. We begin to see life less in terms of our comfort and happiness and more in terms of our role in eternity—and as a result, suffering's perceived impact in our life diminishes.

When we live our life with this greater purpose in mind, we set our minds "on things above." Colossians 3:2–3 puts it this way: "Set your minds on things above, not on earthly things. For . . . your life is now hidden with Christ in God." When we set our minds on eternal things—or things above—we no longer feel tied to this "between" time or the suffering it holds. Instead, we start to see it as an **opportunity** to prepare for our time in eternity.

Let's look at just a few of the ways that we can see our current life as preparation for our life yet to come:

- **This "between" life is an opportunity for us to grow in familiarity and connection to God.** God's Word tells us that He created humans for companionship. In fact, He physically walked side-by-side in conversation with humans until sin and suffering entered the earth. Now, sin and suffering act like a barrier that keeps us from seeing and being with God fully, which means that we will not be physically present with Him again until our time in eternity. Until then, we have an opportunity to learn more about this one who created us and who will love us for all eternity. And the closer we become with Him, the less threatened we will feel by suffering.

- **This life gives us an opportunity to become more like the perfect example of Jesus.** Because God created us in His image, we all share certain characteristics with our creator but to a lesser degree. This "between" time gives us an opportunity to improve on these characteristics by following the example of God's perfect human son, Jesus, who lived on this earth. Jesus was the perfect example of one who endured the suffering of this "between" world. At the same time, as we strive to be like Jesus, we are not obligated to "get it all right," because this life is not the end.

- **God's healing presence in our suffering shines a bright light into this dark world.** When we walk through this "between" time with Jesus, His light shines through us. The more we release the push-back we feel against suffering—whether present or potential—and the more we absorb His healing, the more His beauty and healing flow to others. This is an opportunity for us to express the image of God, by reflecting His eternal light into the temporary darkness.

  > Therefore . . . we do not lose heart. . . . For God, who said, "Let light shine out of darkness," made his light shine in our hearts to give us the light of the knowledge of God's glory displayed in the face of Christ. (2 Corinthians 4:1, 6)

  Again, shining God's light does not require us to "get it all right." It simply means remembering God is with us and embracing hope, even as we live with the awareness of suffering:

  > We have this treasure in jars of clay to show that this all-surpassing power is from God and not from us. We are hard pressed on every side, but not crushed; perplexed, but not in despair; persecuted, but not abandoned; struck down, but not destroyed. (2 Corinthians 4:7–9)

3. Finally, here is what the eternal perspective tells us about *the time after this life:*

   We can face suffering because we have the sure hope of eternal joy. In the same way that Jesus "endured the cross" because of "the joy set before him" (Hebrews 12:2), we can endure the suffering of this life when we are convinced of and focused on the joy of eternity—that place where all suffering will cease and where we will forever be with Him. Jesus knows from experience that this perception of time beyond is what will carry us through the difficulties of the present world toward the dependable hope of the eternal joy to come. It is what will give us the type of hope expressed in Romans 8:18: "I consider that our present sufferings are not worth comparing with the glory that will be revealed in us."

So, now that we have talked about what it means to have an eternal perspective, let's revisit our original question: As we arrive at this place where we want to courageously look toward peace but fear the potential for more suffering down the road . . .

how do we now live?

We now live with "our minds set on things above." We live in the realization that while life is here and now, it also stretches beyond our current world. We now live with an eternal perspective that shifts our focus from the things we see now onto "things above." And we live this way because it helps us to acknowledge and come to peace with *all* of the experiences on this journey—past, present, and future. This includes crisis and suffering and uncertainty, but also joy and hope and beauty, because even as we set our minds on things above, God gives us glimpses of beauty in this present world.

In fact, God's beauty is all around us right now. We see it in nature, in music, in art, in science, and in fellow image-bearers of the creator. And because its presence in this world is an expression of His love, grace, and mercy toward us, it reminds us that although this world is broken, it continues to carry the imprint of God's creative hand. And so, in this same world where we acknowledge the muddy road and the storm clouds, we also acknowledge the warmth of the sun and signs of new growth in the earth.

This acknowledgment that God's beauty and Spirit are present even during our times of pain makes us more willing to remain open to suffering's arrival. It assures us that, no matter the struggle, our companion, the redeemer and creator of everything beautiful, will be there. So, we can be ready to absorb *whatever* life has to offer. Jesus Himself gave us this assurance when he said,

> "I have told you these things, so that in me you may have peace. In this world you will have trouble. But take heart! I have overcome the world." John 16:33

God's beauty and glory cannot be destroyed. So, whether they are in full view or waiting to be discovered amid the ruins of suffering, at some point, they will make themselves known to us—in this world *and* in the world to come. This truth enables us to live in a way that we can embrace the mysteries of hope, peace, eternal identity, and a God who is always with us and then move ever forward with courage and peace. And as we do, the tapestry of our stories will grow in beautiful, complex, and expressive ways that are only possible as suffering and healing intertwine.

REFLECTION AND APPLICATION

Let's think about how this eternal perspective can give us the courage in our day-to-day lives to move toward peace.

I have a short list of questions to ask you that will help you to reflect on the concepts we discussed today and to think about how you might apply these concepts to your personal life. I will read one question at a time and pause after each one, so that you have time to write your thoughts in response.

> Read the questions below out loud. Pause after each one to give participants time to reflect and to write their responses.

- How do I respond to the eternal nature of my existence—the before and the after? How does this truth help "life" come into perspective?
- How will I now live in a way that is different from before?
- Is it possible for me to see—or even to look for—beauty interwoven with my suffering?

COURAGE AND PEACE

We have acknowledged suffering as a natural, expected, and unavoidable part of life. This is a difficult concept to accept, and your heart may still be wrestling with it. Yet, you are healing—one step at a time. And there *is* hope and peace to be found.

> God did this so that . . . we who have fled to take hold of the hope set before us may be greatly encouraged. We have this hope as an anchor for the soul, firm and secure. (Hebrews 6:18–19)

A NEW PERSPECTIVE
PART 1

YOUR NAME

A NEW PERSPECTIVE
PART 2

> In His mind before
> one of my days
> came to be,
> my name engraved
> on the palm
> of His hand

YOUR NAME

> Eternally
> with the LORD

SESSION 35
OUR EMOTIONS: WHERE DO THEY TAKE US?

GOALS FOR PARTICIPANTS
- Identify common emotional destinations
- Identify well-worn pathways to particular emotional destinations
- Discover the presence and possibility of peace
- Learn how to re-route to peace from any emotional location

MATERIALS
- This lesson
- Participant worksheet: Emotional Destination Map
- Plain paper; pencils and pens

VOCABULARY
- **arena** (uh-REE-nuh): the central stage; a field of conflict or activity
- **catalyst** (KAT-uh-list): something that causes a response or activity
- **response** (ri-SPONS): an answer or reply, as in words or actions
- **realization** (ree-uh-luh-ZAY-shuhn): the act of understanding clearly
- **regret** (rih-GRET): to feel sorrow for one's actions or words

GREETING

Each session begins with a greeting. This will be unique and personal to each group.

REVIEW

We have considered many layers of our suffering and many possibilities that can help us move toward healing. What truths did we discuss in our last lesson that can help us live out our new eternal perspective?

Allow a few minutes for participants to respond to the question.

We have learned to expect suffering—even embrace it—even as we set boundaries on the negative effects. We also now have tools that can help us face the future with hope and courage.

LESSON SCRIPT

The experience of suffering brings many emotions. We have talked a lot about those emotions in our journey together. We have expressed them and written about them—even drawn pictures about them—and over time, as we have come further along this path, these emotions have changed. They have changed because of new perspectives we have taken and new truths we have learned. And they will continue to change as we continue our journey into the future.

So, now that we are here, we need to have another conversation about our emotions. This is important because emotions have an effect on our direction. Whether we realize it or not, our emotions do not just happen and then go away. Rather, they take us somewhere.

We have done a lot of work to get to this point, so we want to ensure our feet stay on this path toward healing. But to do this, we want to get into a regular habit of asking ourselves two important questions:

- Where do my current emotions lead to?
- Can I change the destination if I need to?

Imagine a car with a driver and a passenger. The journey begins with one person driving, but as the car travels down the road, it comes to a particularly treacherous place and stops. The driver and the passenger both get out and switch places. What happened in this scenario? The conditions of the road changed, and a new driver took over.

This is similar to what can happen with your emotions. Picture yourself and your emotions in a car. Who do you think is most often in the driver's seat? In other words, do you feel that you are most often in charge of steering your life, while your emotions are just there for the ride? Or are your emotions usually the driver, while you sit in the passenger seat, with no influence over where they will take you? Do you, perhaps, start in one position and then switch places whenever the road gets rough?

It is not uncommon for us to feel that we are in the driver's seat until a rough patch stops us—and then our emotions take control of the wheel and drive us to a place we never intended! This is natural, and it does not mean that our emotions are bad. In fact, our emotions are a gift from God and are a part of what gives us His likeness. We can, however, keep emotions in their proper place, so that they don't continually steer us off-course. And when they take over, as they are known to do from time to time, we can redirect ourselves and get back on track—even if they have led us somewhere we don't want to be.

This car ride that we take with our emotions is the emotional journey. And we take several such journeys each day. So, if we want to stay on-course, it is in our best interest to learn exactly what these journeys entail. Although one journey may involve different emotions than the next, each journey is made up of two main parts. These parts are the *catalyst* and the *response*.

It all begins with the **catalyst**.

A catalyst is something that *causes* a response. Think of it as the first spark that causes a fire. In an emotional journey, the catalyst is anything that nudges, pushes, or pulls us into some form of emotional response.

In a negative emotional journey, the catalyst is something perceived as negative. This might be something that is commonly seen as negative, such as a natural disaster, a death, or a serious physical diagnosis. Or it might be something that only you perceive as negative; perhaps, a particular person is coming to visit, for example, or you are assigned a job that is difficult for you. We can feel a spark ignite within us simply because of the way someone looks at us or because of something we hear on the radio or television.

But no matter what causes the spark, the result of it is that we feel a sense of loss. This might be a loss of our own value, a loss of control, the loss of a relationship, the loss of a dream or ideal, or even the loss of our physical well-being. And the loss might be real or perceived. Remember that to *perceive* is to see something in a particular way. So, in this case, a perceived loss might come from a story or explanation that we unconsciously create in our minds. For example, when someone looks at us in a certain way, we might unconsciously create the explanation in our mind that they are looking down on us or being critical. Even if the other person does not feel this way at all, we can still feel loss as a result, simply because of how we perceived the situation. In this case, we might feel the loss of our self-worth or our friendship with that person. But whatever loss we feel, it feels real—and so it causes us to respond with the same intensity and emotion that we would have with a real loss. And when we respond to this loss, whether we are aware of it or not, a gate swings open.

We don't consciously open the gate. We don't need to turn any knobs or push it forward. The catalyst simply sets things in motion, opens the gate, and we walk through. This is the second part of the emotional journey, after the catalyst: our **response**.

We don't often stop to think about our response. In fact, in most instances, our response is involuntary —which means that we do it almost without any awareness at all. We just move through the gate and down one of the many emotional pathways on the other side. There are actually some well-worn pathways here that tell us we have been this way many times before. And the more times we have traveled a particular path, the more involuntary each successive trip down that path becomes.

This involuntary motion continues until we reach a moment of **realization**. We become aware of the negative emotions that have taken control of our journey. Perhaps, we also become aware of wrong choices we made along the way. And we realize that we are now at a place where we don't want to be.

When we look back on our emotional journey, we feel **regret**. We wish we would have done things differently. We wish we would have stopped to think more carefully about whether to walk through that gate, to take that path. We wish we could have made a different choice.

But the reality is, we are *here*. We *did* take the chosen path, and now we are off-course. So, we need to find a way to get back on track.

We need a road map.

Hand out copies of the worksheet and then continue with the script that follows this information box.

As you use this worksheet for reflection and application, note that the intent of this worksheet is not to point out *shoulds* or *should nots*. We only want to acknowledge that these potential destinations are real in all of our lives. Often, participants will begin to shake their heads or smile as they recognize those destinations that are familiar to them, because it reassures them that these experiences are common and that they are not the only ones to have them.

The following list tells you the destinations on the map and provides explanations for a few of them that participants may question.

- Rewrite the story (This indicates when someone changes the details of an event to make it feel or sound better to them or to others.)
- Physical coping mechanisms (This includes actions such as eating or not eating, watching television, drinking alcohol, doing drugs, exercising, working, shopping, and so on. Not all such actions are bad but can quickly become addictive—which causes harm.)
- "I don't care and I don't need anyone."
- Take out my emotions on others (This indicates when someone expresses anger, mistrust, or vengeance toward others, especially those who are not involved in the situation.)
- Bitterness
- Anger
- Justify my response by blaming others for my baggage (This indicates when someone blames others for their problems. For example, "My mother mistreated me, and so now I mistreat others," or "My boss doesn't appreciate me, which is why I don't do well with my responsibilities.")
- Confrontation / Accusation
- Anxiety
- Shame
- Regret
- Defensiveness
- Loneliness
- Despair
- Fear
- Sadness / Tears
- In hiding or denial
- Physical violence
- Revenge
- Mind conversations: Play the loop again and again (This indicates when someone repeats conversations over and over in their minds, either to recall what was said or to rehearse what they would like to say.)

- Dig the hole deeper (This indicates when someone continues to make the problem seem larger and larger, by adding details and "fueling the fire.")
- Fill the time / Keep busy

This road map will help us to be more prepared for the emotional journeys that tend to lead us off-track. It shows many of the destinations that we tend to find ourselves at after we respond to the catalyst and walk through the gate. Some of them may sound familiar to you.

The intention of this activity is not to say that any of these destinations is bad or evil. We will all find ourselves in these types of places multiple times per week, maybe even multiple times per day. But when we become more aware of them, we can begin to make choices in the future that will keep us off the well-worn path that leads us there. And at those times when our arrival at these destinations seemed unavoidable, we can use our maps to help us leave—because these are not places where we want to settle in and stay.

We want to get to know our well-worn pathways. And then, we want to discover another way.

REFLECTION AND APPLICATION

Let's look at the emotional map in a personal way. Take some time to think about where you most often tend to go. What locations feel comfortable or even make you feel good when you are responding to an emotional catalyst? Feel free to note those areas on your map. You may also write down thoughts on the map or even provide examples of common catalysts that tend to send you down well-worn paths to some of these destinations.

Give the participants time to study their maps and to think about their own emotional destinations.

We can all see ourselves on these maps, can't we? Maybe you haven't thought of your emotions in quite this way, but it helps when we can put words and images to our everyday experiences.

Now, we have some good news! Did you notice that there are multiple shelters of peace on the map? These can be very helpful for us when we find ourselves in one of these destinations. And the reality is, no matter where we are on the map, there is always a shelter nearby. Whenever we find ourselves in an unhealthy place and want to get out, we can locate a shelter of peace to go to and find safety and calm and renewal. These shelters of peace can take us off of our well-worn pathways and offer us a good and healthy place to stay until we are ready to move forward from the situation.

If you remember from our previous discussion about peace, it is possible for us to live in a shelter of peace—even in the midst of conflict. Peace is a sense of well-being and a feeling of completeness from our trust in God, who is close by in any emotional struggle.

> It would be a good idea to return to lesson 32—PEACE—and review how we nurture peace in our lives. Discuss how to act on those truths about peace whenever we find ourselves in a destination on the emotional map. Allow time for this discussion and encourage participants to be honest and open with themselves.

What is our conclusion to this conversation? What do we want to accomplish?

Whenever we sense that we are being nudged by an emotional catalyst toward a response, it is good for us to . . .

- slow down,
- observe our surroundings—or determine where we are on the map,
- uncover the well-worn pathways that we tend to follow when we are emotionally upset, and then
- run to and linger in a shelter of peace, until we are ready to move forward.

COURAGE AND PEACE

Our emotions are a gift from God. Our emotions are a part of the way we are created in His image. We are wise to take time to know ourselves so that we can express our emotions in ways that are healthy for us and for others. There is no need to hide what is happening inside. God sees you. He knows you. And He loves you.

EMOTIONAL DESTINATION MAP

SESSION 36
LET THERE BE JOY

GOALS FOR PARTICIPANTS
- To open our hearts and emotions to the possibility of joy
- To recognize the strength that comes with joy
- To listen for and recognize the sound of a new song

MATERIALS
- This lesson
- Plain paper; pencils and pens
- Extra paper or cardstock for the End-of-Study Testament Activity (3x5 inches or 4x6 inches is suggested, but any size will do).

VOCABULARY
- **jeopardize** (JEP-er-dyze): to put at risk or danger
- **perplexed** (per-PLEKST): puzzled; in confusion
- **wonder** (WUHN-der): admiration; awe; amazement

GREETING

Each session begins with a greeting. This will be unique and personal to each group.

REVIEW

Our last lesson was quite interesting as we used our map to follow the pathway of our emotions and to "find ourselves," so that we could begin to make wiser choices that would move us toward peace.

What destinations surprised you? Which were familiar to you?

Allow a few minutes for participants to respond to the question.

LESSON SCRIPT

You have turned my wailing into dancing; you removed my sackcloth and clothed me with joy, that my heart may sing your praises and not be silent. LORD my God, I will praise you forever. —Psalm 30:11–12

This is what we long for, isn't it?

At first glance, joy seems to betray the suffering. We are unsure if it fits into the story. We hold it at arm's length, as if allowing it in could **jeopardize** the true telling of our story. As if expressing it could nullify the contradictory ache.

But is this fear true? Does joy really make light of the pain? Or, maybe worse, does it imply that everything is now "fixed?"

Joy is unique. Different from happiness, it is not dependent on circumstances. And so, yes, it belongs in our narrative. Even in those who have suffered, there is evidence of joy: it is the golden thread woven into the multicolored tapestry that tells our story.

In a life of suffering, joy is evidence of . . .

   a soul that has been wounded but is not crushed.

   a spirit that has been **perplexed** but is not in despair.

   a body that has been struck down but is not destroyed.

Another word for *joy* is *wonder*, once again suggesting mystery—something unexplainable, yet undeniable. This comes as no surprise, since joy arrives most often when I feel the wonder of God's care.

At times, I have experienced His intimate provision: a gift that meets a personal need still unvoiced—sometimes, a need I had not even recognized! In those times, I open my arms and embrace the profound mystery that He is present, and joy washes over me.

And joy does not travel alone.

The book of Nehemiah tells us about a time when God's people were disconsolate. Ezra was reading the law of Moses to them, and they were undone—weeping because of past events in their own lives and in the lives of their ancestors. Then Nehemiah spoke clearly and told them to stop grieving. Why? Because "the joy of the LORD is your strength" (Nehemiah 8:10).

This tells us that joy has a traveling companion—*strength*.

Think about it. We all know the weariness of depression. Exhaustion, listlessness, emotional and physical fatigue—these feelings flourish when we are downhearted and anxious. "Be strong!" people say. Yet, strength seems evasive and out of reach.

So, where do we find strength when we are undone? Strength grows and flourishes in the presence of joy. And so . . .

- We look for God's care and provision, and we rejoice with gratitude when we find it.
- We open our eyes to beauty and allow it to penetrate our heart.
- We enlarge our perspective to see our value and purpose beyond this "between" life, with its muddy roads.
- We smile to acknowledge I Am on the journey with us.

We may not suddenly get the strength to leap mountains in a single bound—but we may find the energy to accomplish that one difficult task facing us that day. And as we feed the joy, we will grow stronger.

Joy is open to all of us. But, as we have learned along our journey, we alone choose to embrace the moments of healing that we are offered. This includes the choice to accept joy.

To be without it is a loss—an empty place that is *felt*.

Do not be afraid of joy. Your joy is not a betrayal of the suffering. Joy is part of your new song.

REFLECTION AND APPLICATION

> Ask participants to get into pairs or small groups to discuss the questions below.

For this activity, we will break out into small groups, and then I want each group to come up with examples of the following:

- First, give some examples of how happiness is different than joy.
- Second, give some examples of how joy produces strength in us.

Designate one person in your group to write down the examples you come up with. When everyone is finished, the designated writers will share your examples with the class.

> When the participants are finished, ask each one to share their responses, and then move onto the question below.

We discover joy unexpectedly, when we are reminded that

- We are valuable.
- We have purpose.
- We are not consumed.

Think of a time recently when you were reminded of one of these truths. Did it bring joy?

> Allow time to discuss the questions above.

The end of this course will soon be here. This activity will help us to reflect back on our journey and to think about some of the changes that we have observed in ourselves since the beginning.

Some of you may have a difficult time seeing or expressing the positives that you have observed over the previous weeks. As with joy, we often hesitate to acknowledge or speak about the positive things—especially with others—for fear that it means all is now fine. But we have talked together about this and come to the realization that this is not the case. We can have joy and peace and other positives even in the midst of negatives. Positive and negative can both be present and come alongside each other.

With that in mind, it is important that you allow yourself to see how you were as you came into this group and then to see the progress you have made during our time together. Yes, you *have* taken steps forward. And this card will be a testament of your growth.

1. Give each person a clean piece of paper or card stock (3x5 inches or 4x6 inches is suggested, but any size will do).
2. Ask them to write "I came in" on one side of the paper and "I will go out" on the other side. (Alternatively, you could label the cards before the session and then distribute one to each participant.)
3. Use the script that follows to explain the activity. Note that it would be a bit difficult to think about and complete this exercise quickly, so the idea is to explain it to participants now and ask them to complete the exercise after they leave class. Ask them to bring the completed exercise and be prepared to talk about it at the final session.

| I came in... | I am going out... |

So, on one side of the card, I want you to write these words: "I came in." On the other side of the card, write, "I will go out."

Take this card with you and, in the time before our next session, consider with honesty and compassion what changes you sense in yourself. Ask yourself these questions:

- How would I describe myself when I first walked into this group?
- What is different, new, changed, redeemed in me as I walk out of this group?

Think about your emotions, your state of mind, your sense of well-being—then and now—then write them down on the appropriate side of the card. For example, you might write "I came in . . . numb" and "I will go out . . . able to face my emotions." We all know we are not at the end of our journey, and no one's journey is perfect, so avoid extreme contrasts like, "I came in . . . suffering" and "I will go out . . .

healed." Rather, just look at yourself carefully in the mirror, so to speak, and notice the contrasts that are there. It may take time, but you will find answers to these questions if you look long enough.

We have learned that the pathway to resolution is not a straight line. But there is still clear forward movement. We can see it in ourselves and in each other. So, bring your observations with you to our next session, and together, we will share what we came up with. We will give testimony to our growth.

COURAGE AND PEACE

As you go on your way, remember that the joy of the LORD is your strength. Yes, you are *worthy* of joy and you are *capable* of strength. Your pathway of healing is opening those doors to you. So, walk through with confidence.

SESSION 37
A NEW SONG

GOALS FOR PARTICIPANTS
- Embrace the idea of new hope, new joy, and a new song
- Learn how to identify the time when God awakens the possibility of healing
- Share evidence of forward movement

MATERIALS
- This lesson
- Plain paper; pencils and pens

VOCABULARY
There are no vocabulary words for this lesson.

GREETING
Each session begins with a greeting. This will be unique and personal to each group.

REVIEW
We are on well on our way. We continue to move forward. We are not fully healed, but we are stronger than when we began. We have given suffering its place and not allowed it to take over our identity. We are equipped with tools that can help us live courageously and wisely. We still weep but we also have begun to sing. So, let's end our sessions together with some encouraging words about our new song.

LESSON SCRIPT
We were introduced to Naomi early on in our journey. If you remember, Naomi moved away from her home, family, and culture into a strange land. She lost her husband, and then, as a widow, faced the loss of both her sons.

We now return to Naomi's story because, in her journey of suffering, she lived out this awareness of God that we recently discussed—the awareness that He is with us and has a bigger purpose for our lives than what we see in this "between" time. This is the awareness of God that can bring us peace.

Naomi might have given in to the numbness and despair of her circumstances, but *she did not*. She did not have every answer. She did not know what new challenges awaited her. She just kept listening to the quiet voice inside that called her forward—out of the numbness—and then she took steps into and through and eventually away from her pain.

And then *Naomi told her story.* As we listened to that story, we learned much about Naomi and God. Remember, she didn't wrap up her pain in a pretty package and pretend to have all of the answers. Rather, she told her story of sadness and loss with honest emotion and truthful words. She opened her heart and let it spill forth:

> "Don't call me Naomi," she told them. "Call me Mara, because the Almighty has made my life very bitter. I went away full, but the LORD has brought me back empty. Why call me Naomi? The LORD has afflicted me; the Almighty has brought misfortune upon me." (Ruth 1:20–21)

Naomi spoke the raw truth of the situation while she *also* expressed her understanding of God. As she expressed her suffering, God became a natural part of that expression.

Essentially, she said,

"My loss has left me empty."

"The events of my life taste bitter to me."

"I feel afflicted, burdened."

"I remember how I used to feel, and now the blessing is gone."

"And it all happened by the hand of God."

In response to this passage, there are those who say that Naomi *blamed* God; but it is more accurate to say that Naomi *placed the responsibility* for the suffering on God. There is a subtle but important difference. Blame is often cast upon someone with an accusation of unfairness or neglect. Naomi, however, spoke of God with the highest and most profound worship, while at the same time acknowledging her pain through His hand.

To this point, notice what Naomi did *not* say:

"Why has God allowed this to happen to me? I don't deserve this suffering."

"God is not fair."

"I will no longer trust God because of this suffering."

"This suffering proves to me that there is no God."

Naomi did not blame God. Rather, she saw her suffering clearly—and, even more importantly, she saw God's hand in it!

Seeing that God was in her suffering did not frighten her. In fact, understanding that her affliction had passed through her Father's hands is what gave her the confidence to launch out again into the unknown. Her awareness of God in her suffering is what kept her in conversation with Him. And it is that awareness that made it possible for her to hear His voice say, "Move forward."

Naomi felt suffering to the depth of her being. But she knew to that same depth that God was there. God, the Almighty. The LORD. *Her* LORD.

Likewise, the conversation we have with God during suffering is extremely important. God is aware when we are simply saying what we think He wants us to say or what others dictate to us. But it is our honest conversation with Him that will eventually lead us to a place where we can make peace with the suffering and peace with God.

REFLECTION AND APPLICATION

Spend time on the following conversation. This is a very important end to this study. It is important for the participants to see and feel the change that has happened to them over these weeks. And it is equally important that they share their experiences of healing—or at least forward movement—as it is to share the original pain.

NOTE: Leaders in training may or may not have thoughts to share in this discussion, based on how their previous practice sessions have gone. If they do *not* have anything to share, then this discussion is not as necessary.

You may or may not remember that, at the beginning of this course, we read this verse from David, which has been the foundation for our journey forward:

> I waited patiently for the LORD;
> he turned to me and heard my cry.
> He set my feet on a rock and gave me a firm place to stand.
> *He put a new song in my mouth*, a hymn of praise to our God.
> Psalm 40:1,3 (emphasis mine)

Some of us may not quite feel ready to sing a new song. That is okay. The anticipation of a new song is enough. This anticipation is evidence that you have a renewed purpose and identity and that you have gained some awareness of your value.

However, some of us may already hear notes beginning to form. Maybe we have even begun to gently hum.

Regardless of our place of readiness, our new song is more possible now than it has ever been on this journey, all because we have taken steps forward. So, let's share ways that our hope for a new song has become evident in our lives. Let's take this time to share from the cards you received at our last session.

- How would you describe yourself when you first walked into this group?

- What is different, new, changed, redeemed as you walk out of the group?

COURAGE AND PEACE

> Instead of presenting the following words as loosely scripted text, please read the message word-for-word, as it includes a personal letter from me, the author.

As we draw to a close, the author would like me to read you a personal letter from her. *This message is from her to you as you move forward from your suffering, toward courage and peace:*

Dear Fellow Travelers,

I want you to know that I thought of you as I wrote this study. I also suffered greatly through unexpected events and betrayal from those I trusted. As a result, I doubted my value and purpose, and I thought that I would never sing again.

So, I connect with you in your pain. But I also connect with Naomi and David, for I now have a new song. This new song is different from the one I used to sing. It comes from deep within. In fact, it is rooted in the soil of suffering. It rises out of the pain and is filled with my expression of gratitude to God—because He is with me in my suffering, He heard my cry, He set my feet on a rock, and now there is sweetness once again in my life. He put a new song in my mouth.

I do not know when your awareness of a new song will come; perhaps, you already hear the notes faintly. But when it comes, the melody will be your own. It will tell your story, which came to life before you were born and will continue into eternity. It will be a tale of suffering mixed with hope, pain mixed with beauty, and a God who is with you through it all.

When it comes, don't be afraid to let it flow from you—whether it's a few notes or a full chorus! Don't worry about what others think or say. After all, your new song is for you alone, given to you by your trusted Traveling Companion: Your Good Shepherd, your Savior, your I AM.

Together, we can:

Sing to the LORD a new song; sing to the LORD . . . (Psalm 96:1)

With love,

Susan

APPENDIX A:
OPTIONAL SESSIONS TO COME ALONGSIDE CHILDREN IN SUFFERING

Adults are not the only ones who suffer. Children feel pain, as well. Particularly in crises that affect whole families or communities of people, children's suffering comes not only from their own pain but also from the pain of the adults they look up to, literally and figuratively. But children are further disadvantaged in the healing process than even their adult counterparts because they do not have the vocabulary, the life perspective, or the coping skills to interpret and respond to the events that cause them pain.

As adults, many of us feel the desire to help children in their suffering, but we are unsure how to connect with them or just generally feel unequipped to help. For this purpose, the pages that follow contain six additional sessions for those who want to learn to help children through their pain.

- The Personhood of Children
- A Child's Responses to Suffering
- Open a Safe Door For Children to Share Their Story
- Nonverbal Ways to Open the Door
- Body-Based Ways to Cope With Anxiety
- Spiritual Reassurance
- Discussions for Deeper Understanding

SESSION 38
THE PERSONHOOD OF CHILDREN

GOALS FOR PARTICIPANTS
- Understand that children have an identity of their own
- Understand that children have value of their own
- Learn to interact with children as individuals who have identity and value

MATERIALS
- This lesson
- Plain paper; pencils and pens

VOCABULARY
- **personhood** (PUR-suhn-hood): the state of being an individual with human emotions and characteristics that make one unique and separate from others
- **purposeful** (PER-puhs-full): full of purpose; intentional
- **respect** (ree-SPEKT): concern or regard for another's feelings or wishes; honor

GREETING

Each session begins with a greeting. This will be unique and personal to each group.

LESSON SCRIPT

Before we talk about how to *help* children, let's discuss how we *see* them. Why? Because our view of children determines the way we respond to them, especially in their suffering. If we see them merely as possessions of their parents or as little "people in waiting," for example, then we might not believe that they even experience suffering or that, if they do, it is not necessary to call it to attention.

To truly understand how we can help children, then, we must first understand how to see them for who they are—God's creations. Earlier, we discussed what it means in our own lives to be created by God. So, before we go further into this lesson about children, let's briefly review that earlier discussion and see how it applies here.

To start, we can recall that this conversation took place in our lessons on identity and value. Those lessons showed us that God's hand in creating us is what gives us our special identity and value—because God not only created us in His own likeness; He also created us with a purpose.

By the end of our lessons on identity and value, we had gathered three main truths:

- I am a unique and purposeful creation of God, the Perfect Creator.
- Because God created me in His image, I can find my true identity in Him.
- I am valuable because God declares me to be valuable.

Together, these truths form our real identity. Do you remember what that means? Let's review together:

- **This identity never changes.** Every minute of every day of every year, this truth remains: You have always been and will always be a unique and purposeful creation of God, the Perfect Creator.
- **This identity is not dependent on you.** Your unique identity is yours simply because you exist! It will not change based on how you think or feel or act. Neither will it change based on anything you do, whether for God or anyone else.
- **This identity is not dependent on others**. Because your identity was given to you by God and is in God, no one can take it from you. Some might not believe this or might not treat you as if this is true, but that does not change the reality.
- **This identity is not dependent on events or circumstances**. Neither the harmful events that put you on this journey of suffering, nor any current or future events and circumstances can change your true identity. These events and circumstances are part of your story, but they are not your identity. Even the pain that you have experienced is not your identity—it is only a part of your story.
- **This identity is an expression of God's own beauty.** Beauty is named in the Bible as one of the characteristics of God. It is also a description that we often use when we talk about His creation. When we witness a sunset or a mountain range, for example, we might say, "How beautiful!"
- **Finally, this identity gives you value.** You are valuable because God declares you to be valuable—and your value never changes or diminishes.

These truths about our real identity apply equally to children. Think about this: when God creates us in His image, He gives us this image at the time He conceives of us, *before* we are even born. This means that even infants still in the womb carry God's likeness and, as such, they have value even *before* their first breath. Likewise, babies, young children, teenagers, and people of every age have value just because they were created by God.

In addition, because God is **purposeful** in His creation of each of us—that also includes children. He chooses to bring us to life in the womb, He sees us before we are born, and then He watches us each moment of our lives, from infancy into adulthood.

This means that the truths we learned about ourselves extend to young people as well. So, we can also say that . . .

- Children are a unique and purposeful creation of God, the Perfect Creator.
- Because God created children in His image, they can find their true identity in Him.
- Children are valuable because God declares them to be valuable.

Inherent in these truths is the idea of **personhood.** *To have personhood is to be an individual with distinctly human emotions and characteristics.* But it is more than that—because to have *personhood* also means that . . .

- our individual emotions and characteristics are what make us unique and separate from others
- our individual emotions and characteristics are what give us value

Every human has personhood. Adults have personhood, and so do children. This means that children are individuals with feelings and characteristics that make them unique and separate from others and that give them value. In other words, children are persons in their own right—their importance and identity are not attached to or under the authority of anyone else, including adults.

Jesus Himself recognized the personhood of children. The way that Jesus treated children and the things that He said about them made it clear that He saw them as persons in their own right, with their own value and image that were independent of the presence or authority of any adult. We see evidence of this attitude of Jesus in two specific passages:

> People were bringing little children to Jesus for him to place his hands on them, but the disciples rebuked them. When Jesus saw this, he was indignant. He said to them, "Let the little children come to me, and do not hinder them, for the kingdom of God belongs to such as these." (Mark 10:13–14)

In this passage, Jesus says that the kingdom of God belongs to children, in their own personhood. This suggests that they are important in the kingdom of God and that this importance is not dependent on any parent or adult. Now, let's look at a second example:

> He called a little child to him, and placed the child among them. And he said: "Truly I tell you, unless you change and become like little children, you will never enter the kingdom of heaven." (Matthew 18:2–5)

In this passage, Jesus holds up children, in their own personhood, as examples for adults to follow. He says to "change and become like" children, which implies that children are unique from adults in a *valuable* way. This verse also reinforces the idea that their importance in the kingdom of God does not rely on anyone else—in fact, their ability to enter heaven is attributed solely to the fact that they are children!

When we go back to the time before Jesus's birth, however, we see that Jesus's view of children was simply a reflection of His Heavenly Father's perspective. We see God express this perspective in the words He speaks to His people about the commandments He gave them:

> These commandments that I give you today are to be on your hearts. Impress them on your children. Talk about them when you sit at home and when you walk along the road, when you lie down and when you get up. (Deuteronomy 6:6–7)

Here, God says that children, in their own personhood, deserve His teaching and truth *now*—not just when they become adults.

This truth that children have personhood is foundational to our ability to walk alongside them through suffering. It tells us that children are individuals with whom we can connect personally, especially when we have the shared experience of pain. It also tells us that children are individuals with their own unique identity and value, which means that each one is worthy of love and respect. As such, this truth equips us to provide children with the necessary care they need to move forward on the path of healing. Let's look at a few of the ways this happens.

The truth of personhood shows us that children need assurance about their identities and value. Children often attach their identity to a parent or another adult. This means that the child's sense of identity changes depending on circumstances and the reactions of others. That loss of identity leads to a loss of value. Children may often believe the lie that they are no longer valuable because of particular events in their lives. Children need to know that their value does not change or diminish due to suffering, trauma, or abuse from others. We must speak truth to them: *You are valuable. You are valuable because God has declared that you are valuable.*

The truth of personhood shows us that children are worthy of love. Children long for love. In fact, a child's longing for love often overpowers any outside threat to their well-being. But many children do not feel worthy of love; rather, they feel that love is something they have to earn. And so they embrace and give love to others readily and with abandon. Sometimes they even love without precaution or when trust has been broken. They give out love over and over again—even when it is not reflected back to them. But as persons in their own right, children are worthy of love—real love. As we interact with children, then, we want to assure them that they are loved—no matter what the situation. When they have done something unwise or even disobedient, we want to assure them of our love. When disastrous events are all around us, we want to assure them of our love. When the future is uncertain, we want to assure them of our love. We assure them of our love through our words and actions, directing our attention toward them and treating them as unique, individual persons made purposefully in God's image.

The truth of personhood shows us that children are worthy of respect. We most often think of **respect** as something that children give to parents or adults. This is right and good. In turn—as individuals with personhood—children are also worthy of respect. Even young children who do not know what *respect* means know the feeling they get when someone shows them—or does not show them—respect. And when they feel this respect from others, children are assured of their value and identity. So how do we show children respect? There are many ways, but one definition of respect mentions the word *notice*. A person feels respected when they feel noticed—and this particularly applies to children. We can be intentional about this when we walk into a room and take special notice of a child. We can be also intentional about this when we notice each child as an individual who responds to suffering in their own unique way.

This means that if a group of children is under our care, we do not simply care for the group; we care for each unique child in that group. Even if all the children in the group have experienced the same crisis, we recognize that each child is unique in how they perceive that crisis and respond to pain. We consider each child's perspective, we see each child's unique characteristics, and we acknowledge that each one is valuable in a way that is different from others.

In turn, each child will sense whether we see and value their individual characteristics. They will know if we are listening with respect. They will comprehend the value we see in them. And they will respond to the relationship that we nurture in a way that will lead them forward on their journey of healing.

REFLECTION AND APPLICATION

Is this way of looking at children new to you? How will this influence the way you speak to children and respond to them—particularly those children who are in pain?

Give participants a few moments to share in response to these questions.

COURAGE AND PEACE

Our children are individuals with a unique identity. We thank God for each one. We accept them as fellow members of His kingdom. We learn from them and become like them in ways that please God. We also share the truth of God with them—in practical ways that reveal our own need for Him, our own trust in Him, and our dependence on only Him. When we do these things, we come alongside the children on this journey. They learn from us and we learn from them. We minister to each other, and we move forward together as we share in our courage and peace.

SESSION 39
A CHILD'S RESPONSES TO SUFFERING

GOALS FOR PARTICIPANTS
- Recognize untruths about children in suffering
- Identify common responses, verbal and nonverbal, from children in suffering
- Intentionally watch for symptoms of suffering in children

MATERIALS
- This lesson
- Plain paper; pencils and pens

VOCABULARY
- **assumption** (uh-SUHMP-shun): something taken for granted or thought to be true without proof
- **nonverbal** (non-VER-buhl): unspoken; without using words
- **passive** (PAS-iv): not actively participating; showing no interest
- **preemptive** (pree-EMP-tihv): an action taken against something anticipated or feared; preventively
- **resilient** (ri-ZIL-yuhnt): able to recover well from negative events; able to stay strong in response to pain
- **status quo** (STA-tus QUO): the way things are or have been; the way things are expected to be
- **trigger** (TRIG-er): something that brings up the memory of a traumatic experience in a way that sets off an intense negative emotional reaction

GREETING

Each session begins with a greeting. This will be unique and personal to each group.

REVIEW

Our discussion about children began with their personhood. Because each child is created by God in His image, each child has individual value and purpose. And because they have personhood, children are worthy of love and respect.

In what ways did Jesus recognize the value and personhood of children?

Give participants a few moments to share in response to the question.

LESSON SCRIPT

Children have personhood and so they each suffer uniquely, just as we do. Yet they face some serious obstacles on their path of healing:

- They are not fully equipped to comprehend the source, the motivation, the consequences, or the significance of particular events or actions that feel hurtful.

- They are not fully equipped to verbally express their concerns and fears. In other words, they do not have the vocabulary needed to verbally express their emotions, and they often cannot speak confidently to others about their concerns.

- In crises that impact groups of people, both children and adults, the pain of children is often overlooked or considered negligible in comparison to everything else that needs attention. This can happen because, as adults who have been consumed by trauma, we can become preoccupied with our own experiences to the point that we forget about the experiences of others. It can also happen when the damage created by the crisis event demands our urgent attention and consumes our resources of time and energy.

- The suffering of children also goes unnoticed or unheeded due to many of the **assumptions** and misconceptions we have about them. Let's talk about three such impactful assumptions in detail.

Assumption 1: Children are resilient. They will survive.

This is a mix of truth and untruth. It is true that children *are* **resilient**—their inbuilt instinct to survive helps them find ways to adjust and adapt during negative times. And so, we might believe that they have a handle on their suffering because they show no signs of upheaval and despair. But the reality is, the outward expression of calm does not always represent what is happening inside—thoughts and emotions may be in turmoil. In addition, even when children find ways to cope, they often do not choose *healthy* ways to cope.

We know this is true because many adults now deal with pain that they experienced as children. They found a way to survive in the aftermath of the event, and this served them well in the moment, allowing them to get through the immediate pain. However, they never actually experienced true healing because, as children, they had no way to express or confront their difficult emotions—and as a result, their pain was never allowed to surface.

So the truth is, although children may "survive," the temporary adjustments they make to cope with pain may not survive long-term: eventually, their pain will rise to surface.

Assumption 2: If children don't mention pain, they are okay or have moved on.

There are many reasons that children don't mention their pain—but hardly ever is it because they are okay. Most often, it is for one of the following reasons:

- *They do not know how.* Many children are not able to find the correct words to express their negative emotions. This is especially true of very young children who have a limited vocabulary and a limited understanding of their own emotions.

- *They might worry about others' responses.* Children might not share their negative emotions out of concern that others will react in disbelief or even criticism.

- *They desperately want things to be okay.* Often, it will appear that children have adjusted to a crisis simply because their longing is to move on and past the pain—to a place where all is well. This could result in a couple of different reactions:

    They might believe that, if they don't talk about their pain, then perhaps that will mean it is not a reality.

    Rather than recognize and think about their pain, they create scenarios in their minds where all has been put back into place as it once was, and they live as if these scenarios are reality.

- *They try to protect their own sense of security by protecting the loved ones meant to provide it.* Children rely on the adults and caretakers in their lives for their sense of security. So, even if one or more of their loved ones was the source of their hurt, children will look beyond the pain in a desperate attempt to regain the sense of trust and safety they once had. They may not even be able to acknowledge that they have pain let alone be able to speak about it.

- *They want to protect relationships.* If their pain is attached to someone they love or to someone who is important in their own life or the lives of others, children will stay quiet simply to protect these relationships. This often means that they will take the blame for the hurt on themselves rather than direct it outward. Further, they will not talk about their pain because they will believe that they were the ones to cause it.

Assumption 3: As soon as circumstances are better, children will forget the past.

This is another mix of truth and untruth. Although children do tend to adjust more readily than adults after a crisis is over, this is often because children are not as concerned with things like retribution, vengeance, or the need for someone to admit wrongdoing—which can promote their healing and enable them to see and accept good and joy back into life. However, this willingness to embrace good can also prompt children to return to people or circumstances that continue to cause them pain. Time after time, these children will reach out for the results they so desperately hope for, only to have these attempts repeatedly end in hurt.

In those cases when circumstances do change, children may appear to forget their pain—and their minds may forget the events that led to that pain; however, the effects of their trauma will remain for years and often even influence their responses well into adulthood.

It is important that we move from *assumptions* about children and their response in suffering to **preemptive** words and actions. To act preemptively is to take action before the event actually happens. Our goal is to think more about preventing a problem than hoping to solve it when it can no longer be hidden.

If we are to recognize and care for the needs of children in suffering, then we must learn to recognize these misconceptions in our own minds. We must also become more intentional to look for and respond to suffering in children. How? There are two main ways we can live out this intention:

1. First, whenever traumatic circumstances are evident, rather than assume that children are okay, we must assume that they have unresolved pain.

2. Second, we can look for specific signs that signal the presence of suffering in children's lives. These signs can be difficult to detect because they are not always obvious. In fact, most of these signs are **nonverbal** responses and behaviors—which means that we will not become aware of them through children's words. This means that we must be alert and actively look for these signs in each individual child, because no two children are alike. We must also be alert to each child within each individual circumstance, because the same child might respond differently to their pain in one situation than they do in another.

So, what signs should we look for? Here are some common responses that signal feelings such as suffering, grief, sadness, and worry, along with a few examples of each:

WHAT TO LOOK FOR	EXAMPLES
Behavior Changes	- A clear change in behavior; for example, from generally obedient to blatantly rebellious, from talkative to silent, or from active to inactive - Tantrums or demands for attention
Changes in Social Interaction	- Withdrawals from conversations and interactions with others - A sudden desire to be left alone - A sudden fear of being left alone; for example, clinginess
Changes in the Ability to Think, Concentrate, or Remember	- A clear change in performance at school; for example, poor work or an unwillingness to participate - Forgetfulness
Mood Changes	- A clear change in outlook, from generally positive and happy to negative and sad - Increased weepiness - A negative view of themselves; for example, self-accusation or feelings of worthlessness or guilt
Physical Symptoms	- A loss of appetite - Trouble sleeping - Headaches, stomachaches, or body aches and pains
A New Fear or Concern	- A fear of going to sleep can relate to fear of death or new crisis events - Separation anxiety from a parent can relate to a fear of losing the parent
Questions That Express Worry or Uncertainty	- "Are we going to move again?" - "What will happen if . . . " - "Have I been bad?"

Interestingly, these signs fit all of the characteristics of trauma that we learned about in session 5, which tells us that trauma affects children in the same ways:

- Trauma impairs their memories.
- Trauma changes their view of themselves.
- Trauma changes their view of others.
- Trauma manipulates their responses.
- Trauma's manipulation takes them to a place of fear.

Like adults, children also react to **triggers**, such as a sound, a smell, or touch that remind them of the initial crisis event. Often, when children react to a trigger, they are not even aware that they have been triggered. They just have a sudden, strong response to something, and they do not understand why. So, this is another sign to look for. Whenever a child responds to something in a way that seems unusual or even exaggerated, we would do well to find out more about what caused this response.

In the same way that children will not discern when they have been triggered, they will also not understand why they display these signs of suffering—these new behaviors, symptoms, and changes in attitude—that you observe. Children lack the ability to be self-aware to the extent that adults are, and so they will not often be able to explain why they feel or have acted a certain way. They will only know that they feel a need to survive and keep the **status quo**.

This lack of self-awareness can make it even more difficult for us to understand and respond to children who we suspect are suffering. So, in the meantime, as we work to observe and detect the signs of trauma, we can help children by repeatedly speaking truth to them.

To offer truth to all children is important; but to offer truth to suffering children is crucial, because these children tend to hold onto two very distinct and destructive assumptions about themselves:

- I am responsible for the bad things happening around me.
- I am powerless; my voice will not change what is happening around me.

In some way, these two statements might even seem to contradict each other, but the reality is that children hold onto both very strongly. On the one hand, they do not see themselves as important enough to impact others to make changes that would specifically help them. On the other hand, they imagine that it is because of them that these outside events have happened—or are still happening. It may seem unthinkable, but children place responsibility on themselves for everything from marriage problems to financial problems to war. They will even blame themselves for the illness and death of loved ones.

The blame, shame, and responsibility they hold onto in secret create a heavy burden for children to carry, and so, as adults, it is important that we speak these truths to children:

- You are not responsible for the bad things that have happened. You did not cause it to happen, and you are not responsible to fix it.
- Your voice has power. Your words and feelings are valuable. I want to hear.

We do not wait for children to ask the question or voice the concern. We speak it preemptively. Once is not enough. We must speak these truths repeatedly because they go against the deep natural tendency of suffering children to believe otherwise. We can do this by looking for opportunities to speak these truths in our everyday conversations with children. And then we can support our words with active listening and connection that allows them to express their negative emotions and find a way toward healing.

We will talk more about how to do that in our next lesson.

REFLECTION AND APPLICATION

Give participants an opportunity to share in response to the questions below.

What truth did you learn about children today that is new to you?

Think about a time when you made a wrong assumption about a child's response to suffering. What assumption did you make?

Can you think of a child who has shown the effects of suffering in ways that you did not recognize before?

COURAGE AND PEACE

Our children long for life to be right and good and safe. As adults, we know that this expectation cannot always be realized. But we also know that, when it is not realized, we can look for signs of suffering and offer truth. Children will be naturally drawn toward healing when we show them love, respect, and attentiveness to their pain.

SESSION 40
OPEN A SAFE DOOR FOR CHILDREN TO SHARE THEIR STORY

GOALS FOR PARTICIPANTS
- Recognize the need to open a safe door for children to share
- Watch for ways to engage children in conversation about their suffering and pain
- Avoid closing the door on children's conversations about suffering and pain

MATERIALS
- This lesson
- Teaching Tool: Open the Door
- Plain paper; pencils and pens

VOCABULARY
- **shame** (SHAYM): the painful feeling of disgrace; dishonor; loss of face
- **nonverbal** (non-VUR-buhl): expressed without words
- **verbal** (VUR-buhl): expressed in spoken words

GREETING
Each session begins with a greeting. This will be unique and personal to each group.

REVIEW
In our previous lesson, we discussed how each child relates and responds to suffering uniquely; however, there are some common signs of suffering that we can watch for. Do you remember a few of those signs that a child might have pain or concern? What do you remember about them?

What two conflicting untruths do children carry that hinder their ability to deal with suffering?

Give participants a few minutes to respond to the questions above.

Once we discover that a child feels the negative effects of suffering, we can take the next step: we can open the door and invite them into conversation.

LESSON SCRIPT

Throughout this course, we have talked a lot about our stories. Our stories are precious and valuable. They include the expression of our fears and joys and doubts, along with our responses to certain events. They are real to us and a part of us. But the reality is that our stories often include pain and suffering.

As adults, we understand this. We know what pain feels like and we have words to express it. We also know the fear of sharing our story *with others. Will they believe me?* we wonder. *Will they think I am complaining? Will they understand the pain I feel? Will they make me feel guilty or shameful?*

Children have the same concerns about sharing their stories. They may not know how to express their concern in words, but they still feel it just as deeply as we do. And so, children put an emotional boundary around themselves to protect them from this worry. This boundary emotionally separates them from others; it keeps their feelings closed off to the outside world. As long as they stay inside, they will not have to worry that their stories will be met with doubt, disbelief, or criticism—because their boundary will prevent them from sharing those stories.

This boundary is different from the boundaries that we have learned to set up throughout this course. Our boundaries were positive. They were intentional, truth-based, and meant to protect our health and well-being. But a child's emotional boundary is something they set up without their own awareness—it is not intentional, it is not healthy, and it is not based in truth. Further, it does not protect their well-being; in fact, it actually *prevents* it. It keeps the child away from healthy behaviors like expression and communication that will ultimately lead them to healing.

Despite these differences, we can use a concept that is already familiar to us to help us visualize this emotional boundary—a fence.

As mentioned, children who have put these emotional boundaries around themselves do not even realize the fences are there. But, as adults, we can observe the presence of fences that prevent their healing.

A lot of times, the presence of a fence becomes obvious when we have a verbal interaction with a hurting child. We might go into such a conversation and expect it to turn out something like this:

Adult: How do you feel? What is wrong?

Child: I feel sad. My friend doesn't like me anymore, and I am afraid I will never have any friends again.

Adult: You are a good friend. You will be fine.

Child: You are right. I feel better. I feel happy now.

But instead, the discussion sounds more like the following:

Adult: How do you feel? What is wrong?

Child: Nothing is wrong. I'm okay.

Or, if they tell us what is wrong and we give consolation, the child reacts as if they heard nothing we said. The problem and sadness remain. When a child appears to be "closed off" in this way, this may signal the presence of an emotional boundary—a fence.

> Show the Teaching Tool, Open The Door, to the participants.

So, what do we do when there is a fence in the way of a child's healthy expression and healing? First, we look for the entrance. Then we open the door. Let's look at each of these steps in turn.

1. **Look for an entrance.** Almost every emotional boundary has an entrance. But to find it, we must be willing to take some time with a child and connect with them. One of the best ways to do this is to include them in our own activity: as we take a walk, as we work in the kitchen or the garden, as we go on an errand. Conversations are more comfortable when we are together in an activity, and children find it easier to share when the attention is not directed only at them.

   If it is not possible or practical to include the child in a personal activity—if you have planned to mentor the child in a location other than your home, for example—then think of another activity to do together; perhaps, you could draw, color, or do a simple game or puzzle.

   When you devote intentional time and attention to a child in this way, you communicate that you see the child as a unique individual with value. You also show that you are someone with whom they can feel safe. And it is this sense of safety and value that will allow you to find an opening to the child's emotional boundary—an entrance that will give you the opportunity to open up a door.

2. **Open the door.** When we open the door to a child's emotional boundary, we essentially show them that their fence has one safe area where they can allow their emotions through. This open doorway gives them an opportunity to release some of their emotions and their story—an opportunity that, if taken, can lead them toward healing.

But how do we do this? The way we open the door is through communication.

Communication can be **verbal** or **nonverbal**. Verbal communication is just as it sounds—it uses the spoken word. Nonverbal communication is expressed outside of speech—it can be written or drawn, or it can be expressed through visual cues such as behavior, facial expression, or even posture.

To connect with children, we must use both forms of communication. However, in many cases, a verbal conversation will not be what opens the door for a child to share. Rather, verbal expressions of pain tend to grow out of nonverbal expressions. That said, we do not want to jump into nonverbal activities until we are prepared for the conversations that may arise from them. So, in this session, we will focus on ways to verbally communicate with children about their pain. Then in our next session, we will discover nonverbal ways to open the door.

So, how do we verbally open the door to help a child share their story?

As we saw a minute ago, "What's wrong?" is not always the best way to start the discussion. Here are some suggestions that might be more effective:

- **Point out a sign of suffering.** Perhaps, you observed a child exhibit some of the symptoms mentioned in our last session; for example, maybe they have shown intense anger, extreme quietness, tiredness, lack of appetite, and problems at school. You might start a discussion with, "I have noticed that you don't seem very hungry lately." Then follow with, "When I feel that way, there is usually something bothering me. Is there something you are concerned about?"

- **Bring up an event but put the focus on yourself.** You might say, for instance, "I feel sad that Uncle John died. Sometimes I miss him so much. How do you feel about it?" Or, "The storm last week frightened me. I wanted it to stop. How did you feel?"

- **Offer the reassurance that it is okay to share.** If a child looks especially burdened or appears uncertain about whether to share, you can make it clear that you notice them and sense something is wrong. Then reassure them that they can share whatever is on their heart. For example, "There might be something on your mind that you think would upset me. I am here to listen and help if I can. You don't need to protect me. We can work on problems together."

- **Consider one of the following alternative conversation starters.**
    - When have you felt angry recently?
    - What is something that you like or don't like about yourself?
    - What do you think others like most about you?
    - What is the hardest thing in your life right now?
    - Do you ever worry? What makes you worry?
    - Do you ever feel lonely?
    - Tell me about one of your friends. What makes a good friend? What makes a bad friend? Has anyone been a bad friend to you?
    - Is there anything you wish were different in your life? If you could change one thing, what would it be?

Avoid asking such questions as an interrogation. Rather, weave them into the conversation naturally. Once you have opened the door to a child's sharing, you can work to keep it open by making the doorway safe. To do this, you must respond in a way that does not show anger, accusation, disbelief, or shame. Such negative responses will send a message to the child that the doorway is unsafe, and the door will begin to close. Not only will the child stop sharing, but their closed door will become more difficult to open the next time you try. In fact, there is a chance that it may never open again.

With this in mind, we must mentally prepare ourselves to respond in a way that will keep the door open—regardless of what the child might share. This is important because it is not unusual for a child who is suffering to say something that shocks or surprises us or even makes us angry. But if we are prepared, then we can stay calm and positive and safe on the outside, regardless of what we may feel on the inside.

So, let's prepare by taking a closer look at anger, accusation, disbelief, and shame, along with a few other negative responses that can close the door to a child's sharing.

- **Anger** might seem like an appropriate response, especially if the child shares that they have been harmed or mistreated in some way. However, a child will not respond well to an outburst of anger—even when that anger is directed toward someone else. For example, if your anger is directed toward a family member or school friend who mistreated the child, the child might be afraid that you will confront the offending person, which could cause retaliation against and further mistreatment of the child. The child might also fear that your anger outburst will draw attention to their story, when their intent was to share this story with you alone. Either way, strong emotion does not calm.

    So, if you feel angry at what a child has shared with you, pause and take a deep breath and calm yourself before you respond. Then simply express your concern and assure the child that you will defend them. This will keep you from adding intensity to the event and fear to their heart.

- **Accusation** often slips into our responses unexpectedly. If a child shares, "John took my book, and now it is torn," your first reaction might be to say, "I told you not to play with John. I knew this would happen!" Although this may be true, and there may be lessons to be learned from a situation, the time to point this out is not during your initial response. Rather, the immediate focus of this time is to allow the child to share their pain.

- **Disbelief** is expressed when we respond with questions and comments such as, "Are you sure that's what you saw?" or "I can't believe he would do something like that!" We can also unwittingly imply that we don't believe a child's story if we ask too many questions—as if it is an interrogation.

- **Shame** should never be a response to an open door and, if given, will close the door for sure. But shame is tricky. It can sneak in through responses that we may think are innocent at the time. For example: "You thought the storm would carry the house away? That is silly—anyone knows that could never happen!" Or, "What if your friends heard you say that? They would think you are a baby." We also shame a child when we laugh in response to what they share. When they share something that is very serious to them, and we laugh or make fun of their feelings, we cause shame.

Shame is often what a child fears most—even though they do not have a label for it. So, we must avoid this response at all costs. If we do not, we will surely close the door and stop the child from sharing more of the story.

- Another response that will close the door to sharing is to **break a child's confidence**. No one likes to have their private thoughts and emotions shared with others. So, we must protect what a child tells us rather than talk about it with others. If the child cannot trust us to protect their feelings, then they will not continue to share them with us.

- Finally, we close the door when we attempt to **talk the child out of their feelings**. Like shame, this response can sometimes sneak in when we do not expect it. Often, it comes from an instinct to reassure the child, but it results in minimizing their feelings.

We might say, "Stop being afraid of the storm because it won't hurt you," for example. This only undermines their fear. It also tells them how we think they *should* feel, which suggests that they are wrong to feel how they really do. A better response is to acknowledge and confirm the emotions they do feel. We can say, "The sound of the wind was frightening. I understand that it sounded as if it was so strong that it could carry us away. But the wind that we heard is not strong enough to pick up our house. Next time you feel that fear, come tell me and we will talk about it."

Finally, know when to draw the conversation to a close. If the child has shared with you and you have connected with their feelings and given them realistic reassurance, then that is enough. *Avoid pushing the conversation to some kind of perfect ending*—because if the conversation goes on and on, and the child becomes bored or begins to feel like sharing is a chore, they will be more likely to avoid it next time. Children have shorter attention spans than adults, and so a brief interaction is fine. You can always return to the discussion later. Above all, follow the child's lead. If you sense they are ready to move on to a different conversation, move with them. If they seem to want to share further, keep the door open.

To listen and respond well is not always easy. We will not always get it right. But we can always lean on and learn from God, who listens perfectly. We can see a good example of how God listens to us in these different translations of Psalm 116:2:

> Because he turned his ear to me, I will call on him as long as I live. (NIV)
>
> Because he inclined his ear to me, I will call on him as long as I live. (ESV)
>
> Because he bends down to listen to me, I will pray as long as I have breath! (NLT)

These translations give us visual pictures of how God listens. They show us that *He turns, He inclines,* or *He bends down*. These are all words that indicate that God cares enough to hear what we say that He will actually change his position to focus on us when we share with Him. He bends down to our level to hear what we have to say.

In the same way, we can put ourselves in the right position to listen—physically, mentally, and emotionally. We can bend down or sit on the floor so that we can be with the child as we listen. We can turn ourselves to face the child rather than look at our phone or book. We can put our minds in a position of readiness, so that we are prepared to respond in way that is calm.

Sometimes, it only takes an eye-to-eye smile and a response of "I hear you." Each child wants to know that they are heard, believed, and valued, and each child will know if we are truly listening. If we are, their door will remain open. And so, we listen carefully. We give verbal and nonverbal encouragement. We reassure. We will not always say the right thing, but we can always be aware and focused, so that we provide the best possibility for open conversation.

One of the greatest gifts we can give children is simply to see them in their pain, make a connection, and reassure them of the truth that they are not on their own. As we do these things, the doors of sharing will remain open, and one conversation will lead to another and then another. And the more we practice, the more comfortable we will become with this wonderful opportunity—until eventually, we will find ourselves on the path of healing together.

REFLECTION AND APPLICATION

Plan a time to connect with a child. Look for an entrance and then use one of the conversation starters mentioned to try to open the door. Be mindful to keep the doorway safe and the door open. If you are able to participate in such an opportunity, write about the experience and plan to share it during our next session.

COURAGE AND PEACE

Our children have precious and valuable stories to tell. When we open the door to help them share those stories, we might even find that some of their emotions connect with ours. Both adults and children can grow stronger as they include each other in the healing journey.

OPEN THE DOOR

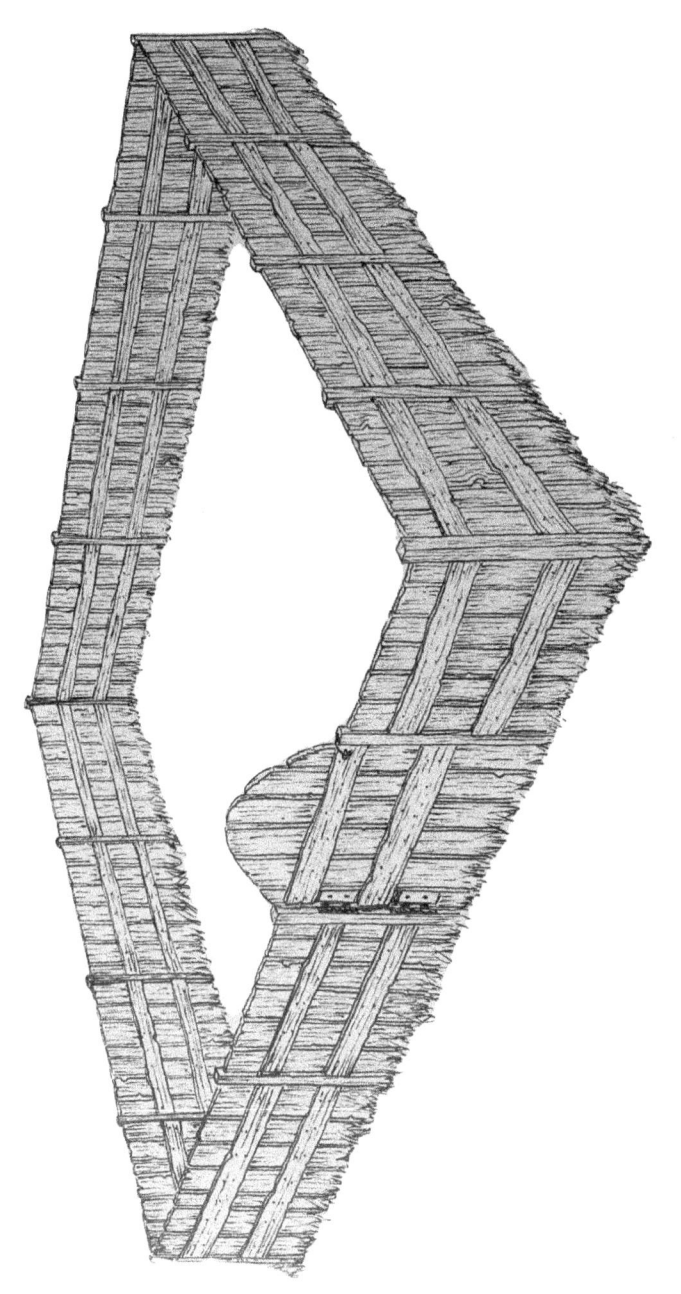

SESSION 41
NONVERBAL WAYS TO OPEN THE DOOR

GOALS FOR PARTICIPANTS
- Recognize the need to provide nonverbal connections to help children share their story
- Become comfortable with the nonverbal tools explained in this session
- Use nonverbal tools to help children express pain and suffering

MATERIALS
- This lesson
- Participant worksheet: Activities to Help Children With Nonverbal Expression
- Plain paper; pencils and pens; crayons, markers

VOCABULARY
- **script** (SKRIPT): the words that can be used to teach the lesson

GREETING

Each session begins with a greeting. This will be unique and personal to each group.

REVIEW

In our last session, we discussed ways to initiate verbal conversations with children about their pain. We also talked about what things to do and what things to avoid to keep the door of communication open.

What do you remember from that discussion about how we can express disbelief, accusation, and shame without intending to?

If you had an opportunity to speak to a child this week, were you able to apply some of what you learned in our last session? If so, how?

Give participants time to respond to the questions above.

LESSON SCRIPT

Today, before we start, let's remind ourselves of what we've learned so far about children. First, let's remember the wrong assumptions we tend to make about children:

- Children are resilient. They will survive.
- If children don't mention pain, they are okay or have moved on.
- As soon as circumstances are better, children will forget the past.

Next, let's revisit some of the more common obstacles in a child's path of healing:

- They cannot fully comprehend the source, motivation, consequences, or significance of hurtful events or actions.
- Their limited vocabulary makes them less equipped to express their concerns and fears verbally.
- In crises that impact groups of children and adults, the pain of children is often overlooked or considered negligible compared to everything else that needs attention.
- Their suffering goes unheeded because of the many wrong assumptions we make about them.
- They assume shame and responsibility for their suffering and feel like their voice is powerless to change it.
- They worry about others' responses to their stories, and they desperately want to maintain the status quo.
- They feel the need to protect relationships and their own sense of security.

If you recall, it is because of these obstacles that children tend to put an emotional boundary around themselves. They keep the painful parts of their stories hidden behind this fence, because they want to avoid the fear and discomfort that comes when they share—but as a result, they also avoid the opportunity to heal. As adults, we can help them find an entryway in their fence by connecting with them personally and then we can use communication to open the door.

In our last lesson, we discussed verbal ways to open the door and keep it open. However, it is not often that a verbal conversation will initially open the door for a child to express their story. Because of this, we need to be creative to spark nonverbal expressions of their story, which can lead to verbal expressions later. That will be the focus of this lesson.

> If possible, make a copy of the worksheet for each participant so they can have this as reference. Distribute the worksheet now. If this is not possible, encourage the participants to take notes so they can use these exercises later in interactions with children.

The following activites are important for interaction with young people and children. Take time to consider them carefully and role-play them with the participants.

We are ready to consider a series of activities that you can use to engage young people to think about and express their stories. These activities use nonverbal keys to open the door to possible verbal communication. In other words, these activities provide the opportunity for a child to share some part of their story or feelings without using words. This sharing may lead to "words" or it might remain as a nonverbal expression—and this is okay. The goal of this time is to build trust and gain some insight into what is happening in the child's heart and mind. Some of these activities will be the same as those used in our adult discussions, while others were created to connect especially with children.

Each activity includes instructions and a **script** that you can use to communicate verbally with the child. The script is in *italics*. In many cases, it will help to do the activity with the child so that they see what is expected. This also keeps you busy so that you do not watch them too intently, which can make them uncomfortable and prevent them from sharing openly.

Note that, in many of these activities, the words *anxiety* and *anxious* are used. If a child asks you what these words mean, you can find their definitions, along with a short discussion of what anxiety is and how it affects us, in the next lesson.

Spend time on the activities on the following pages. When it is time to close the lesson for the day, return to this point and share the closing sections.

REFLECTION AND APPLICATION

Plan a time to connect with a child. Look for an entrance and then use one of the activities from this lesson to try to open the door. Be prepared for the conversations that may arise from a child's nonverbal expression and, as always, be mindful to keep the doorway safe and the door open. If you are able to participate in such an opportunity, write about the experience and plan to share it during our next session.

COURAGE AND PEACE

Children *want* to interact with us—they either just don't know how, or they fear they will not be heard. We can open the door for this interaction with simple activities that give children a way to express their emotions. When we do, we give them the ability and courage to have that interaction, which is often all they need to come through the door.

ACTIVITIES TO HELP CHILDREN WITH NONVERBAL EXPRESSION

A PICTURE OF ME

Provide the worksheet with the outline of a child. (Give each child only the appropriate figure—boy or girl.) Use this outline to open the door for the child to express emotion and concerns. Be sure to give the child ample time to fill in the details.

Let's imagine that this is a picture of you. It doesn't really look much like you, does it? But we can add details that will help the image come alive! Let's do that.

> *Maybe you could add hair color.*
>
> *Add a favorite dress or shirt with colors that you like.*
>
> *Next to the head, draw a picture of something that you often think about.*
>
> *Near the feet, draw a picture of a place where you like to walk.*
>
> *Next to one or both of the arms, draw a picture of something you like to do.*

You can also use this picture to show some of the things you feel.

Maybe you feel pain or discomfort somewhere. Draw a circle on the area of the picture that doesn't feel well. It might be a part of your body like an arm or a leg or your stomach. Or it might be something inside—like your heart or your thoughts. Maybe your eyes hurt sometimes because of things you see—maybe those thoughts bring tears. This picture can show how you feel inside when you draw it on the outside!

You might be surprised by the creativity of children to show what they feel in this way, and their marks on the page can lead to further conversation. However, be gentle—don't push for more details unless the child is open to share.

A PICTURE OF ME

A PICTURE OF ME

CONNECT COLORS TO EMOTIONS

Provide the child with the Colors of My Emotions worksheet. Talk about these emotions with the child and explain that, just for this activity, particular colors will represent particular emotions. (In other words, these colors do not generally represent these emotions.)

Color in the rectangles with the colors you agree on for each emotion. Then encourage the child to color the image with those colors that they feel. Feel free to vary the instructions to make them age-appropriate and relevant to your specific conversation; for example, you might ask them to color the image to show the emotions that they feel most often or the emotions that they felt at a particular time or event.

Here are some examples of the colors you might use for each emotion, but feel free to choose your own:

- red = angry
- yellow = happy
- black = afraid
- gray = sad
- green = confused
- brown = anxious or stressed

The children can add colors of their own, as well.

This creative, nonverbal expression of a child's emotions may also lead to verbal expression, so be observant and ready to apply the ideas from our previous lesson to conversations that may arise.

COLORS OF MY EMOTIONS

329

COLORS OF MY EMOTIONS

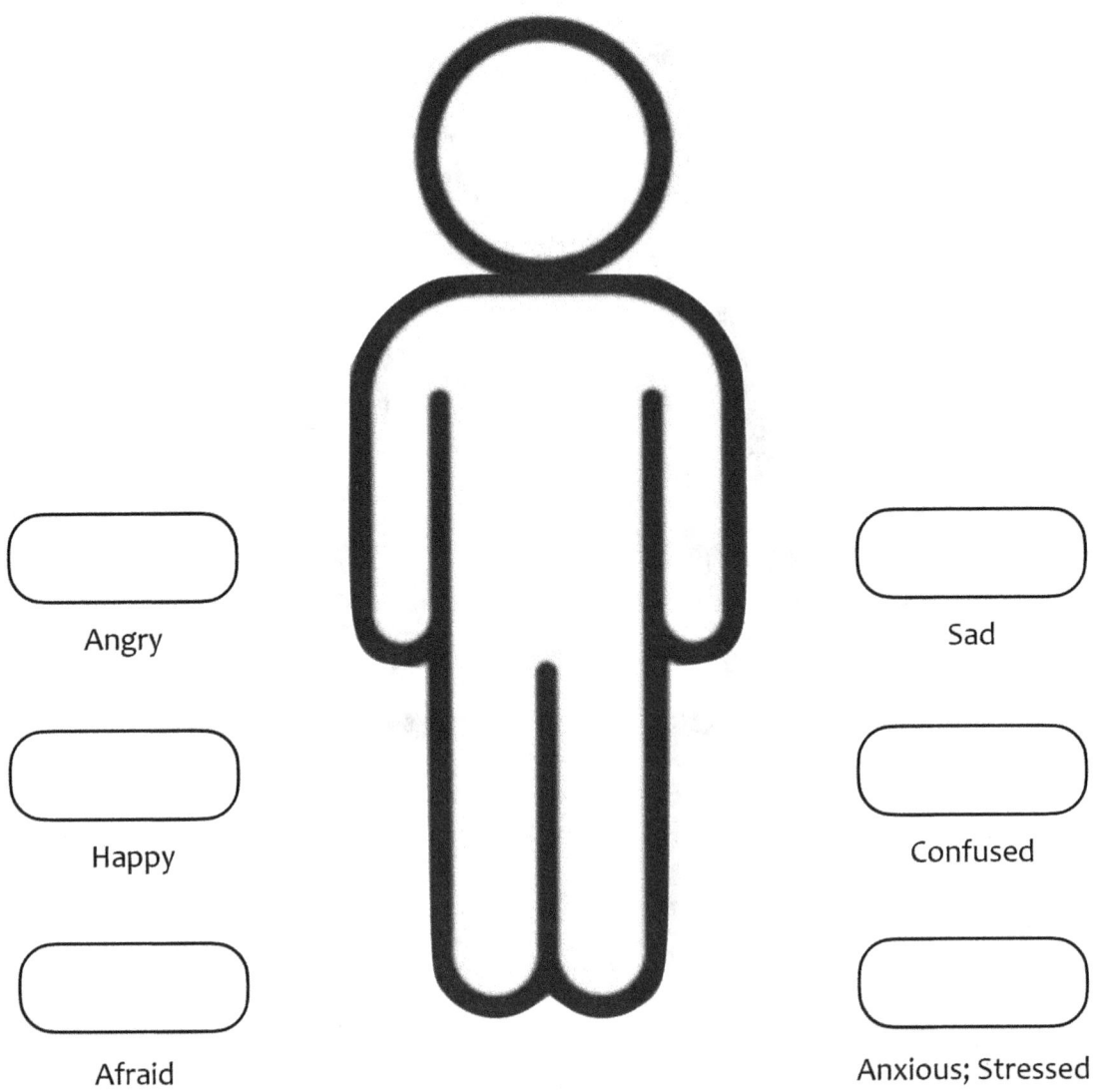

330

A PICTURE OF SUFFERING

Children think in images and pictures more often than in words—especially when they are suffering. We give them an opportunity for expression when we ask them to draw the images they see in their minds.

For this activity, simply provide each child with a plain piece of paper and a few colored pencils or markers. Then give them the following instructions:

> Sometimes we have an experience that is difficult to share with others.
>
> There are some things that I find very hard to talk about. I see painful events in my mind, and I don't know what to do with them. One way I can express the pictures in my mind is to draw them on paper. The picture I draw might not look exactly the way it does in my mind, but it tells the story for me so that I don't have to hold it in my thoughts so tightly.
>
> Maybe there is a story in your mind that is hard to talk about. You can use the paper and pencils and markers you have to tell a story. You don't have to say one word with your mouth. You can just speak with your pencils and markers. There is no right or wrong way to draw your story, and you will not need to explain it to anyone. This picture is just for you, and you are the only one who needs to understand it.

After the child has drawn for some time, add this encouragement:

> You are doing such a good job of telling your story. As you look at your picture, perhaps there is a place where you feel hurt, fear, or pain. Circle that part of your picture to give it special attention.
>
> Sometimes, it can be hard to think about the places that hurt, but they are important. Your pain is important to care for. So, let's give it some attention so that it knows we see it.

The child should not be required to explain the picture to you, but you can offer to listen if you see an entrance—an opportunity to open the door.

Remember that this is the goal of the activity: to open a door for the child to share. No child will come to peace and healing with their pain until they can first express it safely to someone. So, if the child shares, listen. Do not correct them or try to change their story. Hear the story just as the child experienced it and as they feel it. Sometimes, this is all they need—the chance to express how they feel. Once they take this chance, you can discern whether further conversations are necessary, based on what they have shared.

A MAP OF MY FEELINGS

Children may have difficulty saying, "I'm angry"—especially if the emotion is connected to a family member or friend. This emotional map helps the child express negative feelings. Speak to the child:

We may have trouble expressing our emotion when we are anxious about things that are happening around us or to us. These feelings can come to us when we do not even expect them. One minute, we are in a good place, with good feelings, where we are happy and everything is fine. And then something happens, and we suddenly find ourselves in a different place—a place where we do not feel so happy! Maybe we feel sadness or anger or something else, but it does not feel good. We can feel confused and wonder, "How did I suddenly go from a happy place to this not-happy place?"

Has this ever happened to you? Maybe you were in a good mood, and then you saw or heard something that bothered you, or maybe something even happened to you, and then off you went—to a place of fear or anger or sadness? This happens to all of us at one time or another. And when it happens, it can be hard to say how we feel because we are confused and maybe even anxious. So, this map can help us.

> The following script is optional—if the concept of a map is not familiar to the child(ren).
>
> *Do you know what a map is? A map shows you a picture of something from up above—it is as if you are a bird in the air looking down on it. The map shows you the whole area and all of the things in that area. So, if you have a map of your town, it will show where the streets are and the shops that are on those streets. This helps you find your way to the place you want to go!*

A map can be very helpful. It helps you know where you are, so you can find a way to where you want to be. Our map is like this too—except that this map does not show us a town or a lake. It shows us our heart—or what we feel inside.

It is true for all of us that our emotions take us to various destinations—just like when we travel on the road. The difference is that we might not choose where our emotions take us! We experience the event and then off we go—to a place of fear, or anger, or sadness. And just like on the road, we might find ourselves lost—and we don't know how we got there. A map can help us see where our emotions take us. This helps us express to others how we are feeling. And then we can make some decisions about whether we want to stay or find another place to settle. This worksheet shows the open gate at the bottom of the page. When something negative triggers us—a thought, an event, something we see or hear—the gate opens and our emotions go somewhere—even if we don't want them to. Let's look at the map together and see if any of the destinations seem familiar to you.

Encourage the child to look at the images and then point to one or more that connect to their feelings. This may be a feeling they have at that moment—or one that they remember feeling recently. Allow the child to tell you why—do not interpret for them. They may see something different in the image than you do. This is not the time to say, "You should not feel that way." Nor do we want to talk them out of their feelings. This is a way to open a door for the child to tell some part of his or her story, or at least to express some part of their emotion.

IMPORTANT: Draw the child's attention to the love messages on the map: *God sees me. God knows me. God is with me. God loves me.* These are truths that can help us to be strong even when our emotions take us to confusing or difficult places—perhaps, we are not even sure where we are.

WHERE DO MY EMOTIONS TAKE ME?

A TIMELINE OF POSITIVE AND NEGATIVE

This activity will help children give a visual to their story. This is the same activity we did together at the beginning of the course, but in most cases, children will not be able to make their timelines as precise or detailed as adults. To add events to their timelines, children may just write a few short words or draw a picture. (For young children, you may write the words for them. Be careful to write exactly what they say—do not add your own interpretation.) Don't push them to be exact in the representation of the event; the goal of this activity is just to help them express a part of their story—it is for them, not for us.

To do this activity, provide the child with a plain piece of paper and a pencil, and then use the script below to help you guide them through the steps. Pause after each of the numbered items to give the child time to complete that step.

> *Our life is a story—a very special story. A story is like a series of events. One thing happens and then another thing happens and then another. Some of the things that happen in our life story are good, and some are bad.*
>
> *So, think about some of the good and bad things that have happened in your life. Once you think of them, you can put them on your paper, and this will tell part of your story!*
>
> 1. *Take your piece of paper. Draw a line across the center of the paper.*
> 2. *Add a mark at the beginning of the line; this is when you were born. Add another mark at the end of the line; this is today.*
> 3. *It is a short line for such a long time, isn't it? Now you can show some of the good and bad things that have happened in your life. Start with one good thing that has happened and put it ABOVE the line. You can use words to tell about it or draw a picture of it.*
> 4. *Now, think of one bad thing that happened. Place that BELOW the line.*

Continue this for two or three good and bad events. The goal of this activity is simply to help the child see that both good and bad things have happened in their lives. Do not spend a long time talking about the details of the events.

> *Look at the events on your timeline. Are there one or two that make you feel anxious or afraid or sad? Circle those events. This is a good way for us to see what is causing stress and anxiety.*
>
> *You have now told a part of your story in a safe way! This is good. we usually feel better when we talk about these things rather than hold them deep inside.*

EXPRESS EMOTIONS ON A TIMELINE

This activity can help children discover if their fear or pain is caused by things in the past or by things that might happen in the future. It can also open another door for them to share the pain or fear they feel.

In this activity, the child will use a simplified version of a timeline to discover where their emotions come from. Give the child a piece of plain paper and a pencil, and then encourage them in the following way:

Draw a straight line in the center of the paper.

Now make a mark in the center of the line. This mark is today.

Everything to the left of this mark happened before right now. Everything to the right of this mark will happen after right now. (**Note to mentors**: When you use this activity with younger children, you may need to point to the part of the line indicated by *left* and *right*.)

Imagine that you are standing on the center line, which is right now. Next, think about a time when you feel anxious or afraid or sad.

Point to the place on the timeline that causes you to feel this way. Is it something that already happened—before today? Or is it something that you worry could happen after today?

Sometimes, we mix up these two things—we think that what already happened is the same as what could happen. So, we worry about them in the same way. But if we want to feel better, then we must handle each one in its own way. How?

When things that already happened to us cause pain, we can't change those things. We can think and think about them, but we cannot make them go away. So what do we do? It is hard, but we can accept that the painful thing happened to us. This means that we do not try to make it disappear. We do not try to make it "not" happen. Sometimes, we feel like we want to put the pain somewhere else on the timeline—maybe even after today in the future—so that we can stop it from happening. We want to make it better.

But it already happened and we cannot change it. So, we accept that it happened, and then we learn to live bravely with any changes caused by that painful time. After a while, we begin to realize that we will be okay and we start to feel better—even with our painful memories.

When things that could happen cause us to feel anxious or afraid, they can seem even bigger and stronger than the things that already happened. That's because things that could happen are in our imagination—and we usually imagine that they will happen in the worst way. But in real life, the things that we worry will happen almost never actually happen. And the time we spend in worry about these events is harmful to us. It can make our bodies tense and our minds feel afraid, and it can even make us feel tired or sick.

When we feel afraid or anxious, it is good for us to ask ourselves, "Am I afraid of something that did happen, something that is happening, or something that could happen?" If it is something that "could" happen, we can remind ourselves that there is a very good chance that it will not happen.

Whenever we feel sad or anxious, it is good to see where those emotions come from on our timeline. Do they come from a time before or after right now? Once we know, we can care for and speak truth to ourselves.

SESSION 42
BODY-BASED WAYS TO COPE WITH ANXIETY

GOALS FOR PARTICIPANTS
- Recognize the need for children to find nonverbal ways to cope with anxiety
- Become familiar with body-based coping
- Comfortably teach children how to cope with anxiety in nonverbal ways

MATERIALS
- This lesson
- Teaching Tool: Anxiety = A Place of Fear
- Plain paper; pencils and pens

VOCABULARY
- **anxiety** (ang-ZIE-ih-tee): a feeling of distress or uneasiness of mind caused by fear of danger
- **anxious** (ang-SHUHS): full of mental distress or uneasiness because of fear
- **cope** (KOHP): to face or deal with difficulties in a calm manner
- **exhale** (EX-hayl): to breathe out
- **grounded** (GROUN-uhd): a feeling of being mentally or emotionally balanced; connected with the present moment and focused on reality
- **inhale** (IN-hayl): to breathe in
- **nausea** (NAW-zee-uh): a feeling of sickness in the stomach
- **reason** (REE-zuhn): to form conclusions or think in a logical way; to think through a problem
- **senses** (SEN-suhz): the capabilities of sight, hearing, smell, taste, and touch by which we perceive the world
- **sensory** (SEN-suh-ree): related to the senses

GREETING

Each session begins with a greeting. This will be unique and personal to each group.

REVIEW

We discovered some simple activities in our last lesson that would help us to open conversations about suffering, pain, and fear. Pictures and colors are things that do not require the perfect words and, thus, can open the door for sharing. These small steps can help children express their pain and begin to heal.

What was new to you in that lesson?

If you had an opportunity to speak to a child this week, were you able to apply some of what you learned in our last session? If so, how?

> Give participants time to respond to the questions above.

LESSON SCRIPT

This session provides short activities that you can do with children to help calm anxiety. These activities are simple, but they work—and not only for children, but for adults as well. Before we learn how to do these activities, however, let's talk about what **anxiety** means and how it affects each of us. This will help us better understand how the activities work to settle both our bodies and minds.

Anxiety is distress or uneasiness of mind, usually caused by a fear of impending danger. For example, if we are alone and there is an unusual sound outside the house, we might be afraid that something dangerous is about to happen to us. However, there are other times when anxiety settles in without a clear reason. There is no loud sound or frightening experience. There is no fear of impending danger. We could be involved in our normal everyday activities and then suddenly and unexpectedly feel unsettled—and when this unsettledness grows, we become **anxious**.

This second type of anxiety, which comes by surprise and seems to happen for no reason, is often caused by a trigger. We talked about triggers earlier in our sessions. A trigger is a sound, sight, smell, or other sensory experience that reminds us of something negative and causes us to react strongly. The trigger most often moves our thoughts and responses from our immediate situation to a moment in the past, which makes us fear that the moment could happen again. In other words, that connection to the past makes it feel like there is potential danger in the moment—even when there isn't.

We all have anxiety at some point in our lives, but for those of us who have suffered, anxiety seems to hold a much larger role in our stories. Further, this anxiety disturbs the potential for peace in our lives, so it is important that we learn how to **cope** with it. To *cope* is "to face or deal with difficulties in a calm way." When we cope with anxiety, we protect ourselves from being carried away by it into distress or despair; we learn to stay in a safe place where we can more readily make wise decisions rather than act out of fear.

It is particularly important that we help children who have suffered to cope with anxiety, because they often don't even know how to recognize anxiety or how to say, "I am anxious." But this task is not as easy as we might think. We cannot simply talk a child out of their anxiety.

> Show the Teaching Tool: Anxiety = A Place of Fear.

One reason for this has to do with our visual of a child who sits inside a fence. The child's fear can become so strong that it is like a fence around them that keeps them in a place of anxiety. It is that emotional boundary that does not allow the child to express their anxiety or to hear or connect with any reassurance that is offered.

Another reason helping children cope with anxiety is not easy is because, as we have learned, trauma lessens our ability to **reason**—and this is particularly true for children. That's why it is often not effective to say things to a child like, "Tell yourself not to be afraid" or "You are okay. Just believe that you are safe." Words of reason are powerless when the grip of trauma has already set in, because the child cannot think clearly.

When verbal reassurance does not help, then, we need nonverbal ways to help children cope. One such nonverbal method that can be effective is body-based coping. Let's talk about why this works.

Although anxiety takes place in our thoughts, it also affects our physical being. When we are anxious, our heart beats faster, our breathing speeds up, and our muscles tense. We might even feel dizzy, break out in a sweat, or experience **nausea.** These are all ways for our body to ask for help. The problem is, words will not often calm these physical sensations, especially in children, and so we need another way to "talk" to the body. This is where body-based coping comes alive.

Body-based activities allow children to communicate a sense of safety to their bodies during times of anxiety, which calms their bodies down. And when the body calms, so does the mind. It is as if the body expresses emotions and asks for help in a nonverbal way, and then the child responds with a nonverbal language that the body understands—through sights, sounds, smells, touch, and hearing. As a result—in the same way that the mind triggers the body to be anxious, the body can then trigger the mind to calm down. And once a child is calm, they can make better choices about how to respond.

Children cannot use these body-based ways to cope, however, until they first realize that they are anxious. Yet, most children do not naturally connect their own emotional and physical reactions to anxiety. So, we must help them make this connection. One way to do this is to notice how children express anxiety during our interactions with them—such as during the verbal and nonverbal activities we learned about in the last two chapters. When we work to open the door to children's sharing, they often will help us discover how they express anxiety.

But another thing we can do is to teach children to recognize the signs of anxiety in themselves. The following ideas will help you get started.

- **Help them discover the physical feelings of anxiety.** Draw an outline of a body. Tell the child to circle areas of the body that feel strange or uncomfortable at times. You might give a personal example—"Sometimes when I am anxious, I feel like I have a lump in my throat. I feel like I can't swallow!"—followed by other possibilities, such as an upset stomach, a headache, or legs that feel like they won't work. Once the child understands what you are asking for, they will begin to express their own physical feelings. Some of their descriptions might seem strange to you, but avoid negative comments or ridicule.

- **Help them discover the thoughts of anxiety.** Make an outline of a person's head and draw a simple face on it. Then ask the child, "What kinds of thoughts go through your mind when you begin to feel fear?" Give a personal example, such as, "Sometimes when I feel afraid, I think that if I tried to run, I could not move."

    Then point to the area of the eyes and forehead on the image: "What kinds of pictures do you see in your mind that cause you to feel anxious?" Again, you might give a personal example of seeing an image: "When I feel anxious or afraid, I imagine that I see everyone looking at me."

As you communicate, you can explain that many of these thoughts and physical feelings come from anxiety. If the child shares their own thoughts and physical feelings, you can tell them that these experiences are ways that their bodies and minds talk to them—perhaps even ask for help—and reassure them that they can learn good ways to respond.

Then walk them through a few of the body-based coping methods below. You can even use some of the explanations from this lesson to show why these methods help—children often understand more than we think.

BREATHING

How we breathe impacts how we feel. Let's think about how we **inhale** and **exhale**. To inhale is to breathe in and to exhale is to breathe out. Inhale = take air in. Exhale = let air out. When we feel anxious, we breathe more quickly, and sometimes we even hold our breath. We need reminders to breathe in and breathe out, slowly and intentionally. This helps to calm our bodies and our emotions. The following methods can help children take control of their breathing during times of anxiety. For all breathing exercises, the inhale and exhale should be gentle and slow—not rushed.

Deep Belly Breath

Place one hand on your belly and one hand on your chest. Take a deep breath in for four counts and then exhale slowly through your nose for four counts. Notice how your chest and your belly rise and fall when you inhale and exhale. (Continue this breathing for three minutes or as needed.)

Inhale
1-2-3-4

Exhale
1-2-3-4

Smell the Flower and Blow Out the Candle

Pretend to hold a flower in one hand and a candle in the other. First, smell the flower—take a deep breath in through the nose and fill your lungs with air. Now, exhale through your mouth and blow out the candle in the other hand. (Continue this breathing for three minutes or as needed.)

Inhale

Exhale

Shoulder-Roll Breath

The shoulder roll is a good breathing exercise that also releases tension and tight muscles. Sit comfortably. As you take in a deep breath, raise your shoulders up toward your ears. Now, drop your shoulders down while exhaling. (Continue this breathing for three minutes or as needed.)

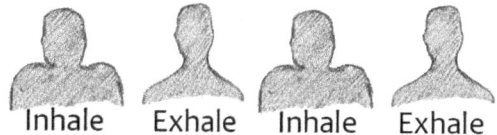

Inhale   Exhale   Inhale   Exhale

Five-Finger Breathing

Hold up one hand, palm faced out, and fingers spread apart. Put the index finger of the other hand at the base of your thumb and breathe in while you move your finger up one side of your thumb. Then breathe out as you move your finger down the other side of your thumb. Do the same thing with the remaining four fingers. Take a deep breath in as you move your finger up and blow a deep breath out as you move your finger down. This will take you through five complete deep breaths. (Continue as needed.)

BODY MOVEMENT

Physical activities such as walking, playing catch with a ball, or swinging are good ways to cope with anxiety. Be sure to plan such activities each day for good physical and emotional health.

Butterfly Hugs

- Cross your arms at your chest, so that your hands are shaped similar to a butterfly's wings and your fingertips sit just below your collarbones.
- Take a deep breath and slowly tap the collarbone areas with your fingers.
- Imagine that your hands are the gentle flutter of butterfly wings.
- Continue for one minute.

GROUNDING

During times of anxiety, we often lose our sense of stability and safety. It is almost as if we are drawn outside of our body, and we begin to imagine all sorts of things that can happen, including all kinds of danger. We are not able to think logically about where we are and what is actually possible—or not possible. In situations like these, we need to help ourselves feel **grounded** again. Suddenly our fears and imaginations take over. We need to bring ourselves back into the current moment so that we can make wise choices. And to do this, we use our senses.

The following grounding activities can be particularly helpful for children who need to regain control when their imaginations and fears threaten to overwhelm them. These activities help the child's mind focus on something neutral and nonagressive. The mind is given a task that distracts it so that the child is not overcome by anxiety. Be aware, however, that each child will be different, and some children may respond to particular activities better than others.

SOUND

- Stop and listen to everything around you. Try to identify all the sounds that you hear. Be patient. It might take time for background sounds to come to life.
- Make your own noise: read something out loud, sing, make a quiet sound that only you can hear, or hum a favorite song.
- Listen to music. Try to hear the instruments and voices separately and then together.

TOUCH

- Touch something close to you and notice everything about how it feels. Think about the shape, texture, and temperature.
- Touch something like a bracelet or beads that can act as a tether to the present or to a sense of peace and calm.
- Enjoy the soft touch of a blanket or stuffed animal or the smooth feel of a stone.
- Hold a warm drink in your hands and feel the comfort it brings.

SIGHT

- Focus on a nearby object and notice all the details you see. Think about color, shape, shadows, and anything else that catches your attention.
- Play a counting or coloring game. Observe your surroundings and count how many squares you can see, for example, for how many shades of blue you can see. Or how many books do you see? What colors are the books? What colors do you see in the sky?

Now that we have gone through body-based ways to cope with anxiety, let's discuss one final coping method that is often *not* effective for children: distraction. As adults, one way that we cope is to keep busy. We fill our time in order to push the pain and fear into the background. And so, we often follow this same strategy with children. We might try to constantly distract them with television, movies, or technology, with the thought that if we keep them busy, they will not have time to be sad. But this does not solve the problem and can even add harm as we encourage them to push the hurt further away into hiding. It is not healthy to stay busy and distracted with the goal of ignoring the pain and pushing it into hiding.

At the same time, when our bodies and minds are in constant stress because of our anxiety and suffering, we need and welcome times of rest, even as we pursue a path to healing. Especially in situations of war, natural disaster, or the serious illness of a family member or friend, our tendency is to constantly talk about the crisis. Every conversation we have seems to eventually end on that that one topic. Children especially need a break from this constancy of crisis around them. We can provide this for them and we can also provide it for ourselves.

We can play a game with them or bake something that they enjoy. We can go for a walk in nature, which calms and refreshes our spirits as we take our focus off of the crisis for a time and absorb the beauty of God's creation. These body-based methods offer hope because they show us that we have other ways to cope with anxiety when words do not do the job. They also show us that God loves us enough to give us the tools we need—our physical senses— to calm our bodies and minds. When we show children how to use these tools on their own, we give them one less area in their lives in which to feel powerless and out of control. We equip them with the capability to help themselves.

REFLECTION AND APPLICATION

If you previously connected with a child and opened the door for them to share, think back on that time now. Did they express any of the thoughts or physical feelings of anxiety discussed in this lesson? If so, look for an opportunity to show them some of the body-based coping methods you learned. As always, be mindful to keep the doorway safe and the door open. If you are able to participate in such an opportunity, write about the experience and plan to share it during our next session.

COURAGE AND PEACE

God created our physical bodies with senses. He can speak to us and calm us through these senses, just as He did with David, who wrote these verses:

> The Lord is my shepherd, I lack nothing.
> He makes me lie down in green pastures,
> he leads me beside quiet waters,
> he refreshes my soul. (Psalm 23:1–3)

These beautiful words that connect to our senses of sound, touch, and sight reassure us that God can be our help and our peace whenever we feel anxious.

A PLACE OF FEAR

SESSION 43
SPIRITUAL REASSURANCE

GOALS FOR PARTICIPANTS
- Open the door for children to connect with God in their suffering
- Provide relevant spiritual reassurance
- Introduce tethers as a reassurance of God when the storm threatens

MATERIALS
- This lesson
- Participant Worksheet: Tethers
- Plain paper; pencils and pens

VOCABULARY
- **abandon** (uh-BAN-duhn): to leave behind; to forsake or withdraw from
- **tether** (TETH-er): something used to hold an object closely to a particular location

GREETING

Each session begins with a greeting. This will be unique and personal to each group.

REVIEW

Body-based coping activities might have been new for you. Did you have opportunity to use any of the exercises for yourself this week?

If you had an opportunity to speak to a child this week, were you able to apply some of what you learned in our last session? If so, how?

Give participants time to respond to the questions above.

LESSON SCRIPT

Our concern for children, their experience of suffering and their response to it, is the foundation for our discussion. To this point, we have focused primarily on physical and emotional ways to connect to children in their suffering and open the door for them to express their thoughts and feelings. But, just as with adults, there is a spiritual aspect that is key to our healing.

Spiritual reassurance can be a challenge. We want to speak truth but sometimes that truth sounds as if we are pushing the pain aside or making light of the concerns.

We, as adults, know the characteristics and attributes of God that can be of great assurance during times of suffering. We want our children to grasp these truths, hold them close, and depend on them during times of uncertainty and anxiety. However, it can be difficult to express these concepts in relevant and concise words that are easy for children to quickly pull to mind. Our adult session about tethers can help us. We discovered that we, as adults, need tethers that hold us during unexpected storms, times of confusion, and threats to our safety—emotional or physical.

Children thrive when they feel safe, and so, events or persons that pose a threat to that safety cause anxiety. Because children connect and respond to visual images or concepts, we can use the image of tethers to provide a visual of safety. Children understand the fear of being swept away and will respond to the reassurance that there is someone who can hold onto them when that threat comes. We will express these tethers with words that connect to them in a personal way.

> The following script in italics is written as if being spoken to children.

Think with me about a small boat that is sitting on the shore. It seems safe enough until some gentle waves begin to push against it. The waves get bigger and before long the boat begins to shift until it is pulled out into the water and floats away from its safe place. The boat now seems to be at the mercy of the waves that rock it to and fro.

There may be times when you feel like that small boat. All seems safe enough and then the waves come. They are not so scarey at first until they cause more trouble and you begin to feel unsafe—unsure if all will stay the way it has been on the shore. The waves can be many different things—sickness, school troubles, war. Perhaps your parents seem stressed and distracted—you are not sure what the waves are—but you know they are powerful. It feels like you are being pulled into the waters that are unfamiliar and you are not sure how to respond. You probably just want the storm to stop.

When we feel this uncertainty, our emotions begin to take control. We feel anxious and fearful. Then we begin to imagine new fears and before long we are sure that we will float away from all that is safe and good. What will become of us?

When this happens, we need something to hold us fast. Listen to this word: **tether**. *A tether is something that holds another thing fast so it will not float away—perhaps a strong rope! We would love to know that even if our boat floats away from the shore, it is still held fast by a strong rope.*

I want to share a very important truth with you now. We have some strong, unbreakable tethers that hold onto us during unexpected storms and times when we feel unsafe. These tethers are wrapped gently—but firmly—around us and no matter how high the waves or how strong the wind, these tethers cannot be broken. The tethers cannot be broken because they are held by God, Himself. And there is no storm that is stronger than God.

Let's talk about these strong tethers that can hold us. Once we know the names of these tethers, we can remember them when we feel like we are floating away. These tethers will reassure us when we feel anxious and fearful.

The following expresses each tether in the simple way we want the child to remember it along with additional conversation you might share to explain it more fully.

TETHER	ADDED CONVERSATION	SCRIPTURE VERSE
God sees me.	Sometimes you may feel that no one sees you. You might fear that in the middle of the storm, others have forgotten you and will **abandon** you. God sees you. There is nowhere that you can be that God does not know where you are.	The eyes of the LORD are everywhere, keeping watch [over you]. (Proverbs 15:3)
God is with me.	Not only does God see you, He is always with you—even when no one else is around and you feel alone. He never runs out of time and He is always interested to hear your story—you can talk to him anytime and you can say anything to Him. He is never distracted by other troubles. He does not just watch from far off, God is right beside you.	Do not fear, for I am with you . . . I am your God; I will strengthen you and help you . . . (Isaiah 41:10)
God knows me.	God knows you because He created you. He knows your fears—even when you do not speak them out loud. Because He knows you, you are valuable to Him. Nothing you do can change that value—nothing others say about you can change that value. God knows you better than anyone does and you are valuable to Him just as you are—with your fears and doubts and questions.	You have searched me, LORD, and you know me. (Psalm 139:1) Are not two sparrows sold for a penny? Yet not one of them will fall to the ground outside your Father's care. And even the very hairs of your head are all numbered. So don't be afraid; you are worth more than many sparrows. (Matthew 10: 29-31)
God loves me.	God was the first one to love you—even before you were born. You can do nothing to earn His love or to make Him stop loving you. Even when you don't feel loved by others—or you feel unlove-able—God loves you.	For God so loved the world that he gave his one and only Son, that whoever believes in him shall not perish but have eternal life. (John 3:16)

When you feel that you are in danger, remind yourself of the strong tethers that hold you safe—no matter what is happening around you. You can say to yourself:

God sees me.   God is with me.   God knows me.   God loves me.

As we give spiritual reassurance to children, we speak truth that reassures, but avoid making promises that we cannot keep. We answer questions honestly. We say, "I don't know" when we have no answer. We admit that we also feel uncertainty at times. We hold them close and we remind them that their heavenly Father holds them close even when we cannot.

We remind our children again and again: God sees you. God is with you. God knows you. God loves you.

One of the most important gifts we can give to our children is to teach them to invite God into their experience of suffering. Our children's relationship with God will grow as they include Him in their pain and their fear. He will become *their* God—an ever present help in time of trouble.

God is our refuge and strength, an ever-present help in trouble. (Psalm 46:1)

REFLECTION AND APPLICATION

Children are visual learners and so it would be good to give some visual representation of the truths taught today. Let's think creatively about some ways we could bring the idea of "tethers" to life for children so they can remember it more easily.

> Have the participants work together on this project. The following are some ideas:
> - Draw a picture of a boat in waves. Add ropes that have the titles: God sees me. God is with me. God knows me. God loves me.
> - Provide a small piece of rope or yarn to remind the child of these truths.

COURAGE AND PEACE

It is difficult for us to watch our children suffer. We feel the need to protect them. We might even doubt at times that all spiritual truth will come to pass as we have taught them. We remind ourselves of this truth:

Jesus Christ is the same yesterday and today and forever. (Hebrews 13:8)

God, Jesus Christ, Holy Spirit—the truth will remain sure for our children as it has for all generations to this point in time.

TETHERS

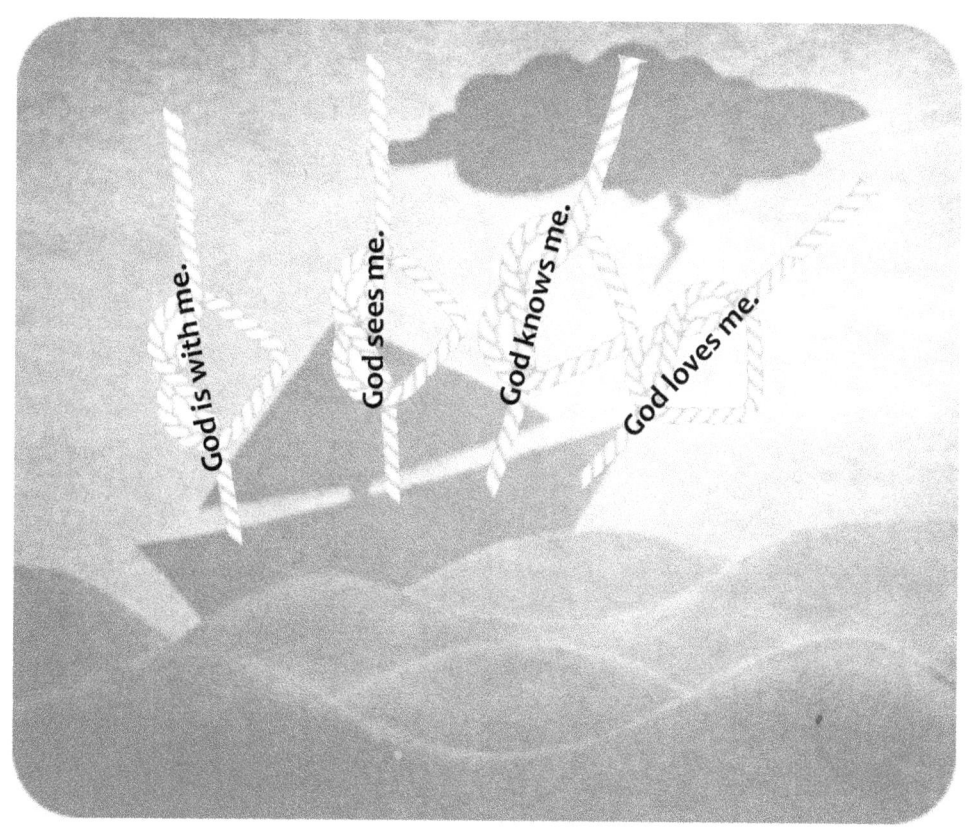

SESSION 44
DISCUSSIONS FOR DEEPER UNDERSTANDING

GOALS FOR PARTICIPANTS

- Speak with clarity about the truths we have learned

MATERIALS

- This lesson
- Plain paper; pencils and pens

VOCABULARY

- **clarify** (KLAR-uh-fie): to make an idea or statement clear; to remove confusion
- **purposeful** (PER-puhs-full): full of purpose; intentional
- **respect** (ree-SPEKT): concern or regard for another's feelings or wishes; honor

GREETING

Each session begins with a greeting. This will be unique and personal to each group.

REVIEW

Our conversation about children has been informative and helpful as we seek to walk with them toward healing and away from painful events. We do not have all the answers, but we now have insight into some of these children's thoughts, fears, doubts and even misconceptions.

If you had an opportunity to speak to a child this week, were you able to apply some of what you learned in our last few sessions? If so, how?

Give participants time to respond to the questions above.

LESSON SCRIPT

> The focus of this lesson is to encourage discussion among the participants. This discussion will help them recall and personalize the truths they have learned in the children's sessions. As such, the majority of your time will be spent not in teaching but in reflection and application.
>
> Discussion prompts have been provided to help you start and maintain this dialogue for the length of the session. Each discussion prompt presents one truth that participants learned about children and then poses thoughts and questions about that truth that can spark conversation.
>
> You may choose to go through all of the prompts together, as one large group, or you may divide participants into smaller groups and assign one or two prompts to each. If you use break-out groups, make sure that you allow enough time at the end of the session for everyone to come back together to share their conclusions. Also note that, for the final discussion prompt, participants will need to work in pairs.

One of the best ways to remember and understand what we have learned is to talk about it. And so, today, we will spend our time together in discussion. This discussion will help us to connect with the ideas we have learned about children more personally. It will give us a chance to contemplate on them, explain them, and listen to others talk about them, so that we can understand their truths more intimately. It will also help us **clarify** any confusion that could keep us from correctly and comfortably applying these concepts to help children.

REFLECTION AND APPLICATION

Discussion Prompt 1: Children are a unique and purposeful creation of God, the Perfect Creator.

- Why is this truth important for children to know?
- How might it help children to deal with pain to know that they are one-of-a-kind and that there is a purpose for their life that is different from all others?

Discussion Prompt 2: Children have personhood: They are individuals with human feelings and characteristics.

We discussed several ways that Jesus views children as persons full of value and purpose.

- Children, in their own personhood, are important in the kingdom of God. They are able to be a part of His kingdom and to work and walk alongside adults.
- Children, in their own personhood, are given as an example for adults. The instruction to "change and become like" children implies that children are unique in a *valuable* way.
- Children, in their own personhood, deserve God's teaching and truth *now*—not just when they become adults.

How can we follow the truths and example Jesus gave to us as we relate to children?

Discussion Prompt 3: Children are valuable—worthy of love and respect.
- How can we show love and respect to children as they express their stories to us?
- One way to show a person respect and love is to notice them.
  - In what ways do children enjoy being noticed?
  - How can we go out of our way to notice the children that are a part of our lives?
  - How can we notice the children who are suffering around us?

Discussion Prompt 4: Children experience suffering. They need help to find healthy ways to move toward healing.
- Why are children often reluctant to share about their pain and fear with adults? What fears do they have about sharing with others?
- What are some conversation starters that might provide an opening for a child to share?
- What do we want to avoid that might close the door when a child is sharing?
- What do we learn from God about being a good listener?

Discussion Prompt 5: Children often need nonverbal ways to share their stories.

> This "discussion" is actually a role-playing exercise to be done in groups of two. This activity is a very important part of this review because it gives participants first-hand experience with one of the nonverbal activities from session 41. As they role-play the child and adult parts, in turn, they will gain a deeper perspective of the impact that these nonverbal exercises can have—a personal perspective that cannot come from merely hearing about the activity. This personal perspective will give participants confidence for when they are ready to use these activities with a child.
>
> When the paired groups are finished with this exercise, you might ask them what they found to be difficult and what was helpful. How did they feel when they were the child participant? How did they feel when they played the adult? What suggestions or ideas did they come up with that might make this activity go smoother next time?

This "discussion" is actually an activity to be done in groups of two. Choose a partner and then, together, pick one of the nonverbal activities from our sessions to role-play. One of you will play the part of the child and the other will play the part of the adult. When you play the part of the child, you should respond with real events and emotions from your own experience—perhaps even a recent event.

Once you have completed the activity this way, switch your roles, so that the person who played the child now becomes the adult and vice-versa. By the end of the exercise, you should have completed the activity twice—once as an adult and once as a child.

COURAGE AND PEACE

Through our discussion, we have reminded ourselves that children do experience pain and suffering. When they are left alone in that suffering, it only grows and deepens and settles in. Although it may be hidden, it will surface one day when they are older, perhaps even in adulthood. By that time, it will have affected how they view others, how they view themselves, and how they respond to circumstances in their lives.

When we help children face their suffering now, we give them a better outlook for the future. We give them the ability to embrace a healthy perspective of pain. We help them to hold onto their value and purpose and protect them from untruths that can lead to despair. We give them the tools they need to move forward in difficult times.

As adults, we see this work as our responsibility and our privilege. And when we take the time to do this work well, we discover that it is also the perfect opportunity to introduce children to our Good Shepherd, who is with all of us on this journey. We can show them that this Good Shepherd, who values them and has a purpose for them, will never change and will give them a way through in the brightest and the darkest times alike.

APPENDIX B:

A LESSON-PLAN OUTLINE AND IDEAS TO HELP TRAIN LEADERS

This section is for those who will train leaders to shepherd others through pain. It provides a list of important considerations and a sample lesson-plan outline to help you organize this book's contents into a schedule that is workable for you.

Your training schedule will fall into one of three categories:

- Short sessions (1.5 - 2 hours) spread over a period of time (weekly, for example)
- Longer sessions (2 - 3 hours) weekly (on a Saturday, for example)
- Concentrated sessions (full-day) to accomplish the training in a shorter period of time (3 days, for example)

Which plan you choose will depend on your participants and your proposed schedule to begin small groups.

Avoid the temptation to begin small groups without this training. Everyone —no matter how experienced— needs to be familiar with the course content and review the basics for leading a group successfully. Everyone needs to experience the activities in order to guide their small group participants with compassion and understanding.

Key Considerations for Your Lesson-Plan Schedule

- ✦ Your training will be expressed from two unique perspectives.
    - At times you will speak to the participants as leaders—as you give information specific to leading a group.
    - At other times you will speak to them as members of a small group—as you model how to share the session content and lead the activities.
- ✦ Present the material in the same sequence as it appears in the book.
- ✦ Be sure each lesson includes time for the following elements:
    - the lesson and its application
    - questions and discussion
    - leadership practice

It is crucial that you take time to go through each session. However, feel free to present the lesson portion of the session in shortened form. The intent is to give leader-participants a firm enough grasp of the basic truths and principles of the lessons that they can go on to confidently express those truths to their own small groups.

Then be sure to have them put the application portion of the session into practice. Guide them through the entire application exercise just as they would lead during their own small-group sessions—*speaking to them as small group participants*; this includes the completion of any worksheets. This part of the training is crucial because it helps leader-participants better understand and deal with the responses that arise in their own small groups, when the time comes.

Experience has shown that many leader-participants begin to process some of their own pain and suffering during this application time. This is okay and should not be rebuked or ignored. Such personal experiences will fuel these future leaders to make their own small groups come alive. The more personally they experience each lesson, the more prepared they will be to comfortably lead others through these challenging conversations.

Time does not allow for the participants to role-play all of the teaching and applications. However, you may use some time for practice as your schedule allows. This can be done as a review after a particular training lesson is complete, for example.

Sample Lesson-Plan Outline

The following outline gives you an idea of how you might organize this book's contents into individual lessons. In this particular example, material is divided into twelve separate lessons. Each lesson covers about two chapters (from parts 1 and 2) or three to four sessions (from part 3). As you create your own schedule, you might choose to mirror this outline exactly or you might adjust it to accommodate specific needs, such as time constraints, urgency level, or number of trainees.

For concentrated training sessions, you will of course combine the training lessons to fit the time period. Make sure adjusted schedules account for the considerations listed above as much as possible.

TRAINING LESSON ONE

Present and discuss:

Preface

Introduction: Help for a Difficult Conversation

How To Get the Best Use From This Book

Chapter 1: Prepare Your Heart and Mind

Chapter 2: Build and Protect a Sense of Safety

TRAINING LESSON TWO

Present and discuss:

Chapter 3: Find Courage, Grace, and Peace

Chapter 4: Logistical Information About the Sessions

Chapter 5: Recommendations for Leading the Sessions

TRAINING LESSON THREE
Session 1: Introduction
Session 2: Begin the Story
Session 3: Our Common Response to Suffering

TRAINING LESSON FOUR
Session 4: How Do I Feel?
Session 5: Become Familiar with Suffering
Session 6: A Picture of Suffering

TRAINING LESSON FIVE
Session 7: Life as It Was; Life as It Is Now
Session 8: Discovering Loss
Session 9: The Emotions of Loss
Session 10: Telling God About My Suffering

TRAINING LESSON SIX
Session 11: Reassurance
Session 12: I Am Not Consumed
Session 13: A Beginning and an End
Session 14: A New Perspective

TRAINING LESSON SEVEN
Session 15: Why?
Session 16: Where Is God in the Suffering?
Session 17: Why Did God Allow This To Happen?
Session 18: Hope

TRAINING LESSON EIGHT
Session 19: Others in Our Story
Session 20: Those Who Caused the Harm
Session 21: Forgiveness

TRAINING LESSON NINE
- Session 22: Move Forward
- Session 23: Truth and Untruth
- Session 24: Discover the Need for Protection
- Session 25: Set Boundaries

TRAINING LESSON TEN
- Session 26: A Strong Protection: Identity
- Session 27: Value: Where Do I Find It?
- Session 28: Tethers
- Session 29: The Reality of Fear

TRAINING LESSON ELEVEN
- Session 30: Along the Way
- Session 31: Redeemed
- Session 32: Is There Peace?
- Session 33: My Guarded Heart
- Session 34: How Should We Now Live?

TRAINING LESSON TWELVE
- Session 35: Our Emotions: Where Do They Take Us?
- Session 36: Let There Be Joy
- Session 37: A New Song

(OPTIONAL) TRAINING LESSON THIRTEEN
- The Personhood of Children
- A Child's Response to Suffering
- Open a Safe Door for Children to Share

(OPTIONAL) TRAINING LESSON FOURTEEN
- Nonverbal Ways to Open the Door
- Body-Based Coping to Help Children with Anxiety
- Spiritual Reassurance
- Discussions for Deeper Understanding

ABOUT THE AUTHOR

Susan Habegger, founder and director of Thrive Life Skills, an international ministry organization, has lived and worked for over 30 years with suffering people around the world. When she unexpectedly met suffering firsthand, her thoughts on healing were transformed, inspiring her to create a cross-cultural guidebook to help lead others along the healing journey. Susan lives with her daughter and family in Michigan, where she explores the Lake Michigan shores. Her constant companion, at home or traveing, is her Good Shepherd.

You are invited to respond to Susan and share how Come Alongside has helped in your vision to create a safe place for healing. Perhaps you have questions about how to use this in your ministry. Simply reach out via email, at susanh@thrivelifeskills.org or through the "Contact Us" option at thrivelifeskills.com.

The conversations in *Come Alongside* are excellent topics for Conferences, Workshops, and Retreats. To request Susan as speaker, go to susanhabeggerauthor.com for more information or through the "Contact Us" option at thrivelifeskills.com.

Finally, if *Come Alongside* was helpful to you, we would appreciate a short review on Amazon.com, so that other readers might benefit from your words and from this book.

Susan is also the author of *A New Song: Our Journey Toward Healing*. A New Song is for all who suffer—before, now, and what is to come. *A New Song* is for anyone who is weary of living under the burden of pain and longs for a way forward toward peace. This book will be your steady companion, leading you through the uncertainty, out of the numbness, and toward healing. It will offer you a safe space, where you can take an honest journey. And, over time, it will be the backdrop against which you will hear notes of hope starting to blend—notes full of courage and peace that will create a new song. A New Song is also available with a Leader's Guide for Small Group Study.

All books are available on Amazon. com or by order from any bookseller.

www.ingramcontent.com/pod-product-compliance
Lightning Source LLC
Chambersburg PA
CBHW080539030426
42337CB00024B/4800